LETTER TO AN
ARAB FRIEND

LETTER TO AN

Arab Friend

BY ANDRÉ CHOURAQUI

PREFACE BY SHIMON PERES

TRANSLATED BY WILLIAM V. GUGLI

UNIVERSITY OF MASSACHUSETTS PRESS

AMHERST 1972

The translator wishes to acknowledge

a Research Grant from the University of

Massachusetts Research Council, which made

sustained work on the translation possible.

Preface

In this second half of the twentieth century one of the most complex and alarming of the problems which keenly interest a vast portion of mankind is without a doubt the conflict which pits the Arab States of the Near East against the State of Israel. World public opinion follows the changing directions of our wars with a sense of identification, dependence almost, as if each citizen of the world felt personally involved in the problems we have to solve and in the battles which under various forms have succeeded each other endlessly in this part of the globe for more than two generations.

The complexity of the conflict is further intensified by the strategic importance of this area which to a certain degree determines the relations between Africa and Asia and by its rich petroleum deposits which invite obvious envy.

Not long ago a French author wrote that "nowhere are such foolish statements made as in front of great works in museums." This sentiment must have been expressed before the time of the Jewish and Arab confrontation in the Near East in a fratricidal and absurd war. Otherwise, the author would certainly have agreed that even more foolish statements are made about the Israeli-Arab conflict than before museum masterpieces. Public opinion and occasionally even statesmen and experts in Near Eastern affairs show a discouraging lack of information concerning the problems, realities and prospects of this part of the world. To make matters worse the press, which thrives on the sensational, adds to the confusion in men's minds, especially since unusual news is not in short supply in our current situation. An additional element of confusion is introduced by the speeches and propaganda of the dictatorships of the neighboring countries which are bent on keeping alive the futile expectations of the masses.

Taking into account the world's image of us and comparing that to our daily lives and hopes leads one to believe in the existence of a true mystification which confuses the issue, discourages all analysis and distorts all plans and prospects.

We must be grateful to André Chouraqui for having again situated the problem of Israel's relations with the Arabs within its vast historical context. By doing this, he places his work at the head of the most necessary endeavor, as the one which leads to a demystification and a clarification which should inform any new creation. The two central figures of his essay symbolize well the societies which confront each other. There are thousands of examples of Jews and Arabs who, like Ahmed and Mattatias, have grown up together, have been separated by our wars and are meeting again today. Almost every Arab can recognize himself in Ahmed, just as almost every Jew sees himself in Mattatias. Their reunion allows the author to give an exhaustive analysis of the relationship between Israel's tradition and that of Ishmael since their beginnings. He recalls the memories of Biblical times when the two peoples emerged from the same geographical, linguistic, sociological and cultural context. He stresses the fundamental similarities of the Islamic and Judaic religions dedicated to the cult of the same God and to the service of the same ideals. He evokes the golden age of Jewish thought developed within the center of the Arab peoples.

Yet, I feel that the most original aspect of his work is his rigorous analysis of the national renaissance of the Jews and the Arabs from the nineteenth century on. No one has demonstrated better than he the similarity of the Jewish and Arab destiny and mission in these pages which have been hailed as among the most beautiful ever written either about Judaism or about Islam. With moving lyricism he speaks of the grandeur of Islam as well as the misery of the Arab peoples, victims equally of colonialism, feudalism and dictatorships whose insane dreams complete the destruction of the peoples they continue to enslave.

By his calling, his training, his personal experience in Algeria as well as in the Near East, and in this chosen place which

renascent and reunified Jerusalem is, André Chouraqui was
in a good position to contribute his share and shed light on
a problem whose solution would be so decisive for the future
of the Near East and perhaps even the entire world.

At the end of his analysis which lends indisputable facts
to the argument, André Chouraqui suggests prospects for the
future. He hopes for the rise of a broad movement which,
in the service of the great ideals we share, finally would reunite the Jews, the Christians and the Moslems in an undertaking of salvation and peace. He believes that the nucleus
of this reconciliation should be in the land of the Bible where
Jews and Moslems should come to terms, create a federation
of states which would end the succession of present conflicts
and settle down to the demands of reconstructing this area
of the world.

Although the historical analysis which this book presents
is undeniable, the reader need not agree with all the author's
conclusions. But if he feels that the program which Chouraqui presents is a utopia, he should keep in mind that our era
is dedicated to the achievement of great utopias which nourished the dreams of humanity from time immemorial. The
State of Israel is itself born of the dream of Theodore Herzl
who often was considered demented by his contemporaries.
Only twenty years ago the French and the Germans seemed
irrevocably divided by an inexpiable hate. Now a new Europe is in the process of coming into being since their reconciliation. Only yesterday the Jews and the Germans, who
certainly do not have the reputation of being easy to get
along with, were opposed in a merciless fight. Here they are
today reconciled and working side by side for a better world.
A short while back was it not lunacy to dream of a trip to the
moon? Thanks to technological progress this is now an accomplished fact.

In contemporary political history utopia has become a
reality to be dealt with. Chouraqui's merit lies in his having
had the courage to say so both with authority and with faith.

As for me, I think that the reconciliation of Israel and the
Arab world corresponds not only to the traditions of the
past but also to the irresistable demands of our present political situation. A United Europe was impossible with dic-

tators such as Hitler and Mussolini. It is likely that the regimes which continue the conflict must be transformed or must disappear before the perspectives for peace may be applied. Nonetheless, it is absolutely certain that the interests of the nations, of the states, and of the peoples of the Near East complement each other and they have everything to gain by peace. The problems which we have to solve then are those for which it is possible to find a solution which will satisfy the interests of each group and at the same time uphold their honor. Territorial problems, the refugee issue, the questions raised by the organization of two societies, Jewish and Arab, which must recognize each other and discover the paths to their new union, will have to be resolved in a spirit of brotherhood. This is possible. The years which separate us from the Six Day War have taught us that not only are the Arabs and Jews "condemned" to live with each other, but that they can do so in freedom, with honor, and in the pursuit of their common good. In addition, there exists a mixed Israeli-Arab economy whose development current realities render hopeful.

Finally, one might say of André Chouraqui's dream of the reconciliation of Israel and the Arab states, what Theodore Herzl already said about another utopia, the creation of the State of Israel itself: "If you are determined, it will not be a dream."

SHIMON PERES
Minister for Arab Affairs
Government of Israel

1 Meeting under a Dome

At dawn on June 7, 1967, not far from our home, the bull-
dozers knocked down the wall of steel and concrete which
had separated Jerusalem from Jerusalem for nineteen years.
Skirmishes continued on the Mount of Olives. There we
were in a city ravaged by three days of war. The mutilated
corpses, the dead bodies lined up along the sidewalks, the
procession of tanks and military trucks, the bustle of the
soldiers and the panic of the crowd, burning buildings, the
roof of the Church of the Dormition in flames, the deafening
noise of the cannons, the hammering of the machine guns—
such was the setting for a reunion we had been dreaming
about for more than twenty years, and which was finally
becoming a reality under the unscathed dome of the Mosque
of Omar.

Since that day in May 1948, when, after the bitter fight
against the Arab armies, I had to leave my family home in
the old city of Jerusalem, not far from your home, halfway
between the Holy Sepulcher and the Mosque of El-Aksa, I
longed for the moment when you and I would have a heart-
to-heart talk. The gulf which separated us grew greater. So
many obstacles had come between us that I feared we would
never be able to pick up our friendship where we had left
off, never be able to go back to the familiar language which
had bound us together, never be able to overcome the barrier
of misunderstanding and shame which separated us and was
destroying us. For seven thousand days, we lived in the same
city under the warming rays of the same sun, and beneath
the same stars, apart and enemies, alone in a world which
made us strangers and prisoners of its frontiers. How jealous
you were of the city which nourished you, the place where I
hoped to forget my suffering in the security of home. What
wishful thinking! I had only to listen to the voices which

echoed from the border, those of Hussein and Nasser, those
of Choukeiri and of all the Arab politicians almost without
exception, to convince myself of my error. Perhaps my
wanderings had finally brought me back to my heritage,
but I still had not found peace. Your silence hurt me. Sometimes I thought about you crossing the street where we used
to play together, and I could picture your cold stare, your
expressionless eyes which looked at everything, but fixed
on nothing. Your look was empty, and so my turmoil grew,
smoldering since the day we were forced to separate, to join
the two armed camps.

The anguish of our affection has never lessened. I had to
understand the enigma of your choice so that I could break
down the hate which separated us. I can still recall my struggle, my resistance to your aggression (a term you will scoff
at), my infinite patience and my relentless fight, once the
war was declared. Victorious, but driven from by birthplace
and home, I was forced to wander in my new country, Israel,
stripped of the heritage of my ancestors and deprived of
your friendship. My loneliness festered and the hate which
separated and disfigured us left a bitter aftertaste. Have you
ever understood why I acted as I did, my bag of tricks, my
sudden stubbornness? Have you ever understood me as I
groped for peace? It was a confrontation with eternity, as
was Jacob's struggle with the angel. Were you aware of my
clear conviction that my victory was as necessary as the sun
in its course, the conviction that my victory was implacably
tied to our reconciliation and salvation?

In spite of my apparent weakness and the formidable
power of eighty million Arabs who controlled the oil wells,
anchored to my Biblical rock, I knew that someday, even
if I had to wait forever, you would realize that I was right,
and that your very salvation depended on my unshakable
resolve not to listen to you, not to follow you. I didn't miss
a single move as you chose your dangerous path of hate. I
was convinced that I, whom your pride almost destroyed,
would be the only one there to reach out to you.

The moment of reunion so impatiently awaited is finally
here. I had hoped that Jerusalem would push away its walls
in the midst of peace and joy. Instead it occurred with

bloodshed and in darkness. Here we are, face to face. You seemed transfixed when I appeared in the half-light of the mosque, as if I were a ghost brought back to life. You came forward and embraced me as you sobbed. A round of machine-gun fire hit against a stone wall just inches away. The moment of confrontation, the explanation of the mystery behind our war was finally at hand. Then your expression seemed to change. Its intensity sought an answer which the decades of hate had made more urgent. What mixed blessings this day of bloodshed and of truth held. For us, Jerusalem was rising above its mourning to reconcile us in silence and happiness. My victory hurt you. I owe you an explanation for the mystery of my obstinacy, as you aptly phrased it. Will you understand the burden of these random memories which I must now talk about as the sounds of the cannons and the last gasps of the battle die away?

You are an Arab. You will not have me forget it. The term did not even exist when we were children. In those days you identified yourself as a Palestinian, or better still, a man of Jerusalem. What a mockery it is that we label ourselves and camouflage our true identity. Palestine, Palestinians—both words go back to the Philistines. The Roman conquerors of Israel were sure they had succeeded in erasing the very memory of the vanquished from history. Israel had paid a terrible price for their victory! The enemy had to be destroyed, so the survivors were deported, and debaptized Jerusalem became Aelia Capitolina. The land of Israel suddenly became Palestine, "the land of the Philistines." Palestinian, stated your identification card, but you knew that you were a man of Jerusalem, a Jerusalemite like me. Our fellow countrymen were Hebronites, Nablusians, Haifans. Conscious identity remained at the very local level in the authenticity of our origins. The British mandate over Palestine had not succeeded in imposing a Palestinian consciousness upon us, and even less, an Arab mystique.

Our regional idiosyncrasies contrasted even more sharply with the outside world. Egypt, Syria, Lebanon, and more so, Iraq and Arabia, remained foreign lands to us. Religion brought us no closer to our rowdy neighbors than it did to the other parts of the Mohammedan Empire which were

3

outside the frontiers of our minds, Turkey, Iran, Morocco, or Pakistan. Probably one of the most unexpected changes provoked by our war has been the imposition by Nasserism of the monolithic myth of Pan-Arabism on Islam with its complex diversity of families.

Ben Bella, in Cairo, ranted and raved at the microphone placed before him and palmed off as a speech the same sentence repeated twenty times, *"Ana Arabi,"* "I am an Arab." The chant did not alter reality one bit. Ben Bella, as is every Mohammedan from North Africa, is an Arabized Berber. For twelve centuries of Islamic history, only a few thousand Arabs had settled in North Africa. If they had generally succeeded in Arabizing and Islamizing it, they had never been able to modify its ethnological structures. Even Nasser is an Egyptian of the Nile Valley, and you, my friend and counterpart, are a man of Jerusalem whose ancestors in Biblical times were certainly brothers of mine, the Hebrews.

Although we were neighbors, we first met at our desks in school. Our families were poor, but wanted to give us as thorough a preparation as possible. I was the eleventh child in my family; you were the thirteenth in yours. We grew up together inside the walls of Jerusalem, city of blue and gold. Its bells, its minarets, its Arabs, its Jews, mingled in the rhythm of our unbounded games. Depending on our mood, we would visit a mosque, a church, or a synagogue. We were cast in the same mold. In our own neighborhood, Jews, Christians, or Mohammedans, we became one at school and at play. We were innocently unaware of the hate which existed among the adults and of the lines of demarcation in our ghettos.

The school day was long for us. It took up almost all our time. At night, we would hurry home. Jerusalem was a small, peaceful city at that time. There were few cars on the road. One of my great-uncles, in oriental turban, used to tell about the arrival of the first automobile in the Holy Land at the turn of the century. He saw it being unloaded at Haifa as the Turkish police casually looked on. In detail he described his terror when the motor started by itself with a frightening clamor. He mounted his horse and returned as fast as he could to spread the sensational news throughout

Jerusalem. His older brother asked him to explain the new contraption, a carriage which moved without horses. Propping himself in his armchair, buried in his oriental garb, he reflected and then concluded that it was all a big joke. He burst out laughing, slapped the messenger on the shoulder and said, "A horseless carriage? No doubt it's your mother who pushes it." This skeptic was to live long enough to see the birth of the atomic era and the creation of the state of Israel. Since that first surprise, the Turks in Palestine had been replaced by the English, the number of cars remained small, and traffic did not hamper the schoolchildren as they scampered home where each one found his ethnic origins.

Once home, you had to forget the school songs and contend with your father, a good Arab, who was totally immersed in his Islamic past and was closer to the men who had built the Mosque of El-Aksa than to our own time. He was well educated and meditated daily on the suras of the Koran. Theological commentaries in the grand old tradition interested him more than the political vagaries of Jerusalem. At his side, you were brought back to your roots, your religion and its traditions, your Arab language and your culture. Sometimes your father would invite me to spend the evening with you, your mother, and your sisters, but rarely did he join us. Everything seemed foreign to him. He would have blended beautifully with Omar's companions. Our century seemed coarse to him. I once heard him give a real diatribe against Islam's decadence. According to him the *imams* and the *cadis* were interested only in their own profit. Islamic thought had become stagnant and adulterated. In the first place, the canonists repeated what had been said a thousand years earlier, masking their own sterility with an intransigent obstinacy. In the second place, the Mohammedan intellectual aligned himself with the Western school and repeated as best he could a lesson foreign to the culture. In both cases, the deep origins of Islam seemed tarnished to him. He suffered more from this than he would suffer from all the struggles he was yet to experience—your wars. Bearing witness to the splendor of Islam, he never stopped enriching himself with the Mohammedan tradition by meditating on the great texts of the seventh and eighth centuries.

He seemed to be living in the golden shadows of the splendid mosques of Jerusalem in expectation of an impossible resurrection. He had so many hopes for you. You deflated them with one tragic blow when you opted very early for Karl Marx and the Communist revolution because you thought they were the last hope for Arab nationalism.

As for me, once out of school, I had to cope with a universe which was completely foreign to the one which our teachers had tried to impose. That was the Jewish ghetto with its rites and regulations, its narrowness, its suffering and its insane expectation of a salvation which always lay in the future. I belonged to a family steeped in the Eastern traditions of Israel. It had settled in Jerusalem centuries ago, in an old house on the Street of Bondage. In the thirteenth century my family had fled from the persecutions of a sultan in North Africa and had chosen to return to the Holy Land where my ancestors had lived for many generations. I could easily locate in the chain of time the humble artisans and small farmers, illustrious rabbis and scholars, shopkeepers and builders, the forebears who had made a Jew of me, a son of Abraham. I discovered my Jewish identity in my father's home. You know only too well our rites, our celebrations, and our clannishness. Sometimes I was caught in the spell of its mystical power—family rites, sacramental gestures of my parents blessing us by candlelight which projected our dancing shadows on the stone walls, the prayers from the synagogue chanted to the ancient rhythm and psalmody inherited from Biblical times, our rabbis narrating the epic of Israel from its origins to the end of time because even the future was history for them in the revealed certainty and knowledge of the ultimate mysteries of the world. This was a strange spirituality which placed its coordinates in the very beginning at the first dawn of the creation of the world, and at the end of time and the last judgment which will assure the reintegration and salvation of all humanity. We were a people anointed in prayer and ritual, carried along by the cycles of the religious calendar. The revealed Word lifted us above time, in a transcendence which could only be satisfied by the fulfillment of the promise. I could vaguely sense the omnipotence of the spiritual universe which engulfed me in its mystery, in spite of the indigence of the world which was its bearer. The humble rabbis and the poor faithful lived on charity or odd jobs, needy people reduced to subsisting on bread and salt while dreaming of the apocalypse. For all of them, living together with the Arab was a basic fact and the opportunity for a happy relationship. My native language, before Hebrew, was Arabic. Both at home and at play, we spoke only this language which was used by our greatest theologians, Bahya Ibn Pakuda, Solomon Ibn Gabirol, and Maimonides. Arabs and Jews, we were really cut out of the same cloth.

In two outstanding works, *Solal* and *Mange-clous*, Albert Cohen had described with sparkling warmth the incomparable fervor of the Mediterranean Judaism in Greece where he was born. Describing the Jewish community in Tunis, Albert Memmi reflected more on his personal problems. He did not succeed in giving an exact picture of the milieu in which he grew up. Nor was he able to describe its preoccupations or render its inimitable flavor. With the exception of Burla, no one has ever captured the poetry of these Jews carrying on the traditions of the East while assimilating modern culture. No one has ever translated the originality of their language and thought, their hearty wit, their tireless humor, or even their depth and courage. One hopes they will have their Albert Cohen someday.

Meanwhile, I would like to give you my recollection of the man who contributed most to my discovery of the Arab world and my love for it, Abraham Mizrahi, my grandfather. He transmitted a double tradition, friendship with the Arabs and, at the same time, an open door to the West. I can still see him dressed in his traditional costume, with his white and gold turban wrapped around the *Shachia* he proudly wore. Throughout his life he held faithfully to the traditional Eastern Jewish dress. His roomy *serul* was a rectangular piece of cloth six yards long which he wrapped around his body. These bouffant trousers held up by a wide linen belt held him in and made him look quite imposing. His vest and bolero were a carry-over of his Spanish strain. To the end of his life, he had the elegance of the torero marching out of the arena and a cheerful aggressiveness which he never lost. He belonged to a long line of scholars who still kept their minds sharp while working the earth for a livelihood. Abraham Mizrahi was a pioneer. He had helped clear the lands of Judea and had planted his own vineyards. I can vividly remember him in his wine cellar close by our house where each year he skillfully directed his workers in the making of a fine wine. I was able to salvage a few bottles from the ruins of the Old City, where he died in 1929.

Growing up, I lived contently in an affectionate atmosphere made even more pleasant by our Arab maids whom my parents trusted to help in my upbringing. My father's house, as my grandfather's, was always filled by our visiting Arab friends. Their strong character showed in their features. Sheikh Mokhtar, the Mohammedan leader, used to visit several times a month. Our greatest pleasure was to accept his invitation to spend a relaxing day on his farm not far from Nablus. I relished the good things our Arab friends served, the famous *eleben* prepared on the farm, the country butter, and sometimes we got to sample the delicious *mechoui*, the foods of the gods. We would reciprocate by distributing the traditional Jewish foods at the holidays. The culinary exchanges were only the outward sign of a much deeper friendship.

My father, too, was a farmer. He owned a vineyard and, as an extra activity, dealt in grain. On Thursday, market-day in Jerusalem, he received his customers and friends. Each week I would take my place in a corner of his huge office where I watched the hustle and bustle of his friends and business acquaintances. The entire day was taken up with discussions about business deals, loans, investments, and sales. All the conversations were in Arabic, in the inimitable dialect of the Jerusalem region. I listened closely to the exchanges which took place in an atmosphere of trust and friendship. Reality, itself, convinced me of our solidarity. The Jews and the Arabs lived side by side strongly influenced by their common condition. They were so harmoniously dependent on each other that I thought nothing could ever change their relationship.

Obviously, we were still Jews, and you, Arabs. The children were still capable of confronting each other in street fights, shouting insults at each other which related both to the individual and the group. These were only children's games. The strong bonds of solidarity were far more deeply ingrained in us. Trust always won out over distrust, and friendship outweighed scorn. Even in times of crisis, this was true.

Yet, from childhood I had encountered the realities of anti-Semitism. In Jerusalem, the population was made up of separate groups which had never really succeeded in merging into one cohesive society. On the one side were the Mohammedans, on the other, the Christians, whether Arab, French, Italian or German, and then totally apart, the Jews. All these peoples had coexisted for ages without being able truly to unite. The Arab, Christian, or Mohammedan children would often chase us playfully shouting "dirty Jew." We got used to the insults, and I learned that I was "dirty" even before I knew what the word Jew meant. In Jerusalem, relationships went on as in the past. We spoke the same language and our habits were similar. Old friendships gave everyone a sense of stability and confidence. Yet, the nature and meaning of things began to change when the British mandate was established.

A curious result of the mandate was the institutionalizing of the Judeo-Arab conflict. The British, eager to replace the Turks in Palestine, had understandably made contradictory promises to both sides. They had taken seriously our conflicting claim to rebuild our country in the land of the Bible, and signed the Balfour Declaration for us. Yet they promised similar privileges to the Palestinians in order to win them over. In good faith, both Jews and Palestinians were to believe themselves justified in their actions—actions which would inevitably clash.

The first incidents of bloodshed between Jews and Arabs took place in Jerusalem in 1921 and more followed in 1929. I was ten years old in 1921. These clashes were of limited consequence and really only concerned the landowners who were uneasy about the Zionists who wished to introduce democratic ways which they neither approved of nor understood. Others almost always kept out of the struggle. Many still hoped that the religious and political differences between the Mohammedans, the Christians, and the Jews could be resolved harmoniously to their mutual benefit. This seemed to apply not only to Jerusalem, but to the entire Arab world, from Iran to Morocco, wherever Jews and Christians happened to be guests of *Dar-el-Islam*. But instead of coming together harmoniously and risking open rivalry, the religious and ethnic groups preferred to withdraw into themselves. As far as the Arabs and Jews were concerned, this contradicted the ageless tradition of cooperation and generosity.

The situation really began to deteriorate when the Germans became involved by sending agents armed with Hitlerian propaganda. In a more indirect way, they put their arsenal of anti-Jewish ideology at the disposal of those who felt they had a justified complaint against the Jews. The conflict which had started at the police level, and then moved to the political one, soon acquired ideological proportions.

Agitators began to crop up in those Arab countries which had a high concentration of Jews. Frequently, they came from the West and offered a curious combination of theological prejudices drawn from the religious conflicts of the Middle Ages and from modern anti-Semitism. They were intent on poisoning the relations between those communities which traditionally coexisted peacefully.

Algeria is an extreme example of this vast undertaking. Here, the first anti-Semitic campaign of great importance followed shortly after the signing of the Crémieux Decree which conferred French citizenship upon the Jews, thereby sharply cutting them off from the Mohammedan community on whose fringes they had lived for centuries. The anti-Semites—not the Arabs, but the very French who were later to become involved in the Dreyfus Case—found the occasion ripe for their activity in the Kabyle insurrection of 1871. To save face after the French defeat of 1870, the colonial administration tried to direct popular Arab discontent toward the Jews. Yet, the Kabyle insurrection had been devised and initiated in that part of Algeria where there were the least Jews. Its promoters did not for a moment think of opposing a decree whose existence was unknown to the majority of the people. It was far more serious business concerning, above all else, the principle of the French occupation. The anti-Semites conveniently diverted toward the Jews a movement which was aimed at them. The debate which followed the Kabyle insurrection was brought before the French Parliament. On July 21, 1871, Lambrecht, the Minister of the Interior, mounted the podium to propose a law which would repeal the decree of October 24, 1870, and again reduce the Jews to the status and insecurity which continued to be that of the Mohammedans. Not a single Arab rose to support the anti-Semitic campaign. The ploy failed and the principle of the Crémieux decree was assured. Its adversaries intensified their fight against the minority which benefitted from it. It was during the electoral periods, especially after 1878, that the latent animosity broke into violence.

By its impassioned rhetoric, the Drumont action was to encourage the polarization of the ethnic groups among which it intended to sow its hate. The Europeans, the Mohammedans, and the Israelites each had their peculiarities. Playing on their political passions would transform what were superficial differences into a hateful segregation. A small clique was going to capitalize on the slightest pretext to attempt something which the clique itself never clearly understood. The restlessness which spread among the Jews seemed to become an end in itself. Hate campaigns in the press, condemnation of the Jewish population, street riots, provocations, confusion, desecration of synagogues, pillaging, murders, nothing was omitted. The anti-Semite movement, exploited in France during the Dreyfus affair, boosted the attack of Max Régis and his partisans. In the principal Algerian cities of Algiers, Oran, Mascara, Mostaganem, Afreville, Marengo, Setif, and Constantine, the year 1898 marked the worst point of anxiety for the victims.

At this point it is suitable to mention the humor of that ghetto visionary, Saadia Perez, who cleverly squelched the anti-Semites. He led a parade of all his friends and servants, Jews and Arabs, and marched throughout the city singing the virulent anti-Semitic repertory composed by certain Parisian songwriters who wished to spread their hate. Those who laughed that day were on the same side, and humor won the day.

The anti-Jewish movement increased in intensity shortly
after the First World War when the anti-Semites denounced
the sacred union which had brought together the three elements of the Algerian population, Arabs, Christians, and
Jews. Hate was deep seated because, since 1921, the city of
Oran had been controlled by the Neo-anti-Semitic Party
of Dr. Molle. The Jews paid dearly for their apprenticeship.
The slogans painted on the walls of the city, the violence of
the election speeches, the insults which had been rampant in
the columns of the *Petit Oranais*, prepared us for the ugly
period which Malraux had already given indications of. The
attack of the anti-Semite party members hit the Jews directly, but through them—and the future was to prove it—
they were also aiming at the Arabs. Their masterpiece was to
pit the Jews and Arabs against each other so that the real
problems facing Algeria would be forgotten. The campaign
of the anti-Jewish newssheet set the stage for the shameful
massacre which took place in Constantine on August 5, 1934.
I remember the consternation in the streets of Jerusalem
when we repeated the tragic toll, twenty-five dead, dozens
wounded, millions of francs worth of furniture and mer-
chandise looted. A Jewish soldier had relieved himself on the
wall of a mosque. In the atmosphere created by the anti-
Semite campaign, the incident was enough to spark the battle between Jews and Arabs while the local authorities casually looked on. The pogrom created panic among the Jews
throughout Algeria. Everybody wondered to what extent
this had been a single, spontaneous incident, and whether it
was a prelude to more massacres. The Algerian Jews were
the first to be implicated in the affair which would eventually affect the entire Arab world.

I remember the anxiety in Jerusalem as we waited for
the coming of the next Day of Atonement. *Yom Kippur*
brought together the men of the city for a twenty-four hour
fast and a prayer which went from one sunset to the next.
That year, contrary to all tradition, the rabbinical authorities
allowed the men to bring their weapons to the synagogue.
I still see the resolute expressions of my brothers, uncles,
cousins, and finally, my father, who solemnly went up to the
place of prayer, each pressing a revolver in his pocket. It was

their duty to defend the synagogue in case of attack. Fortunately nothing happened, in spite of the great tension which existed even in Palestine. Algeria quieted down once more until the period following the Second World War. Together, we feared for our people, for we knew that behind the anti-Semites stalked the deadly hate which would not spare the Arabs once it had dealt with the Jews. The rise of Hitler was a great victory for the Algerian racists. The anti-Semitic Algerians rallied around the swastika. In 1939, it was not unrare to see huge swastikas painted in tar smeared on the walls, especially in Oranie. The reaction against the Popular Front took the form of a general conspiracy against the Jews upon whom a foul-mouthed press heaped its insults. Examples from Germany were a vicious inspiration. The Algerian affair had made us understand the depth of Jewish and Arab solidarity throughout the lands of Islam which were closely linked. A shot fired in Constantine echoed as loudly in Jerusalem as it did in Baghdad.

The rise of pan-German racism was aggravated in Palestine by intercommunity relations. Over and above the local tensions, we saw shaping up before us the profiles of the outsiders who deliberately sought to arm the Arabs against the Jews so they could profit from their divisions. It must be added that Palestine was ripe for discord. The situation was tense. We knew how easy it was to provoke hate and death. Whether we were Arabs or Jews, we felt ourselves the impoverished and impotent victims of a tragedy which was to aggravate the curse of Jerusalem. From generation to generation, the tragic destiny of our city had, nonetheless, allowed the peaceful coexistence of the various communities. The violent conquests of this city which had known so many different masters—the Roman and the Byzantine, the Arab and the Egyptian, the Crusader and the Seljukian, the Turkish and the English—had never hindered either the life or the symbiosis of Ishmael and Israel.

My roots in Palestine went back for generations. Certain Jewish families were proud of never having left the Holy Land since King David's time. I was as much at home as you were. Even the most intransigent of the Arabs could easily agree to a Jewish immigration from the Mohammedan countries. Actually this had gone on continuously. For centuries Jerusalem was the spiritual capital for the Jews of Morocco, Persia, Algeria, and Yemen. They came there to live and die. In their most distant communities they welcomed the messengers, the itinerant rabbis responsible for announcing the Glad Tidings. Your language, Arabic, had become for us, Jews of Asia and Africa, the single language and true foundation of our union. At the highest levels the poets, the theologians, and the spiritual leaders expressed themselves in this one language. The Hebraic Bible and the Aramaic Talmud were taught in Arabic, the language which had replaced Aramean and Hebrew in a large part of the Jewish world. Style is the man, while language is his soul. When our ancestors were in Europe they never spoke Latin. In their Western ghettos they waited for their emancipation for centuries before they gave in and completely adopted the European languages. Our osmosis is as old as our history and is first of all based on the close relationship of our two languages. After having learned Spanish and Greek in order to read Don Quixote and Plato, David Ben Gurion, in his retreat at Sde Boker, began to learn Arabic in order to reread the Koran. He claimed that 90 percent of the terms are identical in Hebrew. I don't know whether this is an accurate statistic, but Arabic and Hebrew are twin languages which have permitted the development of two essentially similar cultures.

For all eternity everything has been prepared for us to recognize each other as brothers, for our mutual understanding in love, courage, and loyalty, so as to assure on this earth the promotion of the kingdom of unity and love. This hope informs not only our vocation but our very life. Everywhere and forever, even during the most serious crisis, the Jews and the Arabs felt very close. The Bible is correct once more when it identifies Abraham as the source of our brotherhood. Jews and Arabs have always carried on close spiritual, intellectual, commercial, and social relations. From Biblical times the Jews had lived in close contact with the Arabs of the North, the Ismailians, and the Arabs of the South, the Qahtanids. From the time of King Ahab, and ever since, the learned men of Israel appreciated, loved, and were inspired by the wisdom of the Arab peoples. Up to the time of Mohammed, relations between the tribes of Ishmael and Israel were close and constant. With the birth of Islam they became even more fundamental. The seventh and eighth centuries were a period of creative symbiosis. When, following the discovery of America, the Mohammedan Empire falls, it drags along with it the decline and fall of the Jewish communities. And even more significantly, an identical and parallel renaissance took place in the Arab and in the Jewish world in the nineteenth century.

What is the basis for the three-thousand-year-old mystery of our relationship?

In 1781, a German scholar hypothesized that the Jews and Arabs must be the principal representatives of a "Semitic race." We know that the Semitic languages, Arabic and Hebrew, belong to the same linguistic family, but why speak of race? This word evokes painful memories for me. Rather than depend upon racial theories based on physiological automatism, I prefer to explore the far deeper spiritual and intellectual affinities. The Bible correctly identifies us as *dodanim*, cousins. I remember the deep conviction with which the old Arabs in our neighborhood used to refer to us as *ben-ami*, the sons of my people.

Not long ago, James A. Montgomery in his book *Arabia and the Bible*, and Duncan Black Macdonald in his work on the common origins of the Semitic peoples held that the literary and religious traditions of the Jews are Arab in origin. The Bene Israel could have been one of the tribes of Arabia which, from there, must have emigrated to Mesopotamia, and then to the land of Canaan. These scholars repeat and adopt the idea of Welhausen and of Robertson Smith, who consider the present Arab tribes the most exact prototype of what Israel was in the Biblical era. They stress the fact that Israel, even after having left Arabia to settle in the Holy Land, remained faithful to its tribal structures. Hence the proof of the Arabic origins. But who will ever solve the enigmas of origins? No theory is ever sure and free from contradiction. The idea of the Arab origin of the tribes of

Israel is argued by numerous scholars and notably by Professor S. D. Goitein in his fine book which he dedicated to *Jews and Arabs, their Contacts Through the Ages.*

What is indisputable, beyond the mystery of origins, is our sociological, linguistic, cultural, and spiritual kinship, and our recognition of each other in the person of the patriarch, Abraham. Sociologists emphasize the similarities between the social organization of the Arabs and the Jews in Biblical times. The Bible frequently mentions the refinement of wisdom of the Arab peoples. This original kinship was confirmed in an almost supernatural way after the appearance of Islam. That we share a single origin and that the cradle of my people may lie in the Arabic peninsula may be debatable. What is certain is that the Jews and the Arabs have lived a unique adventure in the history of mankind. Only their national religions, Judaism and Islam, have had the signal privilege of becoming universal. The national religion of the Jews, through the channels and preaching of the Christian Church, has become the religion of a billion and a half people. The national religion of the Arabs, after the preaching of Mohammed, has four hundred million adherents spread throughout the world. Today two-thirds of the human race recognize the God of Abraham, Isaac, and Jacob, whom the Arabs and the Jews were the first—and for a long time the only ones—to serve.

The mystery becomes even clearer when the astonishingly wonderful and prophetic vocation of Mohammed emerges. The historians of Mohammedan thought have always recognized three sources of inspiration in the Koran. First is the inspiration which Mohammed drew from the spirit of the Jewish and Christian communities, numerous and active in the Arabian peninsula. The rabbis and the monks were his intermediaries for it is absolutely certain that he never read the Sacred Books of Judaism or Christianity. Jewish oral tradition, the Haggadah, or pious legend, the writing of the Mishnah and Talmud, and the teachings of Jesus, prepare the enlightenment which allows him to know, love and serve the God on High. Addressing itself to the Arabs, his preaching utilized the infinite treasure of Arab wisdom. He depaganized and spiritualized it by giving it a monotheistic character.

It is from the Judeo-Christian patrimony that Mohammed draws the essential elements of his thought, the impact of a brilliant teaching which would change the course of history.

"Oh, children of Israel, remember the gifts I have heaped upon you, and remember that I have considered you as the superior people" (Sura 2, verse 44). In these words Mohammed seems to be paying homage to the Jews whom he met at Medina. They must have been the first to introduce him to the meditations of divine matters. In addition, the first biographers of Mohammed considered as a providential sign the fact that the city of Medina, seat of the first community, should have such a large, powerfully-organized Jewish group with such a highly-developed culture. This Jewish community links the Koran to the spiritual heritage of Abraham. Historians are still debating the question of the precise identity of Mohammed's teachers and the Christian or Jewish sect or persuasion to which they belonged. Literature on this subject is plentiful. The Swede, Tor Andrea, Professor J. Obermann, and Professor Goitein* recently raised these questions. Louis Gardet, the very knowledgeable French Islamist has also answered some of the questions which the history of religions raises about the origin of Mohammed's vocation. The theory offered by Professor Goitein is most appealing—Mohammed must have studied and received the Bible from rabbis with an extensive knowledge of Christianity.

Whatever the link which binds Mohammed to the Biblical chain, it is certain that he was very solidly attached to it. In the heroic struggle to convert the Arab world to his new faith, he found his support in the Christian and non-Christian prophets and apostles of Israel, the inspired visionaries who all lived in Israel and in the hills of Judea. So the depth of the phenomenon which inspired the Judeo-Arab symbiosis becomes clear. One God, the God of Abraham, parallel spiritual traditions, and a morality based on the same spiritual laws were to confer on exiled Judaism and on Islam highly similar characteristics.

* Tor Andrea, *The Origin of Islam and Christianity;* J. Obermann, *Islamic Origins;* Goitein, op cit.

Both religions are dedicated to the cult of a transcendent God. Since the destruction of the temple of Jerusalem, this aspect of Judaism became far more pertinent. Settled in their spiritual exile, the Jews were to accept the idea of an absolutely transcendent God who no longer had a home in a temple consecrated to his glory. Nor did they have need of personal representatives on earth such as the high priests and the Levites. The Jews as well as the Arabs adore the Absent-Present, the Most High, the God of Abraham. His transcendence explains the important status of the law in religion, the Jewish *halakkah* and the Mohammedan *shari'at*. In the absence of a single doctrinal authority, the Jews and the Arabs place the source of all authority in the Holy Books. Our religions are those of the revealed Word. The source of religious authority for the Jews was the Torah-which-is-written and the Torah-which-is-on-the-lips. The Arabs made a distinction between the authority of the Koran, *el-kitab*, and the authority of oral tradition, *el-hadit*. For the Arabs, as well as for the Jews, oral tradition could be either juridical or moral. The two religions, and this has far-reaching consequences, were religions of the celestial City. Being missionary in character, they aspire toward assuring God's reign over all the earth. The terrestrial city has to be fulfilled by becoming identical to the spiritual city. As Jesus taught, "thy will be done on earth as it is in heaven." To be full-fledged citizens of the Mohammedan city, man had to participate in the intercession of the Prophet. The Jews shared this view to the limits of their powers during the difficulties of their exile. The Arabs, newcomers on the historical scene, coming out of the desert to intervene in the world, distracted the Jews from their dangerous tête-à-tête with triumphant Christianity.

Between 612 and 622, during the period of Mohammed's teaching at Mecca, the mystical Prophet of Islam ardently hoped and preached for the conversion of all Jews to his faith. He was convinced that the Jews of Medina would be the first to convert to Islam. But Israel, inflexible in its expectation, had a long road to travel alone. Our refusal of Islam's new message unleashed a movement of censure against us which really took hold when the expansion of Islam ceased. Criticism was sharpest during Islam's worst period.

It is most likely at Medina that Mohammed thought about the political organization of the new faith (between 622 and 624). He defined the attitude of rising Islam with respect to Judaism. As you know, the ensuing debate results in a definitive break with the Synagogue. A sign marks this rupture. Initially, Islam had ordered its disciples to turn toward Jerusalem when praying. Having broken with the Jews, Mohammed turns again toward Mecca. It is toward the Holy City of his ancestors that the prayer of his disciples is henceforth directed. The *Kaaba* determines once and for all the *Qibla*, the direction of Islamic prayer. This break is solely on political and social planes. Obviously, Israel and Islam will have different earthly homes. But the Arabs and the Jews will continue to be inspired by Holy Scripture. In the Mohammedan tradition, Jesus is called the Word and Spirit of Allah. Moses is no less favored as Allah's spokesman. Abraham is Allah's friend, *Khalil Allah*, or simply friend, *el-khalil*. All the prophets of the Bible are the prophets of Islam. Within the spiritual heritage of Israel, Mohammed finds the bases and inspiration for his own spiritual teachings.

My friend, you are still surprised by our choice, by the Judaic refusal of the religion of your ancestors. You are still surprised that by their refusal the Jews excluded themselves from the intercession of the prophet and placed themselves in the marginal situation of second-class citizens subject to scorn and persecution.

The break between Islam and Judaism lies along these lines. The Jews, deprived of the support of their terrestrial city destroyed by the Romans, severed from the spiritual help which they found in their now-destroyed Temple, had no recourse but their bitter exile. It was no longer a matter of assuring the promulgation of the faith. Their only hope was to survive until the hour of redemption. Because of this, they were to cut themselves off in the humiliation of the ghettos, to pray for the hour of liberation. The refusal with which the Jews had answered Greek philosophy and the law of Christ was renewed and confirmed with regard to Mohammed and his teachings. What had scandalized the Christians now scandalized the Mohammedans. That the Jews denied the call and the lesson of the purest of its children was not acceptable to the Christians. Jesus was recognized as God by almost half the human race. Through his disciples, he had preached the glory of the God of Israel to the ends of the earth. According to the Christian theologians the Jewish attitude could only be stubborness, callousness, and treachery.

The theologians of Islam, especially Mohammed, were equally taken aback by Israel's refusal of the law of a Prophet who was informed by its Scriptures and its theology, and who based his authority on the revelation of its God whose plan he intended to fulfill. This is clear and no one could be surprised at the Christian and Mohammedan reactions. Our choice, in the eyes of the world, seemed absurd, our loyalty seemed to be treacherous, and our reason—based on the certitudes of our vision—madness.

The Omar Charter, which took on its definitive form in the ninth century, defined the status of the *dhimmi*, the non-Mohammedan protected by the City. He enjoyed a special statute guaranteed by Mohammedan law for the "people of the book," *ahl-el-kittab*. It protected all those who, while not adhering to Islam, remained faithful to the Scriptures which the Mohammedan religion recognized as holy. The non-Mohammedan, whether Christian or Jew, benefitted from a right to privileged hospitality. He was allowed to practice his faith and have his own religious and civil legislation under its own jurisdiction. The Mohammedan state protected his life and his property—an important point because it makes all the difference between the destiny of the Jews who lived in Dar-el-Islam and those who lived in the Christian Empire. The theocratic Christian city recognized no rights, not even the right to life and property, for those who did not share in Christ's redemption and who refused baptism.

The actual status of the Jew in the Mohammedan city varied. The Koran and traditional texts already differentiated the "people of the book" who signed the pact only under duress. Their condition was to be more difficult. Islam is essentially charitable toward its guests whom it protects. The Omayyad and Abbassid dynasties, at least at the beginning of their domination, were particularly merciful. It was from the time of the caliph Mutawakkil that the Omar charter was to restrict the *dhimmi* by a wide range of discriminatory measures which gave him lower status. Excluded from the intercession of the Prophet, in a marginal situation, the Jew was considered a second-class citizen. His situation was all the more difficult as the city in which he happened to be had greater problems. As in Christendom, he was subjected to discriminatory legislation—special taxes, prohibition of the building of synagogues (he was forced to pray in tiny rooms), prohibition of any public display of cult, exclusion from all positions of honor or authority, restriction to neighborhoods set aside for Jews, and prohibition from owning animals for riding. At their darkest hour, the humiliating condition of the *dhimmi* had, by contrast, to show the excellence of the triumphant faith. And, as in Christian countries, the Jew had to wear a special costume which made him stand out before the hostility of the crowd. These measures were taken in those countries and times when the Mohammedan people themselves were crushed by the exploitation of the conquerors of the moment. Then the children of Israel shared the misfortune of their Mohammedan countrymen and added it to the burden which their particular status imposed on them. The Christians marked by their badges with blue spheres could seek the help of their coreligionaries of the West. They stood out in the Mohammedan city, as emigrés from the interior, but at least they enjoyed some degree of protection. The Jews, wearing their badges with yellow spheres, had no recourse but to accept their fate and trust in God. Their lot was not very enviable within the theocratic structure of the Mohammedan city, but they were still far better off than the Jews in Christian countries. Graetz, the author of a ten-volume history of the Jewish people, had recognized this by the end of the last century. Ibn Pakuda, the great Jewish theologian of the nineteenth century, went still further saying that if one considered the Jews simply as another among the Arab tribes, they were decidedly not the most unfortunate. Indeed, Jewish solidarity, its high level of culture, and the outside contacts that Jewish communities succeeded in maintaining, gave them incontestable power and a standard of living often higher than that of the surrounding population.

The Mohammedans never persecuted them in any way resembling the outrages of the Inquisition, the expulsion from Spain, and even less the horror of the concentration camps and crematories in modern Europe. The hate underlying the shameful aberrations of people who had been Christianized for centuries was substituted in Islam by a calm scorn which in trying times the majority could feed upon with regard to the minority it tended to enslave. The Jews probably were consoled to see that reciprocal feelings and attitudes existed. If they were the object of scorn, the Arabs, for their part, had to contend with their own internal strife, torn by tribal rivalries, condemned to misery by an essentially feudal regime.

If, initially, Islam had contracted a debt to Judaism, during the centuries of its development, it generously repaid it by allowing a new era in Judaic history. The creation of an empire which stretched from India to the Atlantic, from Arabia to the Pyrenees, caused significant changes in the structures of the Jewish world. An economic revolution of incalculable consequences begins. The Jews disappear as a people traditionally devoted to agriculture and manual labor in order to settle in the great centers of Islam where they become merchants and craftsmen. In the vastness of the Arabic Empire, the development of business and industry favored the evolution of a rich and cultured Jewish bourgeoisie. Its most gifted children developed a new awarness of the ancient patrimony of Israel. Indeed, the Judeo-Arab symbiosis was responsible for some of the richest periods of the Middle Ages because of its cultural enrichment and the broadening of spiritual horizons. The encounter generated a widespread renaissance of the spirit which forced even Christendom to reexamine its own mission.

The Arab origin of the Bene Israel remains a theory. What is sure is that from the seventh century on, throughout the Arab Empire, the Jews changed languages and adopted the language of the Koran for communication.

From the time of the return from the Babylonian captivity in 586 B.C., Aramean had replaced Hebrew. From the seventh century on, the Jews abandon the language of the Talmud for Arabic. The power of the new language facilitated the discovery of the advantages of Hebrew for the Jews. For the first time, the language of the Bible was methodically studied by Jewish linguists and grammarians who were all born under Islam. Menahem Ben Sarouj published a dictionary of the Bible in the tenth century. In Fez, Judah Hayyuj and Ibn Janah discover the principle of triliteral roots and establish the rules of Hebrew grammar. The rebirth of the Hebrew language was possible because of the richness of Arabic. The poets, the canonists, and the theologians of the Synagogue were all enriched by the Arab language and culture. From the eighth century on, the widespread use of paper, whose production techniques had been learned from the Chinese, allowed an easier distribution of books and favored the cultural upsurge.

Throughout the Arab Empire, the internal organization of Judaism was reshaped. In the Mohammedan Empire, Jews and Christians were equal, both inferior, but both benefitting from an egalitarian legal statute. For the Jews, this situation was without precedent since they had lost their own country. For the first time in the course of history of their exile, they were no longer pariahs but had an official status which makes understandable their strong sympathy for the developing Empire. In Palestine, Syria, and Spain, the Jews helped the Arab conqueror and fought in the ranks of the Islamic armies. In Algeria, they took the side of the Mohammedan against the Christian when the latter tried to establish the Spanish flag over this part of Dar-el-Islam. The best example of the close understanding between Jews and Mohammedans is that while the Christian communities disappear very quickly in Bukhara, in central Asia, in Yeman, in Southern Africa, and North Africa, the Jews survive and ever flourish.

The internal organization of Judaism benefits from the commercial, economic, and spiritual upsurge made possible by the Arab Empire. The exilarch which was in full decline at the time of the fall of Persia, had a new flourishing of vitality and brilliance due to the support it received from the Arab caliphs. The viceroy of the Jews, the *Resh-Galuta*, considered as the heir of David, sat at the court of the caliphs where he had seniority over the Christian officials. The caliph appointed him and it was he who chose the Jewish officers of the Empire. The ancient academies of Babylon took on such a new importance and influence that the Jews call the first centuries of Islam *the Gaonic period*, named after Babylonian leaders.

The intensity of commercial relations in the Empire was a tangible sign of the spiritual authority exercised by the Jewish scholars living in the lands of Islam. This authority spread throughout the Diaspora. The transmission of the works and the decisions of these academies was facilitated by the trips and pilgrimages which the Jews willingly made to the Holy Places. The natural stops were determined by the location of the cities known for their schools, along the commercial routes which joined the East to Western Europe.

For two centuries, the caliphate of Baghdad favored the final attempt made after the end of the patriarchate in order to insure and preserve a central authority for Judaism in exile. The *exilarch* and the *geonim* had no function after the caliphate of Baghdad crumbled under the attack of the Seleucid Turks after 1055.

The brilliant civilization which marked the Fatimid caliphate in Egypt and in Syria, favored the renaissance of the Jewish community of Palestine. The Gaonim whose spoken language was Arabic, tried to revive Jerusalem as a center. The conquest of the Holy City by the Seleucids in 1070, and then by the Crusades in 1099, dashed these hopes. The Jews in Jerusalem were put to death by the Crusaders.

The fall of the caliphate of Baghdad was accompanied by the decline of Judaism in the East as well as in North Africa and marked the end of the Eastern period of Jewish history. The conquest of Baghdad by Mongolian troops put an end to the Abbassid Empire. The caliph and his family were executed in 1258. Eastern Islam's decline parallels that of Eastern Judaism. Cordoba, at the other end of the Moslem world, becomes the counterpart for Baghdad in the tenth century and the beginning of the eleventh century. As did its Eastern rival, it will cultivate the arts, literature, and science, which will come to full bloom, especially under the patronage of Hakem II and his vizir Ibn Abi Amir al-Mansur. The Mohammedans called Cordoba the pearl of the universe. So did the Jews who experienced the most fruitful years of their historic exile while in Spain. Islam's influence encouraged both the anti-Talmudic reaction of the Karaites and the upsurge of theology.

The spiritual teaching of Islam, its extreme liberalism, its receptivity to the very reality of God and the mystical destiny and spiritual avenues of the human soul reminded the Jews of some of the essential realities of faith whose importance they had often forgotten. After the exile, the rabbis had succeeded in giving a strong cohesiveness to Judaism which they had saved from extinction by enclosing it in the steel wall of Talmudic law. This broadening gave the anti-Talmudic dissidence a chance to affirm itself and to compromise for a brief time the results so laboriously gained by rabbinism. The extraordinary spiritual revolution which Islam introduced to the world and its philosophical, intellectual, political, and economic repercussions set the Jewish minds to work. Visionaries appeared to announce the end of the world and the reign of the Son of David. While the reformers waged war against the yoke of the Talmud, a messianic movement spread over the Jewish communities everywhere in Dar-el-Islam. The adventure of Abu Issa comes to mind. Between 685 and 692 he preached an apocalyptic messianism which restored Christ and Mohammed along with an in-depth reconsideration of the doctrinal bases of traditional Judaism. Mystical explosions took place in 720 when Serene of Syria claimed to be the messiah and in 760 when Yudghan of Hamadan was put to death because of his messianic claims.

Islam also inspired the reform proposed by the Karaite movement. The founder of this movement, Aman Ben David, considered the Bible to be the source of written revelation. The Bible was sufficient unto itself and every individual could by his own free examination interpret its rules. Benjamin of Nehavend, in the ninth century, and Daniel Ben Moses, in the tenth century, confirmed the Kara-

25

ite theses and defined its theology. Daniel Ben Moses is still relevant because he preached the return to the Holy Land. For him the most serious sin of the Talmudists had been to adapt the Torah to the accursed exigencies of the Exile. The return to the Holy Land was to free the people from the yoke of ritualistic law and restore it to the purity of its origins.

Islam which itself extrolled a transcendent monotheism, was very powerful in a world largely won over to mono-theism. Thanks to the decidedly convergent efforts of the Synagogue and the Church, it could meet the challenge of the wisdom of Athens fearlessly. The caliphs themselves preferred the translation of the masterpieces of Hellenistic thought into Arabic. The encounter, as you know, was dazzling and profitable not only for Islam but for Judaism and Christianity. The interpreters of the three religions ceased being exclusively exegetists of revealed Scripture and joined the school of ancient Greece.

Kairwan—the Mecca of North Africa, artistic and intel-lectual capital of Islam in its march toward the East—Fez, and Cordoba became the great centers of Jewish thought and development. The work of men such as Saadyiah Ben Joseph of Fayyum who died in 942, Solomon Ibn Gabirol who died in 1050, Bahya Ibn Pakuda, Judah Haley, and Moses Maimonides would have been inconceivable without the mediating powers of Islam and the virtues of the Arab language. Guttman, the famous historian of Jewish philos-ophy, devotes more than nine-tenths of his book to Jewish theology as it developed in Islam and in Arabic. Judaism is indebted to the Arab world which certainly has already re-paid it for the former's contribution at the time of Moham-med and in its earliest history when Mohammedan thought was defining itself in the Jewish academies of Babylon and Arabia.

It is true that Islam inspires a total reevaluation of Jewish thought. The explosion of the ghetto by its contact with Islam had put the Jews in contact with the masterpieces of Greek philosophy in Arabic translation. Pythagorus, Plato, Aristotle, Euclid, and Plotinus became accessible to the doctors of the Synagogue. The works of the Arab philosophers prepare for Islam the synthesis of Greek philosophy and the monotheistic tradition whose faith they had to rationally justify.

It is in this manner that the great philosophical movements of medieval Islam arise. Motazilitism and Kalah, and Sufism as well, will influence Jewish theology. From the ninth century on, following the long line of prophets, priests, Scribes, Pharisees, tannaim of the Mishnah, amoraim and sevoraim of the Talmud, massoretes who established the Scripture, and gaonim, a new man, the theologian of the Synagogue occupied Moses' chair. He breaks away from the exclusive meditation of the internal sources of Judaism, becomes receptive to the outside world, and allows ideas, logic, and even a language foreign to Judaism, Arabic, into his universe. The rabbis of long ago used to express themselves in the collective works which issued from the Sinai tradition which they defined and interpreted. The theologian pursues by himself, by the authority of his own name and his efforts of personal reflection, the work of his predecessors. The result is the relative richness of the intellectual creativity of the Jews in Mohammedan countries aided by the material prosperity of this Empire and the contacts it allows among the thought of the Greeks, the Arab, the Christian, and the Jews themselves. But attempts at elaborating a theology and a dogmatic of Judaism were never encompassed by the religious problem-solving of Israel. Jewish theologians could reach the heights in the area of pure thought, but the river of life flowed elsewhere. It is curious that the Jewish people who received God's revelation and the message of the Bible so enthusiastically had no strictly theological vocation as such. They could not succeed in presenting, by means of a philosophical argument, a truth whose light they perceived. What is essential to them was receiving the Word and living by it. So we have the unusual elaborations on the Mishnah, the Talmud, and the Masorah in a singular and really original language to transmit Israel's vision in the form of thought.

Schools of philosophy stimulated by teachers whose works served as bridges between Islam and Judaism cropped up everywhere in Islam. It is sufficient to cite Saadiah Gaon, Bahya Ibn Pakuda, Solomon Ibn Gabirol, Judah Halevy, and above all Moses Maimonides. After these great names, the memory of the Mohammedan saints and philosophers must be recalled—Houcein Mansour Halladj, the mystic of Baghdad who was born in 922, Abou Bakr el Wasiti, who was almost a contemporary at Ourassan, Abou Bakr el Shibli, and all the great philosophers who inspired the thought of the *Kalah*. Islam and Israel could communicate perfectly on the highest plane where their thinkers and visionaries spoke a common language, drew their inspiration from the same Semitic universe, and sang a mystical chant which mysteriously bound them, not just by common roots, but by the deepest finalities of their common spiritual adventure.

For thirteen centuries, the Arabs and the Jews in the mid-East, North Africa, and even Spain lived both in time and in space in an extraordinary unity of civilization. This unity was the reality of two religions which drew their inspiration from the same text, a civilization and culture which had common sources as their constant reference. This unity was not without sharp differences of course. The mysticism of El Hallaj and the asceticism of Bahya Ibn Pakuda cannot be confused. The theories of Solomon Ibn Gabirol have as their source Mohammedan neo-Platonism from which they differ in many ways. But this made it no less true that throughout Islam, at all times, Jews and Mohammedans considered themselves brothers living in one intellectual universe.

There remains to be written the comparative history of Jewish and Arab thought. Salomon Munk in the last century, and Vajda and Goitein in our time began to touch upon this area. Some astonishing encounters between two currents of thought will contribute a unique chapter to the history of mankind. I would like to underline at this point, the central place that poetry holds in Israel as well as in Islam. In either case, Arab or Jew, the soul seeks to express itself in lyric style. Thousands of poets, known or unknown, famous or obscure, have described their spiritual adventure, some in Hebrew and others in Arabic, confirming the essential bond between metaphysics and poetry. Jewish literature and Mohammedan literature, whether Arab, Persian, Turkish, or even Indian, recognized that this bond is organic. Only poetry is capable of conveying their metaphysical faith which was essentially not a rational written doctrine, but the result of a spiritual fulfillment. Judeo-Arab poetry is destined to reflect in a marvelous way the infinite play of the Word and its creation in the ambitious desire to lift the veil of the ultimate mystery. From Rabi'a al-Adawiya who lived in the tenth century to Nabalousi in the nineteenth, from Bahya Ibn Pakuda to Nahman Bialik in the twentieth century, the same song born of the same inspirations celebrated the same realities about the soul and about man such as they were received and acknowledged by descendents of Abraham.

The Arabs were the people of reconciliation, par excellence.

It is not by chance that the principal school of exiled Judaism was that of the Pharisees. The *Perushim*, as their name indicated, are "those who separate themselves." Strictly speaking, Judaism of the exile was a Pharisaic Judaism whose dominant tendancy was toward separation. It was a question of a fundamental requirement vital to our survival. The sole thought of the doctors of the Synagogue had been to save the vestiges of the authenticity of a people and a tradition which risked disappearing. We had to separate ourselves from everything which was not our profound source, our essential spiritual reality, in order to save the feeble chance for our survival and rescue the fragile spark still shining in us from its darkest hour. We had to refuse everything which might make us deviate from the straight and difficult path. Invariably, everything which was alien to our mission seemed a temptation which it was our duty to repel. After having foreseen the potential of Greek philosophy at the time of the second Temple, the rabbis strictly cut themselves off from it after the victory of the Macchabees. The catastrophe of the year 70 entrenched them in the refusal of all dialogue with the pagan powers. They strongly repudiated any temptation toward syncretism, refusing Hellenism and Latinism. Even Philo of Alexandria was unknown to

Judaism during this entire period. Although he had made
the first great philosophical synthesis of Hellenism and Judaism, he was almost unheard of by the Jews during the
twenty centuries of their exile.

Judaism often defined itself in contrast to Christian
thought and had no communication with Islamic thought
except during Islam's heydey, at the golden age of Spanish
Judaism from the ninth to the thirteenth century. Even then
it fell short of real dialogue. This is the trap in which history
had caught us. Hebraic thought developed during centuries
of constant contact with Greek philosophers, the Christian
faith, and Islamic thought, without feeling the need for the
slightest contact with the surrounding intellectual movement which was developing from our very sources. It is
staggering to think that Athens, so near Jerusalem, was unaware of the intellectual movement which stimulated Jerusalem. Plato does not cite Moses. Plato and Aristotle are
practically unknown to the great masters of Jewish thought.
The Jews who had lived in the heart of the Hellenistic
world without interruption from the time of Alexander, by
one of the paradoxes which fill their history, discovered
philosophical speculation in the ninth century, and that because of the intercession of the Arabs. But the Jewish authors who are influenced by it, such as Bahya Ibn Pakuda,
Solomon Ibn Gabirol and even Maimonides remain, in spite
of everything, marginal to the core of Judaism.

Bahya Ibn Pakuda is a concrete example. His admirable
Introduction to the Lessons of the Heart, is inspired on
every page by the great mystical texts of Islam. He constantly cites the *Encyclopédie des frères sincères* but does
it simply by making a general reference to sages of nations
without specifically stating his sources. He is even bold
enough to cite the words of Jesus, being careful to say that
they are taken from the Bible of the Moslem Haddit describing the acts of Jesus. One must not be shocked by this.
Numerous are the Jews who, in the course of their exile,
discovered Christian thought and loved it. They became
Christians and disappeared as Jews. So it was for those who
were tempted by the splendor of Hellenistic philosophy.

The spiritual sons of Philo of Alexandria were integrated into the Hellenistic world without leaving any issue in Israel. Countless also are the Jews converted to Islam. They also cut themselves off from the Judaic adventure. Only a small number remained Jews, those who accepted unflinchingly the great impoverishment and often bloody humiliation of the Judaic condition for centuries.

The Monogolian invasion and the Turco-Mongol wars weakened the Mohammedan East considerably, while in Spain, the Christian *reconquista* had started. Its decisive moments were between 1085, the date of the reconquest of Toledo by the Catholic kings, and 1248 when, after the decline of Almohades, Seville broke off from the Mohammedan Empire. The principality of Granada, governed by the Nasrides, survived for two centuries longer and fell in 1492, the date of the expulsion of the Jews and the Arabs from the Iberian Peninsula. From the sixteenth to the twentieth century four independent empires divided up the greatest portion of the lands of Islam: the Ottoman Empire which stretched its direct power or its sovereignty over Asia Minor, Mesopotamia, the Balkans, the Crimea, the Islands of the Aegean, Egypt, Libya, Tunisia and Algeria; the Persian Empire, governed by the Safavid dynasty; the Indian Empire of the great Mongols of Turkoman or Mongolian origin and Sunnite obedience; and finally, the Shereefian Empire of Morocco which managed to remain independent from the Ottomans. Throughout its territory and with the exception of its period of cultural glory in Persia in the seventeenth century, the sixteenth century marks the beginning of a period of economic and cultural decadence for the Arab world. The Christians and Jews of the East share in this general movement of progressive sterility of a world which had so powerfully contributed to civilization's great development.

It is from these perspectives that our lives emerge—in the fervor of the walls and streets of Jerusalem. For all of us— Christians, Mohammedans, Jews, Arabs of Palestine, or Europeans settled among us, the English included—the days pleasantly flowed by. The baccalaureat examinations took us by surprise. Only a concentrated daily effort made it possible for us to meet this first academic challenge successfully. After we passed the baccalaureat, our families decided to send us to Paris to further our studies. We were the first in our Old City to enjoy such a destiny. The crusades had changed directions. We arrived in Paris with the souls of conquerors.

2 Twilight

The year was 1933: one automobile picked us up to take us both from Jerusalem to Haifa over the road which passes through Nablus. The boat which brought us to Marseilles allowed us to discover for the first time the eastern Mediterranean. We scarcely noticed the British colonials and tourists who surrounded us. The arid rocks and sand which we had just left, our world of olive trees and cactus, of orange trees and pines, heightened our nostalgia. A line from Mallarmé expressed our joy very well: "Je suis hanté: l'azur, l'azur, l'azur, l'azur" [I am haunted: the blue sky . . .]. We were suspended in the infinite blue between sky and ocean.

For the first time in a long time men of our race were leaving their Asian birthplace to set sail for Europe. During the long family evenings in the courtyard of the house covered with its red stones—sign and glory of Jerusalem—your mother would reflect upon the history of our two families, retracing every branch and destiny from generation to generation: as far as man could remember, nothing similar had happened. Our mothers spoke to each other either in Arabic or in Ladino. When you were a baby, your mother was sick for a time and could not nurse you. My mother nursed you, confirming in the eyes of everyone in the neighborhood the existence of a true family bond between us.

We weighed anchor and pulled away from the gravity of the ages. We were discovering the advantages of being abroad and we marvelled at everything: the rhythm of the ocean, the rolling of the waves, the endless scenery, the biting wind, the schools of dolphins appearing on the seafoam from time to time and trying to race our boat, the light playing in the full fires of the sun at twilight, in the secret of the night or in the sudden bursts of dawn, and finally, the dazzlement of the ports of call. We had chosen the longer route, the Greek islands and Piraeus, the straits of Sardinia and Stromboli, Naples, Genoa, and finally Marseilles.

After so much sun and blue, the pastures, the forests, the vineyards, seemed to be a miracle. So much green after the barren rocks and sand of the hills of Judea! We had never imagined that such a lush and cultivated world could exist. It seemed as though we had entered a new universe. Was it the universe of grace? In the joy of our discovery, we were ready to believe it.

In Paris, we took rooms not far from rue Mouffetard, in a little hotel, rue du Pot-de-Fer. We were very near the quays and only minutes from the Sorbonne and Notre-Dame. From our balcony on the sixth floor we overlooked the roofs of Paris, the city which would let us discover both the world of the intellect and the world of the heart at the same time. Our university studies gave us more than an occupation—they opened wide the doors of knowledge for us. We read anything that happened to fall into our hands. The events which were occurring around us, the rise of the Popular Front, the establishment of Hitler's empire in Germany slid over us as if we were not really affected by every development. Mussolini's invasion of Ethiopia, the war in Spain, Hitler's seizure of power, all seemed secondary by comparison to the awakening of our minds and paled in the light of the intellectual progress we were making. Everything was new in this marvelous universe which offered itself to us. We distinguished badly between light and shadow. At secondary school in Jerusalem, we had been smug about our literary preferences and life had a tendency to become confused with our dreams. Now we were being carried away by our enthusiasm for the sensual fervor of an André Gide or the ontological ecstasy of Spinoza. But our year of philosophy and our contact with our French teachers and friends offered us more solid nourishment. While you were engrossed in Karl Marx, I began to get acquainted with the Bible which distracted me from the seduction of pantheistic thought. It became my guide as I discovered, by myself and for myself, a transcendent reality at the fountainhead of the Infinite.

Books, museums, our long treks across Europe discovering

Italy, Spain, the Scandinavian countries, Belgium and Switzerland, our gambits across France, bicycling over the roads of Provence, our awe at Chartres, the chateaux along the Loire, the romanesque churches of Moissac or Vézelay were less meaningful for us in the long run than the warmth of the Parisians. With what wonder we felt the human solidarity which emerged from a ride in the Métro or an hour spent in a café! Our student evenings in the Latin Quarter or at the Cité Universitaire shook us from our lethargy, tore us from our torpor, and opened the great chambers of our minds. We established so many friendships that they finally broke our atavistic resistance. The authority of our teachers, their merit, and even their contradictions united us with the great currents of civilization. They oriented us to the modes of a new thought and permitted us to understand, from a new perspective, what was happening around us and in the world.

Do you remember Arthur Plessier? We met him at a lecture and soon took a liking to him. With such delight we would often scale the steps of the towers of Notre-Dame to sit by the side of the organist during Sunday mass, you the Moslem, I the Jew, with him the Christian, to commune there, thrilled by the organ music and the solemnities of the Christian liturgy. In spite of the years, the memories remain engraved in my mind. I see you next to Karine, the Swedish friend you met one day in the courtyard of the Sorbonne. She had been attracted by your facial expression, and was to understand you better than you, yourself, ever had. Friendship was not slow to become love. There was such a violent contrast in your personalities that you must have both tortured and enriched each other as you shared everything during the many years of your life together. You were like the alliance of water and fire, of earth and air. The two of you, she the Nordic, the Christian, and you the Palestinian Moslem, were a symbol and an omen in our eyes. To what extent did she help your development? To what extent did she shackle the soaring of the genius we recognized in you?

With the ease of genuine talent, you reached the head of the class. When your father died, a wealthier uncle took charge of you. He also had greater ambitions for you. When you first arrived in Paris, you were far behind the others. We watched you and were dismayed that you couldn't pronounce a single foreign word without a telltale Asiatic accent. Yet in a few months you succeeded in catching up and finished the year with honors. Our teachers recognized a mathematical genius in you. We were sure to have a young Einstein among us. Later, you were to have a brilliant career. Yet, you disappointed us. Was it Karine who was responsible for the conflict in you? Or, rather, was it her presence which tore you away from a strictly book-oriented, professorial career to restore you to your vocation as a champion of people's rights, a democratic leader, a revolutionary?

Our studies in Paris left us enough time to discover the universe which surrounded us—the taste of rain on our lips, endless walks in the forests of the Ile de France, enraptured contemplation of cathedrals and churches, cold chills in the thick fog of the quays along the Seine in winter, the full peal of the bells of Notre-Dame. We experienced the exhilaration which comes with new purposes, and sleepless nights, too, as we recalled the tumultuous spiritual and political conflicts which made our youth so exciting. We were carried away with the discovery of man's thought, his magnanimity, and his feelings. There was anguish, too, as we became aware of ourselves in the midst of the excesses of Paris and of Europe on the eve of the confrontation of the Second World War. In our youthful exuberance, everything alarmed and exalted us: Hitler's rise to power, the revolution and war in Spain, the conquest of Ethiopia by Fascist Italy, the struggles of the Popular Front, the rise of perils in Europe, fascination with the Nazi Moloch. We finally recognized, instinctively, the price we would have to pay in blood for our right to live.

We were discovering the contradictions of the West. We shuddered when we realized the first truth about this civilization which, from the beginning, had conquered our hearts and dazzled our minds. The West was gripped by fear. Our most learned Parisian friends and teachers helped us, by their lucid explanations, to understand what cast a horrible shadow over the West and all its luxury. It was a fear akin to that of seeing worlds collapse, worlds which, nourished

by the past, had not known how to surpass it. The truth of
Valéry's great words had stung Europe: "Nous autres, civil-
isations, nous savons que nous sommes mortelles" [Among
ourselves, civilizations, we know that we are mortal]. Liberal Europe failed in its attempt to avail itself fully of the
plenitude of the finite world. Beneath the drive for power
which served to mask its guilt the West nurtured its anxiety
in the unconscious certitude that all its accumulated splen-
dors would end up being destroyed in some great cataclysm.
Intuitively, we became aware of the vanity of a civilization
which, while being itself ensconced in blind materialism,
purported to be the champion of liberty and of spiritual
values. The terrible fear of the West was that of seeing the
power which it had so patiently accumulated, and which
had made it possible to dominate the world, slip away. In
the darkness and enslavement of war the colonial era was
nearing its end.

Yes, the West was trembling with the discovery that it
was mortal. We soon found out that states, establishments,
nations, families, provinces, individuals were choked by an
unnamed and limitless fear. Fear was everywhere. It was
rotting the gigantic tree of the modern world from tip to
trunk. France was afraid of Germany, England feared Europe, the United States distrusted France and Germany, as
well as Italy and Spain. Everywhere the "free" world fed
on the inextinguishable hate of communism. The awakening
of China made all the chancelleries of the world tremble,
while Hitler, Mussolini, and Franco used the formidable
power amassed by Western civilization for the purposes of
enslavement.

In France, the right feared the left, while the left decried
with hate the fascism which was triumphing in Spain and
in Italy, and had succeeded absolutely in Germany. The
Church, too, was quivering at the threat of communism and
atheism. The class struggle took on a more vicious character
while technological progress widened the abyss which separates generations. We had felt the great force which the
Popular Front had unleashed. For us the triumph of the
Socialist Party led by Léon Blum constituted France's unbelievable and paradoxical response to the hate coming out

37

of Germany. While Hitler was rearming his country, Léon Blum was thinking about paid holidays and was setting up a revolutionary program of social legislation for France. This was France's irony—a Jew, and an esthete at that, was to be chosen by the Church's eldest daughter to oppose the delirium of German National-Socialism. Contradiction gnawed at the foundation of Western civilization whose roots struck deep into the soil of the supernatural peace of the Christian mystery. The entire tree was bending low. The world, choked by a terrible fear, sought escape in the anxious search for power and diversion.

I am still astonished at how easily you, the Arab from the heart of your deserts, and I, the Jew, product of my ancestral ghettos, were snatched up by the whirlwind of Western civilization. We considered ourselves its children. What a phenomenal metamorphosis of our beings, of our thoughts, of our hearts, of our very language—cut off from our roots, we continued to live! Our families had remained in the closed system of our original milieu. Moslems or Jews, they were attached to the Semitic world, to the Arab language, to the religious traditions and folklore of Islam and Judaism which recognized themselves as sisters. By becoming students at the University of Paris, by feeding on French secularism, and by learning Western techniques of thought and investigation, we were accepting, unconsciously, separation from our origins. Our return visits to parents, great-grandparents, great-uncles and aunts, afforded us all the former pleasures, but our heart was far from them. We had become the disciples of Valéry, Rousseau, Voltaire, and the Encyclopedists. "The Passion according to Saint John" thrilled us; the harmony of the "Ninth Symphony" transported us. We continued to be attentive to Jerusalem's history, we followed family developments, we rejoiced in each birth and we mourned each death. We still could laugh at the typical jokes whose humor depended on the flavor of the Arab language and not on its richness of thought. But our soul was far from home.

Such is the magic of French culture: its capacity to integrate men from all over the world. It tries to make them free citizens of the "régions des Égaux" of which Victor

Hugo spoke. We thought that we had become French in the full sense of the word. We felt at home at the university, in the homes of our friends, in every moment of our daily lives. Everything was accessible: the nation, the people, and even the churches which we could attend without fear. In our youth, religious and social segregation had tended to confine us to our respective ghettos. I remember my childhood fears—I had never set foot in a church in my native land. Just passing in front of one made my heart jump into my throat. Christian anti-Semitism had drawn an apparently impenetrable curtain between Israel and the rest of the world. Once (it was either in Paris or Strasbourg) I had spent some time reflecting upon the statue representing the Synagogue. It stands over the threshold of the cathedral, blindfolded and with broken sceptre, next to the statue of the Church triumphant. The medieval sculptor had covered the eyes to symbolize error. I was overcome with the urge to climb its pedestal to tear off that blindfold. I would have liked to unveil the true face of the Synagogue and shout to the world: "See how beautiful she is."

As adults in Israel we dared not enter a church nor cross the threshold of a mosque or synagogue unless we had been born into the sociological framework of which these places of worship were a visible expression. The mosques of Roc and of El-Aksa, the esplanade of the temple, and David's tomb, were off limits for Jews. We were barely tolerated in the other places of worship in the Holy City, and sometimes even turned away when we were recognized. We were hopeless prisoners of a fragile and narrow social system.

In Paris all the artificial barriers were suddenly removed. We had rediscovered our human freedom, and with it our ethnic consciousness and pride. All this seemed perfectly natural. We accepted, as a matter of course, French civilization and the generosity of our new friends who had accepted and loved us despite our race and our religion, simply because we were young, and because we were alive. Consequently, in the struggles of the war and decolonization we found out how much that which had seemed so natural when we were twenty was nothing less than the miracle of human solidarity, just as freely given as life and love.

39

Essentially our experience during this period of our lives was marked by a double transformation. First, we were transplanted from one cultural, spiritual, and social milieu to the Parisian universe, deep in the heart of Christian and Western culture. Then we took an inverse step toward the recognition of our origins, while remaining in the center of European civilization.

As we were growing up, our secondary-school years had turned us into young socialists and revolutionaries. We fancied ourselves atheists, dispassionately detached from family ties. Neither of us could explain why our ancestors had lived and suffered for their faith. We were totally unaware of everything that concerned the religious perspectives of Judaism and of Islam. Western philosophy had won us over. Secular or religious, it constituted the almost exclusive basis for our formation and inspiration. The real treat was to read Pascal, Bossuet, Valéry, and Claudel. Even that respect which we meant to devote to our family world, its beliefs and traditions, depended on our adopted spiritual universe. French universalism encompassed everything, explained everything. Yet, carelessly, we had stopped participating in the universe of our origins. We had forsaken our little garden to cultivate the wonderful park which now sheltered us, a French-styled park, filled with shade and splendor. There we experienced the intoxication and the joy of living.

Three years in Paris, as the Second World War approached, shattered the security we had developed. Two aspects of the situation forced us to reexamine our stand and led us to reevaluate our origins. First, the discovery of the Western sources of thought, of European art and civilization thrilled us. But juxtaposed was the monstrous and soon horrible nightmare which Hitler would subject us to. It still amazes me today to think that by such diverse ways, and by paths so often contradictory, our directions finally converged. You suffered, and were obsessed with the widespread Arab misery which Paris itself had disclosed. Your Moslem brothers were subject to foreign domination in almost the entire expanse of the Arab world. Now you saw what our earliest existence, in the surroundings of our native milieu, had not allowed us to see so clearly. Paris had enlightened you and made you realize that the misery of the colonized Arab peoples was neither inevitable nor necessary.

The ignorance, poverty, and disease which gnawed at your people suddenly was unbearable for you. Your brother's hunger became your own. His servitude kindled your impatience and your revolt. For you, the enemies were your father, your grandfather, your uncles, your Arab friends who played the game which permitted this great misery. *Effendis* and *sheikhs*, *cadis* and feudal lords, were but intellectuals enslaved to their income. You began to hate them instead of the European who had established his dominion in our land. Deep inside, you could identify more with the Frenchman, or with the English liberal, than with the conservative Arab. By the end of your years of study, you and the subjugated, ignorant masses worn by poverty and disease had no language in common. You were further and further alienated from the privileged Arabs who profitted from the colonial regime to ensure their own power and fortunes. I was disturbed that the more uprooted you became the more you hated your father. I was afraid that you might imitate Ahcene, our fellow student, who at Ramallah, one day, loaded his rifle and shot his father in cold blood.

The same drama of revolt against the situation in which we all were trapped, pushed you toward Marxism. With that passion you discovered the world of Karl Marx! How enthusiastically you enrolled in the cells of the French Communist Party! With what impetuosity you followed the awakening of the nationalist movement and its struggle against the colonial regimes throughout the Arab world. Paris prepared you not so much for a profession but for your deepest vocation, that of a leader, a revolutionary who was to direct the fight which would permit the Arabs in Africa and Asia to regain their integrity.

The reasons which made you discover your Arab culture gave me back my Israel with equal force.

In those days we frequently made excursions to the hills of Judea, to the Negev and Sinai, whose beauty was breathtaking. You did not know how the swastikas which we saw covering the walls of our cities and villages disturbed me.

You were unaware of the zeal with which I read all anti-Semitic literature, while you gorged yourself on nationalistic and Marxist books. I was driven by the poison which Hitler and his partisans ceaselessly injected into our souls. We had already learned as children that we were hated because we were Jews—as adults we found out that not only were we despicable, but we were liable to death to boot. Paris showed me the true impact and dimensions of evil. The relentless campaigns of certain newspapers given to Jew-baiting, the echoes which reached us from Germany, Hitler's speeches, the accounts of the Jewish refugees who escaped from persecution in Eastern Europe, and finally the arrival in the European capitals of German refugees whose welcome we took upon ourselves, all removed any remnant of apathy. Again I had to question my beliefs. Moreover, in the whirlwind of so much hate, the discovery of the true face of Christendom, hardly discernable in our Asian deserts, was a revelation. I marvelled at the infinite God whom I found under the arches of Notre-Dame. Bergson, Péguy, Claudel were the masters who made it possible for me to reconsider the cold structures of materialistic thought.

You also know the role which Anne played in my life. She was preparing to leave her home and family about that time, to enter the religious life. She intended to complete her theological studies in the convent and subsequently to go out to live among the lepers in Africa and devote her life to them. She was beautiful, young, and desirable. Our destinies had mingled at the threshold of the convent she would finally enter a few years later. Through her I discovered not only love, but the Christian roots of Western civilization as well. She was a musician. The suppleness of her body, the flexibility of her mind, her keen intellect, the impelling anguish under the apparent gentleness of her entire being, the absolute which was translated by each word and each gesture, designated her as the one to guide me to the heart of Western civilization and, later, to drive me out of it. What she sought and found in me was the Semitic and Biblical East. She learned Hebrew with incredible ease. The Psalms and the Song of Songs became her prayer. Her despair cried out to all of us as dangers mounted on the eve of the Second

World War. Thanks to her, for the first time perhaps, I understood the true meaning of man's freedom. It was also at her side that I discovered the true power of prayer. I began to go to church with as much fervor as I had in my youth when I would go to the synagogue with my father. More than being overcome by the beauty of the liturgy and the music, I was overwhelmed to rediscover in the very heart of French civilization the presence of the prophets, the apostles, the judges, and the kings of Israel. In the play of light on the stained-glass windows, the splendid sculptures, the subtlety of the lessons engraved on the columns, we discovered together our common origins and the values for which her Christian ancestors, just as the Jews the world over, had fought and suffered for a hundred generations. We rediscovered the Testament of Israel, lovingly sustained and protected in the very heart of Christian Europe. And while so many European peoples aimed their weapons and their hate at us, Anne understood that her roots reached as far as our Eastern sources. It was the period when Pius *XI* proclaimed: "Spiritually we are Semites." Her conversion was both an indignant protest against the anti-Semitism of the world and, more important, an offering made to hasten the hour of final reconciliation.

While you led Karine to the discovery of the workers' movement, while you used your vacations to work in factories, to participate in union struggles, riding on the crest of the Popular Front's triumph in France, Anne and I, set out to explore Christian Europe. From church to church, from monastery to abbey, I learned how the Christians had received, understood, and interpreted the teachings of my Hebraic Bible. Contemplating the kings of Israel who mount their eternal guard at the porticoes of the cathedrals, hearing the ancient Gregorian chant which reminded me of the canticles they still sing in the Eastern synagogues, hearing Christian voices expounding upon the ancient Jewish tragedy touched my heart, as Hitler's threats wounded more deeply each day as he delivered his mortal blows.

Colonialism, racism—the roots of the evil which plagued us (the Moslem and the Jew) were identical. In that too, we were brothers. We understood it more deeply one night, at

43

the Cité Universitaire, Boulevard Jourdan, when we heard a shot in Ahmed's room—we dashed in to find the blood-covered body of our friend who died in our arms. Europe was sick, and its malady would have killed us too if we had not chosen to engage ourselves in the heroic madness of our struggle.

The shock of the European crisis ended our round of pleasures and broke the Gidean spell in which so many of our friends had become entangled. My latest attraction, for Spinoza, was consumed by the new fire which the rediscovery of the Bible kindled in me. This marked the awakening of my soul. Paradoxically, the Biblical texts I had learned during my childhood took on a new meaning as I experienced their richness in the atmosphere of the West. Scripture suddenly began to speak to me in a way it never had before. It became for me the way, the life, and the truth. Its words were burning symbols, and my thirst for the absolute which I sought to quench in them became more driving as the reality which we two twenty-year-olds were discovering in Europe appeared more desperate.

The loudest voices to be heard came from Germany. Nazi violence, Hitler's insane speeches, the vile anti-Semitic propaganda of his French emulators disoriented me. I was forced anew to seek out my origins and probe more deeply into their significance. Since 1933 I had become conscious of my Jewishness due to Hitler. The Bible, insofar as it is recognized as a Holy Book, the Hebraic language venerated as a sacred tongue, and the synagogical liturgy, were for me only a past from which I had thought myself liberated. In the broadest sense of the term, I had become a young Westerner of French culture, convinced of the depth of his roots in modern society. Now, a man called Hitler was propagating a racial doctrine which made a pariah of me. The Hitlerian influence began to make itself felt in France. Political parties appropriated Hitler's slogans and Goebbels' anti-Semitic propaganda. Newspapers such as *Candide*, *Gringoire, l'Action Française*, poured out a poison which, paradoxically, acted as a stimulant on us. It was ironic, but we, too, were caught in the trap of anti-Semitism as we probed into the heart of French civilization and the soul of

Christianity. The challenge which I had to face, that of Hitlerian racism, pursued a certain image of the Jew. It was the Jew I tried to rediscover in myself. Again, I chose the way of the synagogue. I accompanied my father there every morning when I was lucky enough to be home and near him. I watched every gesture of the rabbi as I eagerly followed the liturgy. My year became filled with the ancestral rites inherited from the Bible.

For my father, being a Jew was getting up at dawn to gird his forehead and his left arm with leather lanyards to recite the ancient liturgy inspired by the Psalms. For my community, it was keeping holy the Sabbath day, and all the commandments of the Bible. For us all, it was the memory of the old glories of Israel, of the message delivered there by the prophets. It was also the hope for messianic deliverance. Each gesture which defines the life of the Jew reflected and stirred that desire each hour of each day. It was the hope for a final reconciliation when unity, solidarity, love, and justice, would prevail over all humanity. It was the dedication to a certain image of man, the Sage, who had many qualities in common with the Philosopher of Ancient Greece. It was the hope for the triumph of the God of Abraham, Isaac, and Jacob, of the personal God-who-became-Flesh in the course of history and who was to prevail when men would finally be delivered from all tyranny, liberated from all servitude and superstition, free, in a world cleansed of all its idols.

What I saw around me was very different from the portrait of the Jew spread by anti-Semite propaganda. There was no resemblance between the Jews I knew and the money-hungry, blood-thirsty monsters which Nazi propaganda presented for the masses to hate. Alas, I saw the shortcomings of this universe where I had grown up, its fears and shadows, its prejudice and parochialism, and sometimes, as contradictory as it may seem, its intellectual indigence. I understood very well how our Jews had ended up captives of the ghetto, where they had found the refuge which saved them from adversity. The poverty of this society was above all a material one. That was evident in the ghettos where our friends had grown up in Morocco, in the south of Algeria and of Tunis, and in the expanses of Asia. The Arabs were poor, but very often the poorest of the poor were the Jews of the ghettos of the Islamic countries. In Paris, we were to discover together the wretchedness of the Arabs from Algeria and the poverty of the Jews driven from the ghettos of central and eastern Europe. We used to see them arrive, and were saddened by their tattered clothing and their dramatic faces framed by their long beards and earlocks, and their look of tracked animals.

Each day the propaganda media faced us with a hate whose violence acted on us like a drug. A new sense developed in us as we could foresee the blow which was going to hurt us. At a glance, we could detect in a book or a newspaper the phrase intended to insult Jews. At social gatherings we suddenly felt the conversation crystalize on the anti-Jewish theme. I was never able to ease the blow by saying: "Stop, don't hurt me. I'm a Jew." Rather, I remained as silent as I could and showed my reaction only when my pain caused by the scorn and stupidity became unbearable. One day at the university, Condopoulu was boasting of being able to detect Jews by their smell. You saw me become pale. But it was I who made excuses for him and stopped you from striking him. "Let him alone. He probably has had a bad day."

Arab or Moslem, were you better off? The evil from which you suffered was no less deep, but it took on more subtle forms. No one has yet dared to present hate for the Arab and scorn of Islam as a doctrine of universal salvation. Even the fiercest of colonials never has seriously entertained exterminating all the Arabs of the world. But that was exactly what was going to happen to the Jews.

The Hitlerian drive obliged us, willing or not, to reconsider all our values. Progress, liberty, fraternity, equality, justice, all became distorted realities in the din of the anti-Semite press and its repercussions. Hostility affected our sensitivity as salt to a wound. To escape despair we had to find a new meaning for life. You pursued your communist dream, while I, motivated by the Bible, undertook the discovery of the realities of spiritual life. God was no longer an empty notion for me. He became a personal presence, alive and life-giving. My eyes were opened by several examples around me. Swami Siddesvaranander gave me some clues. Our mutual friend Émile showed me the power of losing oneself when he renounced the world to shut himself up in a cloister because of the joy he found in Christ. Renée, whom we had both known, also surprised us when she left the world, professed her vows and departed for the Cameroons to care for the lepers.

And our leprosy, the leprosy of the Jews, who would care for that?

I felt a compelling need to return to my origins to examine the innermost recesses of my mind so that I, too, could give myself to this new God whom I discovered one day in the depths of my being—the God of Abraham, Isaac, and Jacob.

Our life and our studies changed in content but not in orientation. While you were becoming involved with the Communist Party, I was enthusiastically broadening my understanding of the meaning of the Bible and its great Hebraic commentaries, the Talmud and the Cabala. One of our Jerusalem schoolfriends introduced me to Israel's esoteric thought and became my first teacher. He was to guide my first steps and orient my research after this return to my father's house. Involved in our communistic or rabbinical cells, we burned with the same fire.

Anti-Semitism and Jewish suffering, colonialism and the humiliation of the Arab peoples took on their real meaning in Paris. The world from which we came appeared in a new light, in sharper relief and with greater cruelty. It was in Paris under the double motivation of hate and love that we became aware of ourselves, of our Semitic background, you the Arab, I the Jew, both foreigners even though we had been accepted and loved by the people of the West. Even this capital where the great revolutionary ideas had been proclaimed, where the Christian virtues had known their most exalted forms, we heard the Jews insulted almost every day just as we discovered anti-Arab racism. The North-Africans were called *"ratons"* and *"bicots,"* the blacks were *"macaques,"* and we were *"youpins"* [yids]. The horror that we so discovered had the same source and touched us in the same way. You became aware of colonial scars in all the

lands of Islam. You were troubled by the subjection, sometimes even enslavement, of your people, and the subtle forms
it took, as scorn affected the life of both master and victim.
Our absence from our native land allowed us a sharper
awareness of it. Freed of our former complacence, we became personally involved in the tragedy—you, Ahmed
Benghanem, physicist, offspring of a long line of Moslem
sheikhs, raised in the Shyite rite and the spirit of the mystics
of Islam, and I, Mattatias Mizrahi, descended from a line of
rabbis, raised in the shadow of the Middle Ages and under
the vaults of the Stambouli synagogue, in the old city of
Jerusalem. The lash of the West drove us from our placidity
and our somnolence and forced us into a whirpool of mounting peril and blood.

Our uprooting and its anxieties saved us from conformity.
It was easy to detach ourselves from our acquired roles and
to look objectively at the world we had left behind and the
one to which we were eagerly seeking to belong. We hoped
it would allow us to cross the impasse and build the future.
We were brought closer together by an equal repugnance
toward the forms of bourgeois life that we had known in the
Levant. In some circles the supreme commandment was to
"enjoy life," a rather modest enjoyment which consisted
first of subordinating everything, even life itself, to the furor
of making money, then spending it on the consumption of
as many objects as possible, including women. Eroticism
took a brutal hold. The neighborhood Don Juans considered
it in good taste to boast of their conquests and to equate the
excellence of each conquest to its cost. In those days this
was the way in which one tried to place oneself outside the
criteria of good and evil. Paris broke our shackles, gave us
back the liberty to judge more objectively and sometimes
cruelly, our old milieu and the new one which welcomed
us with such total openness.

The Cité Universitaire and the Latin Quarter were headquarters for our exciting discovery. We met less often than
in the streets of Jerusalem, but our relationship became more
intimate. We recognized our fundamental identity and de-
emphasized the differences which formerly used to irritate
us. Our identical reaction with regard to the Parisian en-

vironment brought us still closer. We were both fish out of water.

We had preconceived notions about Western civilization. We thought that it drew its fundamental individuality from the Athenian heritage and knew that its institutional structures were impregnated with the aristocratic spirit of Rome. Our surprise was to find how much the Judeo-Christian element of its spiritual tradition was the secret motivation of its innermost dynamism. Together we discovered and read the books which enlightened us on the triple sources of European civilization. We had learned that the first current, the intellectual one, began in Athens. Rome had given Europe its structures and its law. I was more sensitive to the fact that Israel had provided, through the Bible and the Christian Church, the sources of its mysticism. The taste for logical thought clearly came from Greece and imposed the new norms of thought on Europe. Thanks to Athens the mind was refined. The love of art, the good, the true, and the beautiful, the love of clear and orderly ideas were the ideals received from Plato and Aristotle. We also knew that from this source derived our love of freedom of the mind and body. André Malraux had expressed the proof of this very well in the discourse on the Acropolis when, speaking in the name of Athens, he cried:

> *Jai cherché la vérité, j'ai trouvé la liberté. Je dressais pour la première fois, en face de ces Dieux, l'homme prosterné partout, depuis quatre millénaires, et du même coup je l'ai dressé en face du despote.*
> *I sought truth, I found liberty. For the first time in four thousand years man was no longer groveling and I raised him up before the Gods, and at the same time before the tyrant.*

Subsequently, I discovered that on this point, the pursuit of man's liberty, Athens and Jerusalem were not opponents. The crux of Israel's thought since its Biblical origins has been to demystify the universe, to release man from the illusion of myths, the seductions of magic and the horror of certain forms of slavery. It has constantly worked toward the freeing of the just man from the prison of his animal nature or its thought. The prophets had the heroism to denounce the idols of wood and stone that the nations, including Greece, adored. In spite of the triumph of Judeo-Christianity and Islam throughout the world, the idols have resisted and have never really been completely dethroned. We were to confront these idols under different forms. The idolatry of the modern world and the subtle forms of bondage it justifies soon seemed uglier and more inhumane than the cult of Moloch.

In the universality of the real city that we discovered within the city of Paris, it seemed clear to us that it was fruitless to compare Rome, Athens and Jerusalem. In fact, the three civilizations had recognized and met each other since their earliest origins. Jewish and Arab legalism drew its sources from Babylon and Jerusalem as well as from Rome. Athenian and Jewish thought had already met and evaluated each other in the period of the second temple before the great confrontation at the time of the Macchabees.

The discovery of the depths of Hellenistic civilization made us less complacent about ourselves. When Abraham appeared, Greece had already known the growth of Cretan civilization where metal had been used since the beginning of the third millenium. Troy had been founded and reached its golden age between 2350 and 1150 B.C. In 2100, before the birth of Abraham, the first Cretan palaces already stood. Israel had a seniority over Ishmael which pleased me. But here we were delightfully discovering together the Hellenistic civilization which went back further than our common heritage. This discovery, uprooting us a bit more, brought us still closer together.

A professor at the University of Athens, Piridos Marinathos, contends that very ancient ties existed between the Near East and Greece. It is also his hypothesis that the mythologies of the peoples of the Eastern Mediterranean have a common origin. According to him the earliest populations of Greece are of Near-Eastern origin. Because of the splendor of Athens' genius, we were drawn away from the closed Semitic world. Its history, strongly parallel to that of Jerusalem which survived it only by a century and a half, was part of our interior world. The meeting of Alexander the

Great and the Jewish leaders of Jerusalem in 333 B.C., stands as a symbol and an omen. Greeks and Jews recognize their hour of glory and great enlightment between the eighth and fifth centuries B.C. Their power is shaken from the first century on when Athens is besieged and conquered between 87 and 85 B.C. and Palestine is weakened by internal strife which prepared its downfall and conquest by Rome in the year 63. One hundred and fifty years after Athens, in A.D. 70, Jerusalem succumbs to the attack of Titus. King Areios, who lived between 309 and 260 B.C., recalled in his letter to the Palestinians that "the inhabitants of Sparta and of Judea are brothers and that they are all of the line of Abraham." Twenty-three centuries later, in the streets of Paris, threatened by a second World War, we the heirs of the recipients of that letter could feel this brotherhood even more poignantly.

Athens or Jerusalem? The dilemma which Chestov presented in offering the choice between religion *or* philosophy presented itself in identical terms despite our different persuasions. We were irresistibly impelled to strike out the *or* to substitute *and*. In this—though we did not understand it very clearly—we were the heirs of the Arab, Moslem and Jewish philosophers, who had built the first conceptual systems aimed at integrating the discursive reason of the Greeks with the order of faith. But the option was suddenly to take on a different meaning with the exigencies of the war about to break out.

We had scarcely gotten settled in the happy Parisian soil when we had to move again. For more than twenty-five centuries the psalmist had been chanting:

> *If I forget thee, O Jerusalem, let my right hand be forgotten. Let my tongue cleave to my jaws, if I do not remember thee; If I make not Jerusalem the beginning of my joy. (Psalm 136)*

That my right hand forget how to write and my tongue how to speak—therein lay the risk. Paris might make us forget Jerusalem, teaching us a new language whose genial interpretor was France. In the splendor of the new world which we had chosen and which had so generously accepted us,

Anne and Karine at our sides symbolized our neglect of
Jerusalem.

We were both awakened from our Parisian dream, I by
the clamor coming from Germany and the suffering of the
Jews being driven out by Hitler, you by the stirring of the
Arab world and its struggle against colonialism. You were
suddenly aware of the Calvary of the poor people of Africa
and Asia, especially the Arabs.

Should I admit it? I was hurt when I saw to what baseness
Europe was stooping. Of course, I was even more vulnerable
to everything which concerned what was then referred to
as the "Jewish problem." The increasingly alarming echo of
Nazi Germany's rabid anti-Semitism saddened us. I was
ashamed to see what the reactions were even in France, this
country of liberty, equality, and fraternity, where the elder
daughter of the Church had so many claims to being the
mother of civilization. I remember one night when some
French Catholics had insisted on protesting Hitler's policy of
destroying the Jewish community. Each word, each phrase
penetrated the core of my being. That night I heard Jacques
Madaule pronounce for the first time a violent indictment
of anti-Semitism in general, and of Christian peoples in particular. I discovered the reality of the suffering of the victims of Hitlerian hate, of the general indifference equally
shared by the Christians and Jews who did all in their power
to avoid making conclusions about the most obvious fact,
and I was transformed into a living wound. I suddenly knew
the true character of pain. In these thousands of Christs crucified throughout history, I learned to recognize the face of
the Christ—he too nailed to the cross by hate. I tried to escape
the torture by deepening my awareness of Israel's spirituality. Since I risked dying because I was a Jew, at least I should
know the reasons for my execution.

This marks the return to my sources from which life from
primary school through our Parisian escapade had constantly
diverted us. Jerusalem became a physical presence for me.
Each day I would think about its narrow streets, ramparts,
and towers, its cupolas, belfries, minarets, and domes, its rocks
and grottos. The city's struggles and its sectional boun-
daries where Jews, Christians, and Moslems, Englishmen,

and Arabs confronted each other seemed to be linked to the great conflict which was so visibly developing. I sometimes imagined Christ's death rattle as I walked the heights of Gethsemane. It haunted me at night when I heard the groans of all the victims of the world, victims of Hitler, victims of hunger, disease, ignorance, and oppression. Exploited black workers, slaves, Arabs exploited by the colonials—we learned to recognize the long cortege of misery which slowly moved toward us. We felt it gathering momentum as suffering became more obvious. We instinctively anticipated the horror of the appearance of the still-hidden beast.

Do you remember our summer experiences? Each year since 1935, when we arrived in Paris, I would spend part of my vacation exploring Europe. Once, drunk with sun and freedom, I reached Venice, boarded a freighter and eventually got to Haifa.

Another time I left Paris on my old bicycle. You came too. At night we camped in the fields. On the little tent that sheltered us, we wrote these words: "To live in truth." This axiom seemed to express our deepest need, a need born of the confusion which had overtaken us at the crossroads of culture where we had to live. We could just as well have chosen a verse from the Koran which I had learned from you: "Shall I seek a God other than God?" Mohammed must have put these words on our lips because of our refusal of idolatry and our quest for eternity. Will we be able not to face our brothers to ask them in turn: "Shall you seek a God other than God?" Yes, how could you avoid that question and refuse to live in truth?

Sometimes we would stay in youth hostels where we met young people from all the countries of Europe. None of us wanted to believe that catastrophe was lurking over us. Arriving in Switzerland, we were struck by the anxiety which gripped the people of this neutral country. When they found out that we came from Paris and were en-route to Jerusalem, they would barrage us with questions about peace and about the war which Europe could feel coming. We preferred to think about the clearness of the lakes, the brightness of the mountains, and the heat of the sun. Yet along our way each night we could not help falling into long discussions about

53

the suffering of our peoples. How could we involve ourselves in the inevitable fight for liberation? The causes which
transformed you into an Arab revolutionary and me into an
Israeli soldier were the same. Today I see very clearly what
mixed elements influenced the substance of our mission.
French culture made the suffering of your people unbearable in your eyes. You suddenly discovered the Arab world
totally sunk in a misery which you saw from a new perspective. The spectacle which was familiar to you and to your
ancestors who had accepted it for centuries became intoler-
able. Western opulence superimposed on Arab poverty dis-
gusted you even more. The primary problem, you thought,
was social and political. The reasons for your impassioned
conversion to socialo-communism became clearer the more
radically it cut you off from your native milieu. You considered the Arab problem primarily in its social dimension
for you did not feel threatened either at the religious or
ethnic level. Those who would deny the Jews their existence
as a religious or ethnic group accepted the Arab world with
all its variety of cults, nations, and races. "The better to exploit us," you scoffed, declaring that the crematory was at
least more honest. That is what really infuriated you. You
saw in the *muftis* and the *marabouts* the accomplices of a
regime that appeared all the more hateful to you as you
probed more deeply into solid Marxist thought. The Koran,
the Mosque, everything having to do with the cult or the
spiritual culture of Islam became radically foreign to you.
In their place you discovered the immensity of your people
and its distress. This deepened your break with the spiritual
sources of Islam as your attachment to the most extreme
socialist thought became almost unconditional. You saw
everything in the light of social realities—the Arabs exploited by colonization, Europe, France, the Church, all
Christianity, the Western world were for you only the outward manifestation of the class struggle which you de-
plored. You looked out to all the horizons of Islam, toward
Morocco, Tunis, Libya, Egypt and the Near East where
we were born. I could tell by your silence or your deeply
troubled expression that you were listening to the cries of
the Arab people—deceived, humiliated, enslaved over the

expanse of Dar-el-Islam. You knew about the ancient glory of your Arab fatherland through the books that our French professors had written, but the essence of Arab thought at the time of its greatest glory interested you less than the contrast of this glorious past with the present. You never tired of asking yourself the reasons for this decline, this humiliation, this passage from the freedom of the creator to the enslavement of subdued masses. When the war broke out, you abandoned Karine who was awaiting you in Paris. You soon left for Palestine to prepare for the future. You did not know yet which direction you should take, but you wanted to serve your people at the time of suffering and conflict. After a brief stay with your family, your first stop was a little village of Judea near Hebron, Omum Toura, where you became a teacher.

So you gave up the university career which in a more normal course of events would have been yours. Breaking with Europe, finding anew your milieu and your origins, you would speak no other language but Arabic, and thought of nothing but the liberation of your people. Among your young students in a poor mountain-school setting and surrounded by peasants who from Biblical times had been making the same gestures and using the same primitive tools, you felt the joy of having returned to your people and of offering yourself up to the struggle for your resurrection. The sole traces of the Parisian years: the complete works of Karl Marx with which you fed your hate of poverty and social injustice. It was painful to see your solitude in your new setting. In your thoughts and aspirations you were as far away from the established *effendis* and *muftis* as from the peasants you had decided to educate.

On the whole, you were closer to the British officers and administrators who ruled the country, though you hated them the most. Your Jews, especially those on the *Kibbutzim* and from the colonies remained your friends. Yet it was against them that you were to fight first. Colonialism transformed you, and Nazism transformed me, into beings marked with the seal of infamy, peripheral individuals whom society rejected. We were hurt and finally understood what the word "pariah" meant. Because you were an Arab, all your diplomas and talents were worthless. In spite of your degrees, in spite of the depth of your knowledge and intelligence, in spite of your know-how and courage, you were born an Arab, and an Arab you would remain so long as power in our homeland remained in the hands of our "protectors."

In reality there was no conflict between the irreplaceable, the incomparable magnanimity of Western culture and the interests of those who represented it in this divided country, our native land. But we both were to lose this certitude in the turmoil which was to cover Europe and closely follow in the Near East. I also felt the universe close in on us. At the very beginning I had seriously misunderstood your tension when you had to relate to French society. Even our innate lyrical enthusiam, which was practically indestructible, froze in you as soon as we broached certain subjects. When that happened I could sense that you were pierced to the depths of your soul. Sometimes, I saw something resembling hate appear. I trembled for you, for those around you, and for our human condition itself. I had an abstract knowledge of evil and of injustice but had not personally experienced them with my own flesh and blood. Hitler would make me do that. Suddenly I too was on the side of the pariahs, men whom society brutally cast off before assassinating them. Society was not subtle in its rejection and spat on us because we were Jews, *bicots* [Arabs], blacks, the dregs of the world.

While you dug further into the mountains of Judea in search of your people, I chose to leave the Sorbonne temporarily in order to study in a rabbinical school. I wanted to know more deeply exactly what my heritage meant for me, my Judaic heritage, which overnight, thanks to Hitler, had made a pariah of me. Just as you had fled toward the mountains of our country to prepare for the action which was to lead to the liberation of the Arabs, I felt that I too had to join the army of the destitute fleeing from a Europe in flames.

The Bible worked on me like a spell. I was drawn away from the views of the Encyclopedists, the charm of Voltaire, and Rousseau, the hold of French history and civilization, or of modern Hebraism, to uncover the works and events which for four millenia defined in universal history and in the heart of our civilization the reality of Judaism which religious minds considered a mystery, and freethinkers an unexplained paradox.

My French culture predisposed me to a better understanding of the originality of the thought which my ancestors had bequeathed to me. In its varied manifestations in the course of the four thousand years it encompassed, it possessed a disconcerting originality, a paradoxical and constant tenacity. The combined influences of the ancient Orient, of Hellenistic thought, of the Roman mind, of the Arab and Christian civilizations had not succeeded in making the miniscule Jewish people disappear or even deviate from its course.

I also began to read Hebrew with a new perspective. From boyhood I spoke French and Arabic fluently, but the oldest memories embedded in my soul were of the mysterious presence of the Hebraic language in our home. As far back as I can remember, my father blessed us in the language of the Bible. I still can hear him saying prayers taken from the Psalter or the Hebraic liturgy. Hebrew books were all around us. They held a place of honor—first the Hebraic Bible, but also an important number of works by the prophets or about the prophets, and by theologians who had written their works in Hebrew. My grandfather and great-grandfather had left us manuscripts from the fifteenth, sixteenth, and seventeenth centuries which we owed to the scholars of the family. They too were in Hebrew, even when they had been written in Arab countries. These works of philosophy, theology, poetry, and even a treatise on mathematics written by one of my forebears could not have been conceived outside the countries of Islam and without the deepest knowledge of the Arab's language and thought. They represented the most significant symbol of the historic treasure which evolved from our coexistence. I felt as at home in my Judaic universe as in the Arab world. Realizing the dimensions of our sister languages, I seemed to rediscover part of myself. The powerful verbal structure of the Hebraic and Arabic words and the rhythm of their unchanging roots transpose abstract thought into stark reality. The fundamentally undifferentiated character of Semitic tenses gives them an insuperable strength. The present does not exist. One is endlessly subject to the images inherited from the past and which prefigure the future. Semitic thought imposed itself on me as an imperative. It assailed me by the violence of its images and by the facts—not the ideas—which it presents to the mind, not as an abstraction, but in the relevancy of the Word which triggers the conscience. My moderation inherited from the rationalism of my teachers was swept away. Thought imposed itself as a pure act, thanks to its nondiscursive dialectic. For the first time, reading the Bible in its original text, I felt liberated from the ephemeral. A presence replaced my doubt as the dimensions of universal reality seemed to open out before me without the support of an orderly formal logic. More specifically, I found a refuge from the horrible wound which persecution had caused in my soul by a contemplation made possible by my knowledge of the Bible and its God—the God of Sinai, not the one of the Philosophers. He had become an Eternal Presence for me. I recognized the Master of history in his works—and especially in the book which related his feats, the Bible.

Thus I learned to fathom the meaning of eternity and develop a global vision of reality from the creation to the end of time. It seemed that each of the verses of the Bible encompassed everything, the beginning and the end of every single thing. This thought affirmed itself not as a hypothesis subject to revision, but as a revelation whose truth showed forth the real order of the world. Its vocation was specifically to serve the triumph of the order of unity, justice, and love.

While the flames spread over a Europe dominated by the Nazi regime and the increasing influence of its propaganda, I deepened my knowledge of Hebraic thought, sometimes with delight and even ecstasy. I recognized that the nucleus around which it unfurled in all its manifestations throughout the ages was certainly the affirmation of unity—not the abstract unity of the philosophers, but the loving reality which emanated from a divine presence, from the person of the God of Abraham, Isaac, and Jacob. Beyond the Bible, its commandments, its exhortations, the discipline which finally imposed itself on me as the fruit of its reading, I learned to know the philosophies and theologies which stemmed from it. My mind became more and more attentive to the contemplation of the everlasting. Through silence the presence of

God and his voice are revealed. As I encountered the great masters of spirituality, I tried to practice their lessons.

I would tell you about my pleasure as I discovered in myself all the resources of silence. While the world was crumbling in the tumult of the war, I found this new kingdom which our ancestors pointed out as they enjoined us to be silent and to listen: "Hear, Israel. . . ." Kneeling in my solitude, I tried to practice that command to be silent, not only with my lips but with all my senses. I tried to make myself so small, so receptive, I tried to block out the succession of ideas and images which were an obstacle so that I might attain silence of the mind. I have known my greatest moments of rapture in the loving and adoring anticipation of silence. There were times when I experienced such strength from this communion that my wretched humanity was eventually won over. I really felt, in the pacified conscience of my nothingness, the sovereign presence of a personal God of unity and love.

So I chose the retreats where it was possible for me to separate myself from all human contact to offer myself completely to the confrontation of eternal texts from which my roots drew their vigor. In the desert of Judea, I had been able to make retreats in a grotto with an admirable view. More marvelous still was the kingdom inside me whose vibrant and fervent reality I finally could know. I preferred the solitude of the desert to everything else. I had often lived in the oases of the Jordan and Sinai valleys. Alone I had travelled the roads which connected the oases and each time I rediscovered, in the immutability of the Negev, the infinite presence with which my soul became drunk. Thus, in spite of all my faults, in spite of the freedom in which we had all been raised and which we had sometimes abused, I sensed that it was possible to reach the threshold of a pure contemplation of the uncreated eternal. My instrument of meditation was a text of the Bible, more particularly of the Psalms which were dear to me not only because of the intrinsic beauty, infinitely present, but also because I had received them from the lips of my own father who knew them by heart and daily nourished himself with their prayer.

The more I thirsted, the more I discovered the inadequacies and rigidity of Judaism such as it had come to be taught in the synagogues. I went directly to the sources in order to discover the richest reality which lay beneath the humblest guises. That being so, I could not help affirming the unbelievable spiritual and intellectual indigence of the Judaism of the communities where I had grown up. In spite of the often indisputable human qualities of the rabbis, almost everything was summarized for them in a formalism stripped of substance. The prayers were recited by rote without reference to any real order of thought or knowledge. For centuries the essential effort had been to uphold the strict conformity of traditions putting off the responsibility of knowing and explicating them. At least in the traditional synogogues of the Eastern rite, I could enjoy the music, the rhythm and the rites which preserved their originality and authenticity. This I sometimes sought in vain in Western Judaism which I became familiar with during my stay in France.

While Sephardic and Eastern Jewish thought was lulled in an Orient whose ruin was climaxed by the discovery of America, the intellectual center of Judaism had shifted away from the Moslem lands to establish and strengthen itself in Christian countries. In the henceforth laicized framework of a modern world had risen a new kind of intellectual and rabbi who, without being totally uprooted from the ancient spiritual soil, proceeded from the national culture of the country in which he was born. I discovered Western Judaism at its most critical hour, when Hitler's menace was about to destroy it.

The situation was pitiful—the Hitlerian attack and the miserable display with which we faced up to it. Weakness, cowardice and apathy surrounded us. There was general blindness. Each one looked away from the dangers which were so visibly threatening the world. Even the Jews hoped that the tragedy would really be averted. I remember my shame when one of them sought to convince me that my fears were unfounded as he underscored the Jewish role in the effort which had brought Hitler to power. Jewish bankers could be deceived, be duped by themselves and by the agents of National-Socialism, but it was the entire Western world which remained blind to the triumph of Hitlerism.

"*Les cons,*"—words which Sartre attributed to Edouard Daladier—was an expression applicable, alas, to all of us, cowards who had neither foreseen nor condemned the evils of Hitlerism and who had not even attempted to stop it. At the top of the list were those who knew that they were particularly threatened and who should have foreseen that, inevitably, they would be the first victims.

You left Europe in haste. Nothing could keep you there, not even Karine. With her the break had been without trauma. The years of life shared slipped away without altering you. She had remained a daughter of the North, violent and passionate beneath her serene and cold look. You recognized the catastrophe and you left to rejoin your people. Your departure posed no problems. You only regretted that so many Arabs from North Africa and so many blacks from French Africa were going to be cannon fodder in this imperialist conflict. Hitler's anti-Semitism, his dictatorship— we knew its brutality—horrified you. But that was neither your motivation nor your fight. You suffered from the Arab complicity with National-Socialism, from the use Hitler made of the Palestinian conflict to dupe the Arab chieftans, the *Mufti* of Jerusalem for instance, and to involve them in his cause. But your motivation and your fight were not to be found there either. As the situation worsened, I found myself inextricably trapped. Not physically. When war broke out, September 30, 1939, I was with you in Jerusalem. It was there we parted ways. The world conflict had brought calm back to Palestine as if by magic. I defied my parents and took a ship for Marseilles. Then I went to Paris where I lived out that "phony war" before joining the first resistance movement which was organized in central France. The day war was declared I was hurt in an automobile accident. Scarcely out of my delirium, I opened the Bible which I always had with me in those days. It was stained with blood. The first verse my eyes fell on was this one taken from the book of Lamentation:

I am the man that see my poverty by the rod of his indignation.

3 Agony

The simultaneous discovery of the culture of the East and that of the West went to my head. My drunken feeling became more intense each day and seemed endless. Anne personified all the happiness I had found in France. She was Paris' welcome. More than a woman, she represented my repose in exile. This was not a pause in my Judaic exile, but its goal and fulfillment. For generations, since the day when the Holy Land ceased being Jewish two thousand years ago, my ancestors had known one state—that of exile and of the man on the fringes of society, a stranger to himself and to his country. In that darkness on their very own land, they had recognized their permanent state of transition—true Hebrews, if the word *ivri* implies a state of passage. My ancestors had lived in Jerusalem until the expansion of the Mohammedan Empire allowed them to move along between Asia and Spain by way of North Africa. Then they did not feel cut off from the Holy Land which itself had been Arabicized since the seventh century, nor from Jerusalem which had become a spiritual center of Mohammedanism.

Nazi aggression brought out a trait in me which was part of the very essence of the Jewish destiny and which my Jerusalemite birth had not erased—that of the exile. Throughout the world, even within the bounds of our own country we were subject to a situation which was at once our glory and our weakness. Since the destruction of our land by Roman imperialism, in our dispersion, especially where the Cross reigned, we were forced to withdraw into ourselves for survival.

We believed with the simplicity and ignorance of faith that our wandering would end—the maddest of all Utopian dreams. Endlessly we prayed for the impossible and our obstinacy grated on those who considered us a spectacle. We were very conspicuous, I must confess, and seen through strangers' eyes we, who insisted on being foreigners wherever we went so as to preserve our identity, provoked criminal desires. What did that matter! Only our dream counted. Five times a day our prayer presented the ineffable vision of redemption to us. Nothing could deter us from our transcendent way and our contemplation.

Israel's religion has always been faithful to its permanent characteristic—the participation of an entire people in a historical experience while keeping its relevance to a real situation. Incarnate thought requires active fulfillment. One of the most serious errors of contemporary Jewish thought has been to insist on a systematic apology for Judaism. Too many works speak of the "permanent values of Judaism." But these have become public domain ever since the Bible became the revealed book of the Christians and the principal source of inspiration for the Koran.

You found it curious that we spoke of Abraham, Moses, Judas Macchabee, or Titus as though we had known them. To me our entire history still seems contemporary. This paradox is tied to our historic being itself. I can understand this point better now—the misunderstanding which has separated us for so long is due to a misapprehension caused by the nature of our historic period, so profoundly different for the Arabs and the Jews. In the confinement of exile, an exile for which we had eagerly opted in the hope of the resurrection of our country and redemption of Jerusalem, time had taken on another nature and another rhythm. A year for the exiled Jew became not the time it took for the earth to make a revolution around the sun, but the number of Sabbaths which separate the reading of the first chapter of Genesis from the last chapter of Deuteronomy, the first and last public readings of the liturgical year. Between these two events the Jew—week after week, section after section of the Torah, and from one religious solemnity to another in the moon's cycle—would read the five books of the Torah and celebrate the creation of the world and the last judgment as if he were suspended outside time and space, outside the history of nations. He lived as though physically present in two privileged moments only, the Beginning and the End.

The interim, the time of nations, concerned him only incidentally—happenings along the way. The essential was the moment of the revelation of the Word and, beyond the darkness, its ultimate accomplishment.

This is the irony of history. We were separated from nations and even from the Arabs, not by an incidental refusal, but because we were committed to our time, to our Diaspora. Our suffering did not phase us. We knew that it would last only until the pendulum of history would pick us up in our dispersion to bring us back to port, to our country, the land of Israel, and its capital, Jerusalem.

I would like to share a recollection with regard to this. We were crossing the Negev once when our itinerary included a few days in an oasis. Sheikh El' Arbi, the very lettered *mufti* of the area, knowing that I was there, came to see me and as his religion commanded he extolled the merits of Islam to invite me to convert. I was touched by his sincerity. He wanted to tear me away from my repudiated religion in order to integrate me into the triumphs and the glories of the truth which he served. For him the law of Mohammed was certainly superior to that of Moses for which it was not a substitute but a fulfillment in the light of a new revelation. He emphasized the advantages which would be mine because having the privilege of being a convert, I would enjoy special status in Allah's paradise. I mildly resisted his arguments. I could have added to what he was teaching me about Islam and tell him about the origins of his religion, and confess my unreserved love for the Mohammedan saints. You see, I have loved everything I have ever known about Islam—the romance of the mosques and the minarets, the cry of the *muezzin* which I have fervently listened to daily at the minaret of El-Aksa, and even more, the thought of your scholars and the splendor of the abstract art of your mosques and palaces. For years the Koran in its original was my bedside reading. I loved its irresistible rhythms and I was familiar with its readings in the different liturgies of Islam's traditions. I felt at home everywhere in Dar-el-Islam. What I missed most during the years I lived in the West, was the Arab environment which I found comfortable and indispensable to the equilibrium of life. The discovery of Islamic thought had been an important stage in my spiritual evolution. Nourished by European thought, I felt at home again reading the great theological works which have been Islam's greatness. The historical miracle which has assured the supremacy of Islam in a large part of the world and which has made Mohammed's religion the beacon of such a vast portion of humanity, affected me even more since it is in the shadow of the Crescent that the Jews definitively found their surest refuge in the time of their exile. I listened amicably to my good *mufti* who was repeating everything I already knew. How could I shatter the faith of this man by questioning what he was telling me, which I had neither the intention nor the heart to put into doubt! And how could I tell him he was right and that I accepted each of his arguments, without adhering to the Islamic religion as he wished me to do? One day, wishing finally to speak the language of my converter, I asked him: "You Mohammedans, do you recognize the truth of Moses' Torah?" "Yes, it is the word of god," the *mufti* answered. I continued, "Do the Christians recognize the truth of Moses' Torah?" He answered, "Yes, they think that it is the word of God." I went on. "Do you recognize the truth of the teaching of the Church concerning Jesus?" He answered, "Islam feels that the Church is mistaken in affirming that Jesus is the son of God." "Does the Church recognize the truth of the teachings of Islam as far as Mohammed is concerned?" "No, the Church considers Mohammed to be an impostor," was the reply. I smiled and concluded the conversation saying, "I was born a Jew and a Jew I'll remain so long as you have not resolved your contradictions. I am satisfied with the truth on which the Mohammedans and Christians are in agreement."

While we waited for a subsequent elaboration of a messianic order—such was the principal undertaking of Judah Halevy—criticism of knowledge did not result in the rejection of philosophy but in its subordination, as a science, to theology. His attitude toward Christianity and Islam is completely anticipatory and consists ultimately in an intransigent quest for messianic triumphs. If the spiritual life springs from the communion of man with God, it is realized not by the intellect but by faith—only revelation can show man the way to union with the God of Abraham, not the God of the philosophers. Providence and love characterize the personal God of the Bible. Before it was revealed, divine reality was man's share by causality. After revelation, Israel becomes the theophoric people established in the Holy Land, mystical land of God's contemplation. The Bible makes God's teaching accessible to everybody. Halevy's particularism, different from a number of other thinkers of the time of the exile, points toward a universalism without frontiers. The law of life has been given to all humanity. Salvation is offered to all men who practice this law. Historically only the gift of prophecy is the prerogative of a select few in Israel, the prophets and the apostles of the Bible. The nations may reach the degree of wisdom which the Jews who live their faith have, but all differences are temporary. The time of the Messiah will remove all barriers. The chosen people serve as a force to push humanity toward its accomplishment. As Léon Bloy would later state, "Jewish history intercepts the history of mankind as a dam intercepting a river makes the level rise." History is the great judge which confirms the authenticity of the revelation of Moses publicly and clearly before an entire people. It is what authenticates the supernatural mission of Israel, directly ruled by the particular providence of God. The destiny of Israel, teaches Halevy, was exceptional in Biblical times. Christians and Mohammedans have long since adopted and taught this idea. But this destiny, Halevy continues, remains exceptional in the time of exile which for Israel is the time of abjection. Humiliated, banished, crucified by the exile, the Jews experience, often to the point of martyrdom, the condition of poverty and suffering consented to for the love of God—a condition which the Christians and Mohammedans regard as ideal. No doubt the Jews are forced into this humiliating position by their particular political situation. Each one, simply by adhering to Islam or Christianity could have avoided his Calvary, assumed, after all, for the love of God and in the hope of the salvation whose hour Israel's suffering brings closer. Communion with God is the source of all joy and truth. This is what allows every Jew to participate, primarily by prayer, in the religious life which is an internal phase of supernatural or suprarational prophecy. The spiritual life of the just, enlightened by the joy of obedience and love, is filled with prayer and adoration. The faithful can already savor on this earth the happiness of the beyond. Man is God's associate in the great work of the fulfillment of the Kingdom. Thus, Judah Halevy underscores a fundamental aspect of Jewish thought which results in a personal hope for an imminent beyond and in the perpetual hope for a messianic salvation promised to Israel and to all mankind. In the very frustration of the Jewish condition, Judah Halevy recognizes and proclaims the sign of the authenticity of Israel's thought. The trials were all the more joyously accepted by the Jews as they would, according to their faith, hasten universal deliverance. So the Jew found more than a consolation in his religion, he found the conviction of being an irreplaceable protagonist, God's chosen one associated with the work of redemption in the immense dream of Creation. In Judah Halevy's path, the Cabala was to praise and spread the messianic hope of Israel among the masses from the thirteenth century on. That hope is the life-force which made it possible for the Jews to reach the end of their exile without faltering.

For Israel the exile was characterized by a triple violence. Israel was separated from its God whose temple had been destroyed, its land was under foreign domination, and it was poorly treated by other nations. Such was the essence of the enslaved Jew's condition during the Diaspora. Modern times, with the paradoxical dimension which it introduced into universal history, initiated a third act in their long history. The wall which separated the Jews from the nations has been progressively weakened, while the people, the land, and the language of the Bible have stirred from their long lethargy. These events have not been without pain. While we were studying in Parisian schools, the world crumbled around us. I, a Jew, the son of a Jew, felt this more acutely than you, an Arab, the son of an Arab.

The mystics of Safed, the visionary Jews of Poland, had not been mistaken. The Renaissance had lifted the last barriers and provoked the final breaks which irrevocably changed the direction and meaning of history. The Jews have been the ideal catalyst for the new directions of the modern world. It is not surprising that they were the first to be carried away by the break-through which marked the end of their confinement at the same time as it signaled the close of the Middle Ages.

Growing up together, you and I not only were shared by two worlds, two continents, two types of culture, but, what is more, we lived in different centuries in our native Jerusalem. An outward sign of this truth is in the different way of computing the years of the Jewish calendar which now marks the fifth millennium of its history while Islam is in its twelfth century.

In the synagogues of Jerusalem I, young child that I was, seated next to my father, fervently participated in the liturgy. Thus I contemplated the procession of the scrolls of the Torah carried by devout and loving hands while the assembly of the faithful entoned the Canticles and the Psalms. With my child's eyes I saw concretely how the Word joined with the people to lead it, enlighten it, give it distinction and sometimes trouble it. The Talmud reconciled the meditation of the mystery that of the revealed Word, with the requirements of social and personal life in its two principal types of elaboration, the *haggada* and the *halakah*. It is by Biblico-Talmudic meditation that Israel assured its survival and built the home of the exile in spite of the persecutions of which it was victim.

In order to know this home, to describe its life, the interested theologians endeavored to write the grammar of this language which sang of the exploits of the God-Creator. The philosophers tried to make the following accessible to reason: the mystery of God's justice and love; the secret of his essence transmitted in the Torah, the absolute-in-words; and the foundations of his revelation clear in the history of Israel, the theophoric people. Bahya Ibn Pakuda could teach his disciples the way to spiritual progress and the mystical union with God. Maimonides was extremely successful in defining in verse the thirteen articles of faith, the fundamental dogmas of Judaism. They had to be adhered to under pain of apostasy. Throughout the world the

69

Jews of the East and of the West sang the dogmatics of the synagogue to different tunes, sometimes even to operatic melodies. Yet what made them Jews was more than a creed, be it sung or recited. Never was dogmatic or moral theology totally successful in establishing itself in Israel as it had done in Christendom as an autonomous science. The schemata proper to the spirit of Israel were very close to the Bible received in its original text. Because of this no abstract doctrine, even the most perfect, has ever been able to come between the living Word and the community of Israel. For the most educated Jew, as for the most humble inhabitant of the ghetto, the essential resided in the Torah, in the *Imitatio Dei* which it ordered. The goal was the sanctification of the most humble realities of daily life by the individual and collective practice of the order, the *mitzva*, eternally desired by God, and by the realization of justice and the receptiveness to grace, with gratitude and praise. The dependence of the Jews was therefore absolute. They were to live the will of God to the point of martyrdom if necessary. These theories were not abstract. They intransigently commanded the daily reality of the exile.

These were my thoughts when we left Paris on a warm day in June 1940, as the Germans were entering the capital. You were in Jerusalem while I pursued the roads of my exile during the terrible time of the German occupation in France. You know what the vicissitudes of our fight against Nazi Germany were. We were without ammunition in our underground and had no alternative but to resist the tyranny of a death sentence we could not even question. At the end of our exile we all met again, Jews of the East and of Europe, faced with the same fate. Our very loyalty to our Jewishness doomed us according to the laws of Hitlerian Germany. We were numbed to see the great majority of our co-religionists give in to the *diktats* of the enemy without a fight. When the Jews were ordered to present themselves at the desk of the *Kommandatur* for deportation or extermination, they lined up before the door of their enemy. Men, women, children were doomed (I should say they were dooming themselves) to the most horrible deaths simply because they could not betray their Judaic vocation. I experienced this more than once. From the very first days I worked in the ranks of the Resistance. I had to distribute falsified identification cards to those who needed them either to hide their real French identity or to hide their Jewishness. Not once did it enter my mind that I, too, could benefit from the services I rendered to others. During the entire war I fought my battles undisguised, using my real name. If I had to die, I wanted to do so openly. In our despair death seemed like an emancipation. It still surprises me that death did not come to me. During this period, I lived with the startling confirmation of Judah Halevy's thought.

I was exiled in Christian Europe. The Germans were pursuing us. We were condemned to an unbelievable humiliation. I became dizzy with pain from the barrage of punishment and insults which were heaped upon us. It was cruel to be chased, imprisoned, shut up in concentration camps, and there exterminated in gas chambers. How did I escape this fate which I'm telling you about today? In fact the Calvary was as painful for the survivors, who were there in spirit with those who were murdered and burned in the horror of the gas chambers and the crematories. The awareness of their death is more cruel than the death itself for us who survive and bear witness to it. Each of us died six million times in the concentration camps and in the ovens, and our sorrow is the summation of the inexpiable crimes which haunt us day and night and which we will never be able to forget. I am alive but my nights are filled with the moaning of all the victims, with the death-rattle of all the dying, with the wounds of all those who died in the anonymity of the Nazi charnel-house. I am alive but my flesh is disfigured by the blows, the slaps, the wounds which in the course of this time and for all time the humiliated have undergone, those who have been crucified on the cross of history, those who have been assassinated by the millions, silent bleeding Christs, hanged on the cross of a never-ending Calvary. I stand before you, and I am writing to you just as I spoke to you yesterday. Don't you hear in my appeal the cry, the sound of the last gasp of those who were beaten to death, of those who inhaled the poisons of the gas chambers, of those who were burned, condemned by man's hate? Our sorrow was the sum of all human sorrow. My suffering could not distinguish between the death-rattle of the Jew and that of his German executioner. Our particular destiny, by the intensity of our sorrow, thus took upon itself the destiny of all men. Frequently I would pass a roadside shrine depicting Jesus, that unique Jew, who never stopped dying in the agony of the crucifixion. We were the crucified, the Jews of our century. Our cry joined that of Christ in the dark night of history. Our cry was so loud that it seemed to transform our extreme suffering into fire. I am alive, but my soul will be pierced forever by the cry and by the suffering of all the deaths I have died in the prisons of my exile, in the solitude and the Calvary that were ours day after day, night after night, hour after hour, while Hitler carried on his job of disintegration and destruction. I want you to know it. While you were preparing the revolt of the Arabs, setting up the first cells of the revolutionary movement which would break out a few years later, I, in the depths of despair, backed into a corner, entangled with this mass of humanity which was dishonored, persecuted, killed, ravaged, scorned, exterminated before my eyes, people whom it was necessary to defend bare-handed, gagged and silent. Naked, mute, and unarmed, we were cast before the hate of the nations and of the men who dreamed of exterminating us. How many times have I wished that my heart would stop beating so that I would no longer be witness of the Calvary of my people in the agony of Europe.

Jewish history from the twelfth century to the present era has only confirmed Judah Halevy's astuteness. It is neither in the realm of thought nor in the development of art or technology that Israel has found the true reason for its endurance. If mystical contemplation fortified the will and allowed the endurance of sorrow, messianism constituted the reason and the secret motivation of our life. In the French underground where I soon took refuge, I saw it clearly—the Jew withstood the harshness of the exile only in the hope of a promised redemption. In this process suffering played a necessary though negative role. To suffer was nothing compared to the assurances of the faith and the promise. Judah Halevy lived from 1080 to 1141 in Toledo. Ever since, the Jews have known the rigors of the Inquisition. Their fate has worsened in the successive toughening of Christian Europe. The streets of Jerusalem, nine centuries later, still remembered the massacres of the Jews and the Arabs by the Crusades launched for the conquest of the Holy Places. This taste of blood came back to my lips with a mad violence while we were going through the evils of the Second World War. And in the German charnel-houses I heard Judah Halevy's deafening challenge to history and to God as he cried out over the abyss, "do not seek the truth in philosophy and do not see the certitude of universal redemption except in this, the historical development of the destiny of the Jews. This is what proves God."

The war was all the more cruel to me because it shattered the dream which Paris had allowed: total acceptance in society.

Arriving in Paris, we had passed from a poor and underdeveloped society—its Arab portion still was feudal in structure—to a rich, powerful, educated country well on its way to full achievement. Adopted by the new society, we were to be transformed in mind, heart, and body. My parents had named me Mattatias. In Paris, it did not take too long to change it to the French Matthieu. It was the sign of civil baptism upon my entry to French society. Anne loved the name Matthieu. She was almost completely unaware of Mattatias and the long chain of Isaac, Jacob, Abraham, David, or Nathan which had given him life. They never came up in our conversations. Perhaps she had a secret wish that I would take the initiative and introduce the realities of my Hebraic universe to her. A kind of modesty prevented that. Our friendship resolutely did without my origins. We fed ourselves with the nourishment, both bitter and sweet, which Paris could give us, pre-debacle Paris.

Suddenly Mattatias reappeared. We were on the Champs-Elysees when all of a sudden we saw the German regiments appear. Their proclamations soon followed by deeds left us no doubt. The Jew-hunt was on. I told Anne that I had made up my mind—I would join the ranks of the Resistance to which de Gaulle had summoned us. She made the first move. "I'll go with you." So we both entered the secret world of the *maquis*.

We headed for the mountains on roads filled with mad throngs in confusion over the collapse of France. I shall never forget our night at Orleans. The German artillery battled against a very unequal Allied artillery while aerial combats shattered the night with their fire. We took refuge in the town cemetery. It was an unforgettable sleepless night. We will always remember the huge flames of the city gas-works and the explosion at dawn which blew up the bridges of the Loire. That night death brushed us twenty times. We were surrounded by the unbearable smell of corpses, some of them several days old. We became grave-diggers. The bombed, pillaged city, patrolled by Germans who without warning shot at passers-by, was a vast smoldering battlefield. Homes were abandoned. Germany now ruled over the French. Foreigner and Palestinian Jew to boot, I had and wanted no other choice but to fight. Changing regimes, France forced me to find my deepest personal reality. By random routes and encounters we penetrated into the depths of France. We found refuge in the mountains of the Ardèche where the peasants still could recall other outlaws—the Protestants. From the first days of the occupation the great roundup of Jews had started all through occupied France. Everywhere the survivors pushed toward the free zone where they hoped to be able to stay alive. We were soon to organize to come to their aid. Hiding places had to be found, identities concocted to protect them from persecution, and the means for survival had to be provided. We made immediate contact with the United States which still had an official representation in France and we were able to set up the first cells of the French Resistance. Our work in the anonymity of the *maquis* especially envisaged welcoming and sheltering those whom the persecution had left homeless. Networks spontaneously were set up all over France. The victims of the new situation converged on us with or without the necessary passwords. On principle we never asked anyone the reason for his escape to the *maquis*.

Christians and Jews, communists and gypsies, too, sought us out daily. Their skin color, age, condition, or religion scarcely mattered—they were victims of Nazism. Soon we formed a tattered army with neither house nor home, without money and without ammunition. That was the army of the liberation. We soon learned that in order to organize ourselves our best allies in the French countryside were the local religious authorities. Priests, ministers, monks, nuns, opened the doors of their rectories and convents, and made it possible for us to meet and establish the necessary contacts which allowed us to organize from the outset. Never were we alone. Never did a request go unanswered. We suddenly discovered, especially in our relations with these people, an almost supernatural source of generosity, goodwill, intelligence, and efficiency. Whether we were Jews or communists, the response of the Christians was always positive. This was the way the first steps of the French Resistance began, by an alliance—in some way organic—of the Jews suddenly thrown together with the communists, outcasts of the community, where they both met the Christian élite of France. The meeting allowed an unwritten alliance often sealed with the blood of combat. Before long we had to find hiding places in the less accessible regions for the men, women and children who could no longer live in the occupied cities where they happened to be and where they were the victims of the man-hunt. When we found out, thanks to a code, about the arrival of such groups in our mountains, we worried about the task of hiding these famished and terrorized people. The obstacles disappeared by themselves when we made our needs known in the villages and farms where our Christian friends sent us. Never did I hide the purposes of my fight, nor did I conceal my true identity. Not once did a single individual stand up to denounce me during all those years. There was a challenge to adversity in our attitude. (Since I had to commit myself to being Jewish, I wanted to do it completely, to live and die being Jewish.) I had grown an unmistakably Semitic beard which made even more noticeable any distinctive features which would have stood out in the French countryside. I always carried my Hebrew Psalm-book with me as you well know. Sometimes during the contact missions, I would find myself in the same compartment with German soldiers. Without any false bravado, I felt the irresistable need to read the Psalms and, Judaically bearded, I would take out my Psalm-book and recite for hours on end our ancient prayers. How did I escape death? I don't know. Does man ever set the hour of his own death? My friends worried about my indiscretion. One day they invited me into one of their hiding places where they received me amicably. They had me sit down and, before I knew what was happening, they took a razor and shaved my beard off clean!

In one of his letters Saint Paul writes of the "streetsweepers of the world." That is what we progressively became in a Europe ravaged by war. Soon the refugees filled the countryside, where we had established our underground. The silent children with innocent eyes already marked by anxity from the atrocities they had witnessed, and of which they had sometimes been victims, made us uneasy with their symbolic reproach. Today, I am thinking about Roger who at the age of twelve had already been through twelve concentration camps, or about Jeanine who at eighteen had been the horrified witness of the massacre of her loved ones before being raped and left behind as dead on the mound of bodies where her brothers lay dying. It was in the mountains of the Haute-Loire that these adults and children were to rediscover the taste for life and for combat. It was they, by their crucified and crucifying presence, who gave the others the will to challenge the baseness of the regime which would impose itself on the world should the Germans win.

What touched us most during these horrible years was the selfless and unanimous help of the people among whom we had taken refuge. Everybody simply and naturally put himself at the disposal of the persecuted who needed help, no matter who they were. Each one had the conviction that it was the right of those who were being persecuted to be accepted throughout the areas of refuge which spread around the Chambon-sur-Lignon. The welcome was extended not as a charity, but as a debt which each one had the duty to repay. The sermons of the priests and ministers had stressed this duty especially when it concerned Jews. Here I must tell you about Jean Hatier, a young assistant at the University of Strasbourg (which had been relocated at Clermont-Ferrand). He had specialized in biology. One day he found out that he was wanted by the enemy. Most of his friends had been arrested by the Germans early in the summer of 1942 to be deported and massacred in the concentration camps. He had to flee and came to our area for shelter. He wanted to hide his Jewish identity. The farmers had refused to give him help but changed their minds as soon as they accidentally found that he was another of the Israelites being hunted down by the Nazis.

Soon thousands of people found themselves involved in our merciless struggle. To manage our sector of the Resistance I had to cover thousands of miles across France. By chance stops I would learn of the arrest or the death of some friend. Twenty-five years later I can still see their faces and still hear their words and the sound of their voices. I remember the circumstances which led them one by one to the supreme sacrifice. I hear their death-rattle, their cries in the night. In our adversity, even hope seemed to have declared a moratorium.

We acted outside the realm of hope and reason. All those who were involved in this battle, the members of the underground, the farmers who hid them, the spiritual leaders who sustained them, risked deportation and death at every moment. Daily examples proved it. The number of those who so careless as to let themselves get caught and those who were turned in kept mounting. They were the martyrs of the Resistance against oppression. The fighters had to take a double risk. On principle, I would hide nothing from the people helping me. I always told them that I was a Jew being tracked down by the Germans. When I asked my contacts to help someone, they knew that my errand could have tragic consequences not only for them personally, but for their families.

The circumstances of our action were almost always tragic: convoys of men stolen from the train about to take them to certain death; men and women, old and young, organized in groups which were secretly to cross the Swiss

77

frontier or the Pyrenees to freedom; children whose parents had been assassinated had to be housed, whatever the cost, in order to survive. Soon our area was saturated with fugitives. The longer it lasted, the more difficult the battle became. I remember the day when we got the news of an imminent sweep through our region. During the night we had to bicycle a long way to warn those who risked being deported at dawn. It was in a leper-house near the Pont-Saint-Esprit that I found the hiding place I needed. In the saddest moments, the moments of greatest despair and greatest danger, I could always count on unknown friends who would risk their own freedom to help. I treasure the memory of the joy of the children who after their traumatic experiences saw homes opened up to welcome them. They soon felt at home with their new families which made it possible for them to hope for the end of their torment. No, I never left a village discouraged or in despair because of a refusal. These French people of the mountains and the plains had understood that their human duty coincided with their Christian commitment. They never hesitated to come to the aid of the victims of Nazi barbarism.

Our organization which was open to everybody had only one requirement—courage and the will to win. Due to the course of events, it became above all an instrument for rescuing the persecuted, which in those days meant the Jews. While the apocalyptic massacres which Hitler's regime had launched continued in Europe, the Resistance represented a small spark of love and brotherhood. In our ranks when someone fell, there was always someone else to take his place. We could not afford to give up hope. Tomorrow it might be necessary to accompany a convoy, patiently and heroically prepared, to the Spanish or Swiss border. Tomorrow it might be necessary to attack a train in the Rhone Valley and redirect it toward our *maquis*. We might be forced to kill the guards or the mechanics in Germany's service should they refuse to surrender. Tomorrow we would have to meet clandestinely with our friends to plan the strategy of our common action. Tomorrow might be the time for us to disclose our names and faces revealing the challenge which taught us to understand man stripped of all his masks.

Here I would like to tell you of my memory of Laforêt. He was one of the most active agents of the Christian Resistance of the Haute-Loire. He had organized a series of religious lectures in his home during the most severe period of German repression. Jews and Christians alternately came to relate their reasons for belief or despair. These gatherings, most often on Saturday afternoons, reminded me of the catacombs, but hidden in the woods of this part of France to check the spread of modern paganism. From this urgency developed the movement of Judeo-Christian friendship. Most of those who took part paid for their audacity with their lives. Laforêt, himself, informed that some friends had been captured by the Germans and imprisoned at Puy, impulsively rushed to their aid, worn out by the constant pressure of our fight. Pistol in hand, he entered the *Kommandantur* to try desperately to obtain the release of his friends. He was quickly arrested, disarmed, and taken to Fort-de-Montluc where he was executed. We were able to identify his body only by one intact piece of his shirt and a gold tooth in his disfigured head. That is how we learned to discover each other beyond our shields and our masks. In spite of our religious differences, we felt intimately bound in the day-to-day battles and the new hope which conditioned our existence and our survival. The horror of the times taught each of us to see his neighbor as one to whom he must be merciful, whoever he might be, whatever his origin. The war was the excuse for the worst atrocities, but for many it was also the occasion to open their eyes and minds and prepare for the advent of reconciliation. One night I was aboard a train between Toulouse and Perpignan with eighteen escapees from a concentration camp. Our teams had freed them, but not without paying a price. Madeleine had been mowed down in the course of the operation which had cost the lives of three Germans who were scalded by the boiler of the locomotive. We had to hurry to get the group into Spain because we could expect a prompt reaction and pitiless reprisals. Night fell. The escapees, carrying false identification cards, were dispersed among several compartments of the train. I was wandering about in the corridors when I met an Arab melancholically leaning out the window. He was from Al-

geria. The expression on his sunburned face was one of sadness and hurt. He seemed unreal to me, an apparition from
the depths of time. I was overcome with the desire to embrace him because tonight he was my fellow creature, my
brother, because he suddenly reminded me of the men and
the surroundings I grew up among in Israel, because he ex-
uded the distinct poverty of the Arab fields, because he had
that sovereign art of wearing his rags with nobility, and
lastly, because it was possible for me to chat with him in the
confusion of darkness and anxiety in our language. He told
me his story. For two years he had worked in the mines of
Grand-Combe. His life had been difficult. He was alone
among the Christian workers and did not have the vaguest
understanding of French and of course the other miners did
not know Arabic. He had spent two lonely years forcing
himself to understand what was incomprehensible to him
—the manners and customs of that human community he had
tried to enter. He spoke to me especially about his solitude.
He described his surroundings as rampant with the abuse of
alcohol and empty of all human charity. It was torture. One
could die of thirst and hunger next to the men he had rubbed
elbows with for two years without the possibility of a charitable act. "No, they wouldn't give you a glass of water
even if you were to die of thirst at their sides." Now he was
at the end of his rope. He could not go on. He could no
longer stand the physical effort of his work and even less
his loneliness where, no matter how he looked at it, he was a
stranger. The harshness of life in a Europe at war, the short-
age of food, and the cold were forcing him back to his native
Algeria. Objectively, he knew that conditions there would
be no less harsh, but at least he would be home. When we
said good-bye, we embraced as two brothers. He was supposed to ship out for Oran. I followed him with my eyes
and with my thoughts. When would I see my native land
again, the land of Israel with its palms and olives, and the
incomparable light of its countryside? This time it was with
a happy heart that, after Perpignan, I set out for the Spanish
border. Our eighteen escapees from the death camps crossed
the frontier and started on the road to freedom. That same
day I learned of the invasion of North Africa by the Amer-

80

icans, November 8, 1942. We were irrevocably caught in a
crucial battle upon which depended not only our personal
survival but the future of the world. Again that day Hitler
gave one of his insane speeches. I heard him during one of
our secret meetings in a cave where I was surrounded by
several friends of our sector. He promised us death, but we
had never savored our liberty so much.

This was the absurdity of our times. Never had a persecution been organized more systematically or with more de-
liberate cruelty. But neither had any movements of rebellion
against an established power entailed such risks or been so
resolute.

In the ranks of the Resistance there was a unanimity
which defied all risks and faced up to every danger. Jean
Martin, one of our leaders who preferred suicide rather than
taking the chances of divulging information under torture,
was a symbol but not an isolated case. Each individual was
ready to give his life to assure the safety of his comrades in
battle. The weak, the cowards, were rare and quickly eliminated. They, too, were recruited without distinction of
race or religion. I know of at least two cases of Jews who
were the accomplices of the Germans in the manhunt they
had undertaken throughout Europe. Sammy had been one
of our fellow-fighters from the start. We knew that he was
specifically sought by name by the Germans and the Vichy
who specialized in Jew-hunting. He was obviously being
tracked down and on several occasions he had narrowly escaped the traps laid out for him. We had a hard time convincing him that he had become a danger not only to himself
but to the entire movement. He was to back off for a while.
After a necessary delay to cover his tracks, he would be free
to rejoin the active Resistance in another section and under
another identity. Sammy wasn't easy to convince. I saw
in him the instinctive reflex of men who, feeling the approach of death, revolted with all their being against the
decision which gave them up to their destiny. With a terrible
look which I have never forgotten, he begged us to let him
continue in our ranks and not to interrupt his activity even
briefly. We had to explain to him the reasons which made a
suspension of his service imperative. He had to resign him-

self. So he moved on to join a *maquis* of the Haute-Loire. From Lyon he took a train for Saint-Étienne where I was supposed to meet him with an automobile to take him to an isolated farm not far from Puy. I watched the station exit which was guarded by the Gestapo. When he appeared, I saw a civilian point him out to the German lieutenant in charge. Sammy was quickly subdued and taken to Fort-de-Montluc where he perished under frightful torture. The informer was not only a frightened Jew who had been blackmailed into working for the Germans, but, what is worse we later found out he was a personal friend of Sammy. They had been born and brought up in the same village in Alsace. Poor wretches trembling with terror who sought to save their Jewish hides, misled mothers who were black-mailed into the service of the Gestapo lest they seal the fate of their captive children—I was ashamed to see some Jews make matters worse for their brothers and help our hang-men.

A strange case of this cooperation was the subject of a tale from a city in southern France where a priest had been chosen by the Commissariat for Jewish Affairs to censor the mail of the Jews and to keep the government informed about it. He had been chosen for his competence in Hebrew, a language he had learned from a Polish Jew, Trékowsky, who was a Talmudist of uncommon ability. As chance would have it, Trékowsky showed up for asylum and began to take advantage of his new situation to offer his services to Jews who were being pursued. He took their jewels and other valuables for safekeeping. Anybody who had any-thing to do with him ran into bad luck and was deported. Obviously Trékowsky, a traitor, turned in those who had confided in him after he had taken their possessions. On the first day of the liberation the affair was uncovered. Trékow-sky's guilt was established without any possible doubt by the evidence of the Gestapo archives and he soon went be-fore the firing squad. The priest, due to some upper-level intervention, was pardoned.

The more we suffered from Nazi aggression, the more the cases of Jewish treachery humiliated us. Cowardice was also common enough during this period and it was not bound by race or religion either. The chief rabbi of one occupied country refused to make a formal protest to his government against the deportation of foreign Jews which had been decreed. I had personally intervened so that he would at least save the honor of his office and his community by a public protest. He flatly refused and his reasons were neither very different nor less reasonable than those of Pius *XII* or his defenders who tried to explain the Pope's silence a few years later.

Treachery and cowardice, as well as heroism, were to be found in all camps. Christians shed their blood to save Jewish lives. Germans paid with their lives for the help they gave to the Resistance or to the Jews. If I have learned to free myself of all national or religious pride it was at this time when throughout burning Europe nations and religions found themselves subjected to the pitiless trial of war.

You know how this ended for me. The assault of the French forces which made the liberation of Paris possible had been prepared for a long time by a group I belonged to. In December 1944, I was arrested because of the action of an informer. Who? We were never really sure, probably a Vichy collaborator put on my track one night when I was taking part in the arms transport near the Police Prefecture. I was tied up by the Gestapo, interrogated on the premises of the Hotel Majestic, Avenue Kléber. You know what it cost me—I lost my right eye, squashed by the brute assigned to making me talk. The accident probably saved my life. Had it not happened he would have finished me off. A few days later I was deported to the mines of Silesia. How did I survive? I don't know. My unshakable will to live could not be weakened even by the horrible spectacle of men and women, my people, going to their Calvary in the prisons of Nazi Europe.

Do you remember Mardochée, the Polish Jew? He lived in Jerusalem for years. You must have seen him at our house where he came often during 1938–1939. He also joined the Resistance and was caught in France in February 1943. He was deported and interned at Buchenwald where his robust condition won him a reprieve. One day, though, with forty other Jews he was led to a clearing about fifteen kilometers from camp where the guards ordered them to dig a hole. At the end of the day the grave was ready and the soldiers opened fire on the group. Mardochée was among the first to fall. The bodies of his dead companions piled up on him and around the place where he had crouched as soon as the machine gun fired its first shot. His instinctive reaction had saved his life—he was alive at the bottom of the common grave where the others died. He pretended to be dead for as long as he heard the raucous voices of the assassins. When everything was quiet he managed to climb out of his grave. He was covered with the blood of his friends. Unscathed! He did not have a scratch. Dazed before so many corpses, he chose some unstained clothes—a pair of shoes and trousers from one, a shirt and jacket from another. And paying no attention to the last gasps of the dying which still could be heard in the charnel-pit, he fled. He had covered less than a mile when he met up with a group of German soldiers who called out to him. "Have you seen a hole where a few hours ago a commando group shot forty Jews?" "Yes, it's less than a mile from here." The Germans made Mardochée climb into their truck and be their guide. They were supposed to bring back the forty cadavers to the crematory at Buchenwald. Thirty-nine, there were only thirty-nine! Mardochée also seemed puzzled over the disappearance of the body of the fortieth Jew, his. He advised a search to catch the fugitive and, of course, was the busiest one in the search for his own corpse. How did he have the strength to play this tragicomedy, to come back to the gates of the camp with the soldiers and the thirty-nine cadavers? How did the soldiers mistake him for a local peasant and let him go? That is all part of the game of the possible and the impossible which allowed the Jew to survive the search for his own body. I was to see Mardochée again in Jerusalem in 1961, at the Eichmann trials where he was a witness. It was one of the tragic moments in this trial which turned out to be the trial of all of history's horror.

So Judaism of the Diaspora was trying to save its life in Europe. Six million dead is an abstract figure difficult to grasp, almost twice the present population of Israel. One million eight hundred thousand children under fourteen were assassinated in the concentration camps, children of Anne Franck's age or younger. I remind you once more of these facts which every person in the world should know and try never to forget.

For me the victims of Dachau, Treblinka, and Theresienstadt have the same faces as the Japanese killed at Hiroshima by the first atomic bomb and the victims of the wars for national liberation. I have seen the blood flow from the throat of a black assassinated by a paratrooper. I have heard the last sobs of a Moslem child shot down by machine-gun fire in Algeria. My nights are haunted with the loud clatter of wars, today's in Vietnam as well as yesterday's, the slaughter of the Second World War. I have an absolute horror of violence and war. I had fought in France in the ranks of the Resistance because morally I had no other choice but to oppose Hitler's Germany, the evil of its racism and the horror of his imperialism. The war made hate and violence even more repulsive. I cannot accept the absurdity of the battles to which our generation has constantly devoted itself—I saw too many men, women, and children die.

I would evoke for you the six million assassinated Jews. There are also those who, foreseeing the tragedy, committed suicide—Jean Lévy, for example, the son of the philosopher. That poet of Israel's rebirth who, recognizing his impotence, preferred to disappear into the Seine rather than live out his humiliation. There are those who were killed by the police of the occupied countries, and those who perished from starvation, shame, and despair. There are also the young girls raped and dismembered, the pregnant women beaten, the old people whipped to death as they murmured the ancient *Shema Israel*. There are the fathers who killed their own children to save them from the common fate. There are mothers who put themselves at the disposal of their oppressors in the hope of saving their children. Some offered their bodies and others did away with themselves so as not to be touched. There are the prisoners who fell in the mines of Europe digging coal or salt to help shape the German victory. There are the masses killed with primitive whips and others with automatic pistols. And the agony of the gas chambers! Horror permeated our world.

On night in my German prison I heard the hallucinatory cries of the Jews being tortured. A quarter century later their voices still hurt my ears. This was more than an agony for me. I died with each final breath I heard. I died to myself. Mattatias Mizrahi died six million times in the deaths of his brothers in the prisons of Europe. I was reborn in the bloody adventure of the war, the *maquis*, the Resistance, the German prison. In some ways I had become like the Arab worker who had discovered in his mine at Grand-Combe the cruelty and folly of the West chained to its drive for power. The dreams of my French teachers, dreams of equality, fraternity, liberty, and infinite progress were dashed under the fire of the Panzer divisions and the tortures of the Gestapo. It took me more than a year to recuperate after my escape from the salt mines of Silesia. When I came back, I was practically a skeleton. Only my eyes were visible on my face. The golden reflection betrayed the horror I had seen. For me, the survivor, day and night were a Calvary worse than death. The scenes of the war kept coming to mind and I relived them with an even greater intensity. They finally broke my equilibrium. For weeks I was delirious: I saw myself as victim and executioner, God's truce and the holocaust, the angel and the devil. I was the creator and the destroyer. My preoccupation and my voice would produce images which could with a word be returned to the depths from which I had conjured them. I screamed with pain thinking of the death of my brothers and of the cowardice of a world which had allowed such great pain and dishonor. I thought of the shame not only of the nations which had perpetrated their crimes, but of the Jews, too, who had been the victims. I was enraged by the reasonableness with which the horror had been accepted as a fact, by the misery of the war, the persecution and the massacres, by the horror of the blood-covered man whose murderous and crucified image of God dominated our times. The physicians diagnosed an organic delirium. Time and space lost their meaning as I lived in the eternal presence of a single day. I was torn both by its light and its darkness in the incandescent luminosity of the first day of time. This intensity took hold of me like a magic potion and carried me beyond darkness and despair and illusion. There exists a single light which transcends duality and shares in it. In this light, understand me well, everything is one, only *one*. Challenged by the murderous world I had discovered in Europe, I saw clearly that either a man had to die or take up arms to struggle heroically against that world. I said to my brothers, "you are cowards, cowards for passively accepting your execution. You should stand up before your tombs, arise from your ashes and set out for Jerusalem to rebuild your eternal home there." I thought that the inspiration which had possessed me should uproot and carry along the survivors of my people and lead them back to their native deserts to rebuild man's country. I used to say to my brothers, "take up arms, Israel, and struggle fearlessly against the darkness from which you came." I hoped that the sinister and intoxicating essence of nations at war would turn into incense—the incense of a people of light rising above the unimaginable holocaust to bear ultimate witness for man. Still confined to my bed, I seemed to hear coming from the four corners of the world the tumult of the new scourge of my resurrected people returning to its ancient land. I was exhausted by the intensity of my inexpressible vision. I could not sleep. I was fire and ashes, creature and creator, in the endless cry of the world's agony.

For weeks the doctors feared for my sanity. Their discretion frightened me more than the madness to which I had finally succumbed. One night I was the witness of a strange liturgy. Men dressed in oriental garb gathered in my room. I saw them so distinctly that I had difficulty believing that it was only a vision. "You have reached your crisis. In a few days you will be cured. Come back to Jerusalem. The hour of your resurrection is at hand." The three visitors had the faces of patriarchs. I could recognize my ancestors in them. The apparition calmed me. While my doctors were losing hope for my cure, my fever subsided and my delirium passed. Only an extreme fatigue remained as if my body had been beaten and burned by all the fires of hell. Finally even the fatigue wore off and I was able to leave for Switzerland to enjoy a marvelous convalescence. Near that beautiful mountain, the Jungfrau, I learned to eat again, to breath and to think as a free man. From then on my bedside book was the old Hebraic Bible I inherited from my father. He knew this book by heart. He read it and chanted it with unquestioning faith. The West had taught me its critical methods, and these had for a long time been a wall between the radiant text and my life. The war, its pains, the discovery of the Jewish destiny and its severities had brought me back to the sources of Biblical inspiration. From this moment on I read the Bible as I would a book on current events. Everything in this sacred text related to me. The hortatory chants of the Bible suddenly told the story of our daily existence:

All these curses shall come upon thee, and overtake thee. Cursed shalt thou be in the city, cursed in the field. Cursed shall be thy barn, and cursed thy stores. Cursed shall be the fruit of thy womb, and the fruit of thy ground. . . . Cursed shalt thou be coming in, and cursed going out. . . . Be the heaven, that is over thee, of brass: and the ground thou treadest on, of iron. The Lord make thee to fall down before thy enemies, one way mayst thou go out agianst them, and flee seven ways, and be scattered throughout all the kingdoms of the earth. . . . The Lord strike thee with madness and blindness and fury of mind. And mayst thou grope at midday as the blind is wont to grope in the dark. . . . And mayst thou at all times suffer wrong, and be oppressed with violence, and mayst thou have no one to deliver thee. . . . May thy sons and thy daughters be given to another people, thy eyes looking on . . . and may there be no strength in thy hand . . . mayst thou always suffer oppression, and be crushed at all times. And be astonished at the terror of those things which thy eyes shall see. (Deuteronomy, 28:passim)

We had personally experienced the truth of the Biblical predictions. We had become "the astonishment, the fable, the laughing-stock" of all the peoples of the earth. Neither the Arabs throughout the colonial countries nor the blacks in Africa had ever known such a destiny. The Jews were no longer enslaved or exploited, or secluded as untouchables. They had simply been considered vermin to be exterminated. From this proceeded the heinous concentration camps and practices such as the making of soap from the fat of our

88

cadavers or parchment from our skin. But the skin of the Jew did not deserve this name since according to a Nazi the Jew, strictly speaking, was not a man but an animal with a hide.

All that thought detached itself from the background of a dramatic story which suddenly appeared to me in its full dimensions in its two great acts: the Bible and its splendor; the Exile and its final horrors which were burning themselves out before us. The reservoirs of all human sensitivity had been depleted by two thousand years of tribulation. The Hebraic memory had realized for us the marvel of simultaneity in which all history was lived totally by each of us. We were present in Egypt when the Pharoah slaughtered our infants, present at the wandering in the desert and present at Sinai, present at the struggles of the Macchabees and in the Martyrdom of Bar Kahba, present in the flames which consumed the temple of Jerusalem, present in the shame of our exiles in the East and in the West, present in the expulsion of our brothers and in their suffering in the fires of the Inquisition. The astounding Hebraic memory, from generation to generation, from exile to exile, recorded the implacable truth of the nations and of the Churches in terms of blood. All the accounts, the dramas, the humiliations, and the wounds were noted in full detail. We knew the names of our torturers and our persecutors. Without weapons to defend ourselves, we drew strength to survive from the terrible arsenal of our memory. Christ himself had hesitated to drink the chalice to the last drop. There had not been a torture that the Jews avoided. From the six hundred thousand Jews (according to Tacitus) crucified by the Romans during their conquest of the Holy Land to the six million Jews executed by Hitler—between these two points which mark the beginning and the end of the exile, there is no pain nor any type of torture which we have not experienced—from the most brutal to the most subtle, from the most ordinary to the most unheard of.

One day before the war, I told you about the particular quality of Jewish suffering. The servant suffering from Isiah's vision and the agony of Christ on the Cross seemed to be the essential realities of the exile. There was not a spot

on our body which was not scarred, not a spot on our soul
which was not torn. If the abstract Jew such as history has
shaped him over the two hundred years of our dereliction
should rise up here in front of you, you would flee in fright.
Having lived through the Hitlerian trials in the *maquis* of
Europe, I made up my mind once and for all. As strong as
my Parisian attachments had become, I had to break them
to participate in the building of a new world. My place was
in Jerusalem from then on.

We were changed men because we had witnessed the
burning of Europe, the crumbling of the entire structure of
European civilization, ideological and technical, and the un-
leashing of the hate taught by Hitler. The strife among the
Western nations and the internal struggles among the different parts of the French family, the battles which pitted the
collaborators against our Resistance groups filled us with an
anxiety which weighed on us day and night. So, too, the
feeling of exaltation which we felt in the course of the days
as we risked our lives at each moment in the fight for liberation and that extraordinary tension in which we lived sometimes gave rise to a new kind of enlightenment. The density
of the night had made us *alumbrados*. We could understand
ourselves more deeply and more honestly.

This new knowledge led us both to an identical road: it
made us aware that having a share of Europe, we were not
totally of Europe. An identical spiritual journey made us
realize our relationship, and that we were irremediably foreigners, you the Arab and I the Jew. We were foreigners in
a very different way, it is true. The colonial and Hitlerian
monsters had brutally pushed us out of the society where
we had sincerely thought we could be integrated. Oh, of
course, we were not foreigners to the Christians and Frenchmen who fought at our sides and risked their lives for the
same cause, for the same reasons. We loved them, and the
presence of Anne for me, of Karine for you, represented
more than a symbol—love's truth could overcome all barriers
and assure the victory of a certain image of man. Even those
who fought with us in the *maquis* had to hide from their
people and opt for a camp which was no longer the one in
which they had grown up. We shared the same adventure

with them, but this adventure committed us to something far more basic. The situation which all of a sudden had made pariahs of us brought us very close together, not so much because we were brothers in combat against Germany, but rather because by its racism Germany made pariahs first of me, the Jew, and then of you, the Arab, in your status as a colonized Moslem called upon to revolt or disappear as a free person.

In the course of our years at the university we convinced ourselves that we were young Frenchmen like all the others, Westerners of long standing. The war revealed us to ourselves. Jews and Arabs, we were essentially Semites. This fact struck me with brutal clarity. Those who chased me day and night across the *maquis* of France, those who had sent an inspector of the secret police with orders to arrest me because of my role in the Resistance, those who had set up innumerable ambushes from which I escaped by an amazing set of coincidences, those who deported my brothers and imprisoned them in the concentration camps and executed them in the crematories—they called themselves anti-Semites. What they wanted from me was not just the skin of a Jew, but the very soul of a Semite. I was a Semite because for generations my family, like yours, had spoken a Semitic language, Arabic, and because as soon as my people made the discovery of its Biblical roots, I too began to speak Hebrew, another Semitic language. I was a Semite because of my enemies, because of my parents, because of myself and because of you, my Arab friend with whom I have lived for centuries in these happy places. You were a Semite too, even though you belonged to that branch of the Mosem family where the Palestinian stood out in the midst of the Arab world by his greater receptivity to the outside world and his finer culture. We were Semites by adoption and by choice. We discovered together that the Semitic people had Asia as their cradle. We learned new names: to the north of our Semitic country was the Eastern part of the Taurus chain; to the east, the Zagros chain served as the eastern limit of the Tigris basin. The Persian gulf, the gulf of Oman, the southern coast of the Indian Ocean, the gulf of Aden, the western part of the Red Sea, the isthmus of Suez and the Mediterranean Sea had been the cradle of our Arab and Jewish ancestors and for their cousins the Phoenicians, the Arameans, and the Ethiopians. These were our forefathers who in their Asiatic setting received a message which they had the mission to transmit to the world. Our friendship in our youth in Jerusalem represented a coexistence at the very sources of our ancestral history. We were awed with our rediscovery of that other dimension in us, the desert. Its vision had been blurred for an instant by the lycées and the universities. The war ended our superficiality. The true dimensions of our inner lives finally appeared. Both of us discovered all at once that before anything else we were sons of the desert.

Do you remember our amazement when we took our first tour of the Negev? We put on the old nomad costumes to go camel riding through the endless sands. We suddenly rediscovered our truth in the barrenness of the desert. Until that time our interest was centered in Europe, in France, in Paris, in the theaters, concert halls, and lecture rooms of a world which seemed so marvelously rich to us. On the humps of our camels we were new men. I remember how seriously we took our adventure and the ease with which we shouted the appropriate guttural cries to command our caravan. We certainly were men of the desert. You are an Arab. The very term assigns you the desert as your birthplace. The Arabic word 'arab means any sterile and arid country sparcely covered by meager pastures. The words 'arab and desert designate the same thing, that which is the most strongly anchored in our souls. The Arabs of central Arabia still live in deserts protected against all foreign influence by the sands which maintain a buffer zone between them and the outside world. Their preservation is due to a miracle and is almost unique in the history of mankind. My name too, Jew, designates a geographical place, the mountains of the desert of my native Judea. In the glaring white decor of rocks and sun my ancestors have lived, toiled and suffered. Like yours they also belonged to the desert. They were Jews, that is to say natives of the hills of Judea, frontiersmen of the vast Arabic deserts. Bound to the desert, your ancestors were nomads. Bound to the desert, my ancestors were Hebrews, men in perpetual movement. The word *i'vri* comes from a root which means *to go elsewhere, to go beyond the.* Thus our ancestors, from their most distant origins, were called upon to wander. Exiled from our own country we have been doomed to wander toward oppression and sometimes terrible persecutions. During the war years I had to change residence forty-five times as if to prove that I was a Hebrew, a nomad. Our races, the Arabs and the Jew, are certainly twins. To stress this our Hebraic language writes the Arabic *'vri* with exactly the same letters as the Hebrew word *'vri.* The letters are the same, in similar order—to designate the reality of our eternal country, the desert where the voice which seduced us resounded. The Bible is telling the truth, my friend, when it relates the unbelievable, paradoxical, relevant story of Abraham. It is in his faith that our lives take root. He, too, was a man of the desert, a wanderer, a man dedicated to the Word whose message he was the first to hear. Ishmael and Israel were his children. The story of the relationship of Ishmael, the elder, and Isaac, the younger, and of their mothers Agar and Sarah, summarizes the Arab and Jewish past for the thousands of years of their coexistence. The dispute between the two children of Abraham stems from a conflict of inheritance. It is stated that the younger is preferred by the father and that the elder, Ishmael, steadfast in his right and hurt by the favor given to Isaac, shuts himself off in the isolation of the desert. But Isaac recognizes the brotherhood of Ishmael for all time. In the Bible the Jews already turn toward the Arabs to learn their wisdom and to offer the sources of their own knowledge. Until the appearance of Islam the Jews had been the archivists of Semitic history. It is only in the seventh century that the Arabs discover their Biblical sources and boast of the figures so close to them, Abraham, Job, Solomon. This discovery marks an even more essential rapprochement. The spiritual sources of the Jewish people are immediately adopted by all the Arabs who make our scriptures theirs, who make our prophets into their prophets, our ideals their ideals, our hopes their eternal hope.

Although we discovered this long before, experiencing the European turmoil together, we should have been able to find it in ourselves where it was so transparent. Both our personalities were extreme, subject to outbursts of anger, plagued with irresistable desires, and given to whimsical actions. You were gifted with a noble generosity. But we were capable of true savagery. We felt that we were at the same time selfless and wicked, generous and greedy, equally capable of heroism and cowardice. We were men—disconcerting combinations of very contradictory tendencies, emotions, and instincts. We could pass from one register to the other with shocking ease. Our characters surprised our Western friends.

On the plane of knowledge, we reacted in the same way. Our thinking was intuitive rather than discursive, synthetic rather than analytic. It was really more a question of vision than of thought. We would grasp what we saw. It was a difficult step from understanding to knowledge. For the latter to be perfect, it required the assurance of our vision. This explains the particular nature of our logic. We pretended to be satisfied with the harmonies of the syllogism but the tools of Hellenistic logic remained outside the real area of our knowledge. We could reconstitute all the lines of argument in the world and if necessary invent others, but our conscience could only be satisfied by the powers of intuition. Our thinking reached the powers of vision without ever replacing them. The Cartesian method could help but it did not fulfill us. We all had one little part of us which aspired to the supreme mode of knowledge which comes from intuition and from the powers of global vision. This allowed us the disorderly play of contradictions. We counterbalanced our disorder with a dependable ability for improvisation and with an indomitable energy which no doubt came to us from the harsh realities of our existence in the deserts and the even harsher realities of humanity and history. We finally got used to the juxtaposition of opposites in us. The Bible and the Koran prove with what ease the Arab soul and the Jewish soul can pass from one register to another while still preserving a unity and a constancy of vision and interpretation. Even Arab music and art develop from the infinite repetition of the same motifs, from the juxtaposition of the same forms and the same series of sounds—all made possible by the powers of contemplation which constitute the primary force of the Semitic soul. Yes, we are certainly born of the desert and all the manifestations of our history and our life seem to be inspired by the infinite which fills the desert's beyond. We Arabs and Jews are certainly the children of that desert where Ishmael, the son of Abraham, was left by Agar and where Moses died, contemplating the land of Israel across from Jericho. In this oasis covered with pink laurel and palms, I would often lose myself contemplating the desert. Opposite me on the other bank of the Jordan an Arab wearing a turban also was staring at the immutable dunes. There we were, you and I, children again, like an immutable image of destiny at the sources of our native deserts.

While we were growing up within the walls of Jerusalem, we did not know that our educators unconsciously aimed at cutting the roots from which we had so easily separated ourselves to transplant us in a land which was ours and foreign at the same time. In no country had Jews, Christians, and Moslems lived so closely together as in the time of our youth in Jerusalem. The three communities lived closely associated in matters of economics without completely merging either in their intellectual activities or in their sociological and religious aspirations. Between 1920 and 1940 Palestine and most of the Moslem countries conquered or occupied by European powers experienced a period of radical change. Yet instead of merging, the Jews, Christians, and Moslems continued to live their separate sociological existences. Three camps coexisted without spiritual interaction. The Christians employed Arabs, and the Arabs traded with the Jews who served as middlemen in almost all areas of economic life. But the exchanges stopped there. The communities were introverted. There existed a sort of *apartheid* which no law required, but which nonetheless imposed its bold rule on everybody, even those who would have liked things to be otherwise. One married within his own sociological group. One did not convert, so to speak. Religion enclosed us in a section, in a society, and in a social state from which it was almost impossible to escape. The expressed policy of the mandatory power was to protect the interests of the three existing communities. But they were compromised by a desire for power which instinctively aimed at dividing in order to rule. In the place of an exchange which would have allowed us to know each other better, we were penned up inside the barriers strengthened by the continuation of the practices which were carefully protected. Each group was enclosed in his ghetto: the Christian in his Christian ghetto, the Jew in his Jewish ghetto, and the Moslem in the vastness of his deserts where he was more separated from us than if he were living on another continent. Segregation played a role even in the schools. All those who were part of the privileged group, even if they were Jews or Moslems—colonized people having become themselves colonials—benefitted from the schools which were beyond the reach of the huge majority of young Arabs, mostly Moslem, who were doomed to illiteracy whether they lived in the country or in the city. For those like us who had the privilege of studying the culture and teaching of the dominant class, the experience was no less cruel. I have already stated how the educational system lowered our estimation of our spiritual heritage. I knew nothing about the Bible. I was totally unaware of the Mishna and the Talmud. The rudiments of religion which I studied remained almost foreign to me during the time I was under the influence of our Western masters. My ancestors' past was also foreign to me. I was in the position of many Jewish intellectuals who, integrated into the modern society whose privileges they shared and whose fortune and splendor they admired perhaps more than anybody else, lost interest in the Judaic adventure.

The process of alienation and readjustment operated even more brutally on you. The Jews' long wanderings among other peoples had accustomed us to changing our soul and our culture, to losing and finding ourselves again. Our ties with Judaism in this long and painful exercise had acquired a certain flexibility. For you the break with the Arab world was to be more rapid. Besides, the neglect from which your sociological group suffered was of such proportions that it is impossible to grow up in the camp of those who despised your people without undergoing a break of some sort. Oh, what contempt was heaped on the Arabs in Dar-el-Islam! Of course we Jews were also a target. I grew up, you will remember, among the swastikas which our little friends painted on the walls of our homes and schools. The Jews

96

were used to contemptuous treatment and had come to terms with privilege and habits. They were able to survive the poison of the thousand-year-old practices. For you scorn was a new thing. For the first time you felt as I did, that it was not only humiliating but fatal. It ended up affecting your whole life. I saw it clearly and I trembled for you, for us.

In that too we were brothers. We were both to be pitied, you the *bicot* and I who represented the "dirty Jew" for the mass of anti-Semites, even those who hated you. I could relate an endless series of experiences. We were battered by the hate of man for man. We were humiliated by the pride of so-called Christians who crushed us. One day we were walking together on the square near the Damascus Gates in Jerusalem. A young Arab shoeshine boy offered to shine the shoes of a European seated at a sidewalk café, and the foreigner agreed. When the moment to pay came, the only payment the Arab received was a kick in the face which felled him, his face covered with blood. Another day we had to pick up some wounded men in the city. The police, frightened by an Arab demonstration against the Jews incited by propagandists helped by Hitlerian Germany (that was in 1936), had fired into the crowd indiscriminately killing men on both sides. In this way, little by little, we became strangers to ourselves, to our kindred line, and to the culture which had nourished our ancestors. We became abstract beings whom the Europeans who surrounded us could rightly scorn. For if we suffered from the situation that had slowly developed, the Westerners themselves suffered from it, and no doubt were to be pitied the most. They remained Christian in name only. Their churches had become meeting places rather than centers of cult and adoration. The quality of Christian spirituality in Asia and Africa was a far cry from what it once was in the days of Saint Jerome and Saint Augustine. The most tragic sign of this situation and of the insensitivity which it implied was the almost complete failure of the Christian mission in Africa and Asia. Gradually Christianity became identified with a political regime. The three partners of the monotheistic adventure were basically in a very similar and precarious position. The Jew and the

Moslem were separated from their sociological group and their spiritual source, but their isolation held the Christian in the same situation. The Christian religion around us had undergone the same evolution as the Judaic and Islamic—it had gone dry. The Christians were unaware of their origins and their sources. They were divided into hostile and sometimes warring sects, and similarly cut off from their history. Strange creatures were born, offspring of the hate and bitterness of conflict: an Arab who was no longer an Arab; a Moslem who was no longer completely a Moslem; a Jew who had ceased being authentically a Jew; a Christian who no longer remembered the exigencies of his faith; an Easterner who had forgotten the meaning of his culture and its requirements. When the war came, when Hitler tried to enslave us, that was the hour of truth. We were ready for a more definitive break. The time for radical change had come.

It brought you and your people the same suffering as it brought us. We had known the war, adversity, the concentration camps, and the crematory furnaces. During this time the Arab revolt was fermenting. From the Atlantic coasts to the Indian Ocean it prepared itself to brave the wars whose brutality and savagery history would relate. From the beginning you foresaw the direction Asia was going to take. You left France to devote yourself to the education of your people and to prepare your brothers for their future. The Second World War marked an intensification of the trials of the entire Arab world. The conflict had mobilized and exhausted the manpower, ammunition, and food of the countries at war. Hunger made itself felt in the poorest countries in North Africa and in Asia where men died because of it. They were dying of starvation without any help forthcoming. The revolt started there. Just as the Germans provoked the Jewish revolt in Warsaw and in the ghettos of Europe, and indirectly in Palestine, so did they unconsciously prepare the Arab revolt which was the product of scorn and hunger. In 1945 in Algeria, the Kabyle revolt served as a prelude to the war which resulted in the constitution of a sovereign and independent Algerian republic. The Kabyle revolt had been suppressed with such brutality that the entire Arab world was shaken by it. That was when you left Jerusalem for Cairo where you joined the team which began to plan the widespread Algerian resistance against France. A short time later Abdel Krim was to be freed from his prison to be brought to the Côte d'Azur. He was successful in fooling his guards, despite their vigilance. He found refuge in Cairo and his presence served as a rallying point for you and your friends—which made possible the organization and planning of the revolt of the Moslems in North Africa against French domination. You launched into the undertaking with cold determination. A general plan had been developed which foresaw the successive liberation of Tunisia, Morocco, and ultimately Algeria. No one could foresee at that time what this conflict would cost in blood. In Algeria the war took on terrible proportions causing an incalculable number of deaths. The country created for the joy of living, for the happiness of the honeymoon which Camus has beautifully described, became the stage for the most unimaginable horrors. There war's absurdity reached its most extreme limits, absurdity of a conflict which could have been avoided, absurdity of reciprocal positions. Most of the Arabs and French wanted peace. Absurdity—the position of the Jews who were allied to both groups, tributaries of the Arabs to whom they were bound by a long past, and tributaries of France, too, to whom they owed all their rights and privileges. Between the two parties, they were in an impossible situation, paralyzed by one, and by the other, condemned to silence and heartbreak. One of our university friends, Jacques Lévy, was to be hit by an Arab bullet in the streets of Constantine while his father was shot by French soldiers—this irony symbolized the condition of the Algerian Jews whose community was to disappear as soon as the Algerian war was over. Your road in life had finally been found. Leaving behind the peaceful situation to which your parents destined you, you became an Arab fighter struggling on all the fronts for the liberation of his people. For you the Arab world was not merely solitary, but one, from the borders of India to the eastern banks of the Atlantic. Just as Judaism had changed into Zionism, so Islam donned its modern garb, changing into pan-Arabism. In both cases the

99

movement is essentially identical, provoked by a similar cause, misery, whether Jewish or Arab. Racism and anti-Semitism in the former case, and colonialism in the latter, and a new will for personal and national independence transforms both societies, the Moslem city and the Jewish world, into a distinct and autonomous movement with regard to its religious sources. The prophets of Arabism and those of Zionism, their disciples, may hate and fight each other; but they are still sons of the same Father. The brotherhood of the Arabs and the Jews perpetuates its paradoxical and absurd tradition of enmity that the Bible described in the accounts of the conflicts of Ishmael and Isaac, the heirs of Abraham.

4 Dawn

I made a promise on a December night in 1942 in the Alps at
the frontier which separated France from Switzerland, that
tragic night when Madeleine, hit by a German bullet, died
in my arms. I swore to her, whom I had loved so deeply, that
as soon as the war was over, if I lived, I would return to
Israel forever. For her—a Christian sacrificing her life saving
the Jews, accompanying them once more to the frontier of
freedom—it was like an absolution. The idea that I would
leave Europe to settle in Israel gave some hope to her final
moments. She died happy, thinking that I would finally live
under Jerusalem's skies. I left Switzerland as soon as I had
enough strength for the trip. From Genoa I shipped out on
a phantom ship heading for Haifa. I loved the sea and had
crossed the Mediterranean in every direction. But this time
the trip had a completely different meaning. On the ship
with me I found the survivors of the Nazi hell. They looked
haggard, more like skeletons than men. I hesitated to speak
to them for fear of re-awakening the nightmare they had
left behind. The deep silence which was each one's refuge
was almost unbearable for beneath it lay each one's living
wound, in his body or in his soul. The sea finally took my
mind off the turmoil from which we had escaped. I loved
the taste of salt and iodine, the smell of seaweed, and the feel
of the wind blowing in the sun. Our days of clandestine
struggle were over. Rediscovering the Mediterranean was
the sign of liberation and its baptism.

The real impact came at dawn when I was awakened
by my companions shouting "*Ha Carmel, Ha Carmel,*"
"Carmel, Carmel." I was jolted from my sleep and moved,
as my companions were, toward a sight which left all of us
speechless. In admiration and adoration we faced the sacred
mountain which from now on was a reality close enough to

see and touch. The mountain stood out in a symphony of colors in the rising sun. Dawn on the sacred mountain seemed to touch off an undefinable merriment as we received the sacrament of a new day.

As we drew closer, my friends became more serious. They were crowded in small groups on the ship overlooking the sea, at the edge of a henceforth fulfilled event—at last, the revelation of the land before us. A few of the older Jews chanted a psalm and were joined by other voices. We sang the 126th Psalm which seemed to be written for the occasion, the return of the captives of Zion to the promised land. The country of miracles suddenly offered us the most unbelievable one of all, that of our liberation and safe return after the war's frightful bloodshed. The psalm suddenly had become a living reality throbbing within our wounded lives. We were the captives whom the Lord finally was bringing back to the promised land. The smile on the psalmist's face two thousand five hundred years ago was our smile and our voices were chanting his song. The Bible, its land, its song, and its people, were all present as they had been since the beginning of our exile. The legend became living history. We left our exile to rediscover our country miraculously offered to those who were left after the relentless massacres. I saw it in a new perspective, as if for the first time. Each one of us sensed that setting foot on this land, he placed himself at the source of the purest of poetries. The rocks, the open tombs, the haunted grottos, the desert's screaming solitude, the weight of the cedar's silence, the blue and its harmony, all this was to become the everyday reality of our lives from now on. We were overcome with emotion and with the thought of the indescribable adventure which brought us to this point. We were ready to repeat Judah Halevy's gesture. Arriving in the Holy Land he bent to the ground to kiss the beloved soil. We thought of him and of all those who had lived and died trying to reach this land, inaccessible for centuries but welcoming us now. Our two thousand years of wandering was coming to an end. We were home again. This sentence hurts you, I know. Nonetheless, it is true. For the first time we realized that the land of Israel was our only possible country. I saw a Dominican in a white cassock and with rosary beads in his hand. He seemed lost in adoration. Christ was no doubt present in his heart, but so were David, the prophets and kings of Israel, and even Godefroy of Bouillon, Tancred the Brave, Richard the Lion-Hearted, Saint Louis and, closer to our time, Chateaubriand and Lamartine. Our fervor renewed in the dimension of our own time the acts of the famous pilgrims, Christians, Moslems, or Jews, who knew and loved the country of the Bible. For us the pall of tragedy was added.

We were the survivors of the concentration camps and crematories returning from the great torture of the exile. Here we could hope to heal the scars in our souls, our hearts, and our flesh. In the dawn sky and earth joined in the promise of life on the promontory of Mount Carmel. All Asia offered itself to our resurrection in the happiness of its nuptials with the sea. The sunrise marked the birth of a brand new day. We had lived out the war in the ranks of the French Resistance. We had known the anxieties, the struggles, the horrors of the pitched battle which we had been forced to fight day and night against the Nazis. And now here we were at the shores of Israel—for twenty centuries a hundred generations had not stopped hoping for and announcing this return. We had the privilege of being the first ones to return to the gates of the promised land to rebuild it.

As we drew closer to the shore, we could make out human figures, men who did not stop waving, their faces filled with the joy of welcome. But beyond the living we felt the presence of the dead—they, too, waited for us there on the shore, the Kleins, the Stourtzés, the Levis, Kohns and Guttmans, the Pollaks, the Levandovsckis. And you, Colombe, my friend were there bearing your totem so well. You were all there on the shore to greet us, and along with your welcome we heard the welcome, the moving *barukh haba*, of the legion of our dead and our martyrs. We, the survivors, felt dwarfted by the majesty of the spectacle which included us in its mystery and the intangible presence which filled this place. The land repossessed us as a jealous mistress who clasps her lover in her arms. Our return was her victory. We had no other choice than to give ourselves totally to her.

We arrived in Haifa in an atmosphere made tense by anticipation of the battles which were taking shape between the Arabs and the Jews. My friend, here my wound begins to bleed again. In France we had fought against the Nazis who were moved by a doctrine of hate, Hitler's gospel. We had to risk our lives to prevent its triumph. Having left those terrible battles behind, now I had to take on another fight in the land of the Bible, in the country Abraham made holy. This time the adversaries were not men I detested, but friends, the closet of friends with whom I had never stopped living, growing, and loving, those whose culture and civilization I admired, those whose language had been my native one. My astonishment was the realization that it was possible to fight against loved ones, against those whose friendship you desired, against those with whom you had to live in order to build a new world of brotherhood after the war.

At the port I met some friends who had arrived before we did. Mikhal and Robert had rented a jeep which we borrowed to go directly to the most dangerous front, Jerusalem. We were armed with rifles and pistols, one a light automatic which was Jacob's pride. When we crossed the zones occupied by the Arabs, we were silent and tense. We were more concerned than during the four years of war with the Germans. This battle was more difficult. At every turn we could be surprised by an ambush but managed the whole trip with only a few shots being fired not far from Caesarea. The anguish of this new fight which we had to engage in, while the country which we were to take possession of rid itself of the British, took nothing away from the delight of my rediscovery. What I found was a really strange war. The war and its consequences had driven the Jews out of most of the Arab countries. They had been forced out of Europe by the most dreadful of conflicts. And now, returning to their own land, they still had to face a barbaric and stupid battle. "A war which we did not want," Jacob explained in the command-car as he related the details of the battles of these recent days and the terrible predicament of the Jewish colony surrounded by five Arab armies. In the distance we heard the echo of the bullets which sometimes whistled over us and strayed not far from us.

In Tel-Aviv on May 14, 1948, Ben Gurion, president of

the executive committee of the Jewish Office, announced the establishment of a Jewish State in Palestine. It was a stroke of genius to name it Israel. All the delegates of the Jewish National Council representing both Palestinian and world Judaism were present at this historic moment. An appeal went out to Jews the world over to rally round the state of Israel and help it in the task of immigration and development. The United States and Soviet Russia, with several other countries following suit, had almost immediately recognized the Jewish state against which the Arab states soon unleased the war which had been brewing since November 29, 1947.

The absurdity needs to be explained. The conflict between the Jews and the Arabs developed over a cruel series of foolish misunderstandings. At the end of the last century when the first Jews from Eastern Europe came to settle in Palestine, authority was in the hands of the decadent Ottoman Empire, the "sick man" who was already faltering. Since 1517, in fact, the sultan of Constantinople had ruled Palestine.

For the Turkish police and for the Turkish government, the arrival of the Zionists could only mean one thing—a problem of public order. For them it was not a question of religion or ideology. They looked upon the Jews as agitators drawn toward Palestine where they might set up a socialist regime which would undermine the traditions of their Sublime Porte. The Zionists were first of all Westerners, bearers of a socialist ideal which could have all the virtues in the world, but not have the virtue of pleasing the sultan. Herzl was well aware of it when he went to Abdul Hamid III to propose the redemption of the Turkish debt in exchange for the right to immigrate to Palestine. But at that time Herzl was crying in the wilderness. The road leading to the resurrection of Jerusalem was to be long and hard.

With regard to the police measures which occasionally affected them, the Western Jews did not distinguish very well between those imposed by the Turkish police and those imposed by the indigenous Palestinian Arabs, or ultimately those resulting from the widespread anarchy. It was easy to conclude that the Arabs opposed the Jews. Naturally there had been incidents between Arabs and Jews but they did not go beyond what might be expected in the anarchy which prevailed in all the provinces of the Ottoman Empire. In reality the Palestinians had no say in a country dominated by the Turks since the sixteenth century. They were indifferent to the conflict which pitted the Turkish police against the newcomers. Besides, the Arab population was exposed to the same ill treatment as the Zionist colonials from the police whose tactics were infinitely arbitrary and whimsical. One can still see on the façade of the gates of Jaffa the marks of the hooks where the condemned were hanged. Far more Arabs than Jews met a tragic end there, and frequently for more futile motives.

On the Arab side power rested with the feudal lords who were not in the least interested in having their country spoiled by a socialist regime imported from Eastern Europe by Jewish idealists, pioneers whom they could not understand in any case. The Arabs were equally incomprehensible to the Jews. The Arab world was totally unknown to all these immigrants from the ghettos of Poland, Russia, Rumania and Germany. To make matters worse, the first contacts often took place under terrible conditions. I will give you a single example. A few months after his arrival in Palestine in 1907, David Ben Gurion, who was then a farm worker in Hadera, was going to work one morning accompanied by two friends when he heard two shots. To his right and to his left, his friends fell, assassinated by an Arab hidden in a nearby thicket. The man had only two bullets in his rifle. Had there been a third, it would have been for David Ben Gurion himself. In this way the leaders of the Zionist movement learned to know the Arab world, by shots coming from the irresponsible elements or by the trickery of the feudal lords who at all costs wanted to rid themselves of the socialism which inspired the rise of a Palestine transformed by the Jews.

The Ottoman Empire collapsed at the end of the First World War. The new occupier of Palestine, the British Empire, had received its mandate from the League of Nations. British order replaced Turkish anarchy as the English organized the administration of Palestine. The executive branch had at its head the High Commissioner named by the Crown who exercised legislative authority as well.

The story of this mandate was to be that of a cruel confrontation of certain English, Arab, and Jewish individuals. The war between the Jews and Arabs in Palestine assured British supremacy cheaply. It was easy to take advantage of the famous "divide and conquer" idea and the British administration did not always know how to resist that temptation nor overcome the obstacles which cropped up on the road to peace in Palestine. For the British, fully supported by the native feudal leaders, the difficulty remained the same. These free youngsters dreaming of socialism and revolution modified the social and even geographical structures of Palestine by introducing modern industry and agriculture, and inventing the *kibbutzim*. They could only be one of the avatars of the devil. The attempts at dialogue between the Zionist leaders, almost all of Eastern European origin, and the Arab *sheiks* did not have great chances for success. Once again the growing conflict was not based on a religious or ethnic ideology. It was a police problem—on several occasions Sir Winston Churchill violently condemned British policy in Palestine before the House of Commons.

The agreement signed on January 3, 1919, between Emir Faisal representing the Arab kingdom of the Hejaz, and Doctor Weizman in the name of the Zionist organization, had no results. The different British High Commissioners after July 1920, the date that the first such Commissioners Sir Herbert Samuel took on his duties, assumed the (more or less) conscientious execution of the stipulations of the mandate interpreted by the British *White Paper* of June 1922. But from 1920 on bloody incidents had erupted. April 2, 1920, was a day of trouble in Jerusalem. The Arabs, inspired by the ruling feudality, showed their ever-increasing hostility to the strengthening of the Jewish national home on every possible occasion. In 1921 there were uprisings in Jaffa following an incident during the May-Day Parade. For the rank and file, however, life continued without anything disturbing everyday relations, not even the open conflict which began to worsen from 1929 on.

In August 1929, Jerusalem was the scene of an orgy of

killings and pillages which lasted several days under the indifferent eye of the passive British police. An argument
about the Wailing Wall had been the catalyst. In 1933, 1936,
and 1937 these troubles were repeated.

In 1923, the English had tried to establish a leglislative
council, but the attempt had failed because of Arab obstruc-
tionism. The feudal lords looked suspiciously at the organization of a new state over which they had no hope for
control.

In 1935 the attempt was made again. Again it failed, this
time because of the Jews. In 1936 the Jews and Arabs
reached a formula for compromise which was defeated in
London by the House of Commons and the House of Lords.
That year an Arab High Committee was formed in the
month of April and was presided over by the *mufti*, Hadz
Amin el Husseini. It included the most reactionary elements
of the Arab world and unleashed a revolt which transformed
Palestine into a stronghold occupied by more than twenty
thousand British soldiers. These Arab elements had been
inspired by Fascists and Nazis, a fact since established by the
publication of the secret Wilhemstrasse Archives. The Arab
High Committee had received the financial support of the
Nazis and Fascists who financed the revolt, with the Mufti
of Jerusalem, Haj Amin el Husseini, acting as intermediary.
Hitler and his police achieved in Palestine what they had
attempted throughout the Arab world. In Algeria when the
French administration was in the hands of the Vichy government and tightly controlled by elements commanded
by Hitler's Germany, similar propositions had been made to
the Arabs. The German agents had contacted all the leading
people with any authority over the Algerian Moslems to
propose the organization of a pogrom. For several days they
would be given *carte blanche* to kill the Jews and pillage
their belongings. Considerable sums had been put at their
disposal to organize the pogrom. The Arabs were unanimous. Whether they belonged to the rich and ruling class
(*caid*, *aga*, or *bachagahas*), or to the priest class (*imam* and
ulema), or whether they were the simple elements of the
lower classes, their answer was unequivocal: "We will have
nothing to do with that kind of business." So for the dura-

tion of the war and throughout North Africa, the Jews were unanimously protected by the Arabs. During the Second World War, in the course of the wars for independence in Algeria, in Tunisia, and in Morocco there was never an incident or confrontation with the Jews or Moslems as such. To the contrary, the National Liberation Front in Algeria had given the military very clear instructions, respected everywhere, to protect Jews and to avoid any fight which would set the Arabs against the French army. Here is an example which should be better known and thought about by all of us, Jews, Arabs, and Christians. Just as certain English people had done in Palestine, some Germans supported by their French collaborators had tried to convince the Moslem and the Jews that "Arab anti-Semitism" existed. That seems contrary to the truth to me. The wisdom and generosity of the Arabs of North Africa had foiled the plots of a Germany interested in igniting the tinderbox while its chances for world domination were being played out in Europe. In Palestine the same causes produced different effects. There the feudal chiefs did become involved. They accepted German money and found here and there the equivocal excuses to light the fire and start the war between the children of Abraham, between Israel and Ishmael. Why? The reasons were complex, but the main incentive was clear. It was primarily a matter of preserving their feudal privileges and strengthening their domination of the Arab countries which were traditionally subservient to them. It was obvious that the Jews endangered these privileges and disturbed the foundation of Arab society as it had crystalized under the Ottoman Empire and had become more entrenched since the English had taken over the government. The means mattered little, they were interested in the ends—to stop the Jews from settling in Palestine and to halt the revolutionary changes which necessarily accompanied their arrival.

As the Jewish national home was strengthened, moved by its internal dynamism, by the thrust which the world Zionist organization gave it, and paradoxically fortified by the rabid persecution which Hitler had unchained in Europe, some Arabs took a more rigid stand against the Jews. The English profited from the situation by giving a progressively stricter interpretation to the Balfour declaration. On May 17, 1939, the British government published the *White Paper* which effected a complete reversal of British policy in Palestine. This *White Paper* had a long history. As the conflict between Jews and Arabs became more aggravated, the British had sent commissions which published an impressive number of documents. The *White Paper* published in June 1922 while Churchill was minister of the Colonies, the *White Paper* of Lord Passfield in October 1930, the French report of July 1933, the failure of the attempts to establish a legislative council, the voluminous report of the Peel commission which in July 1937 agreed for the first time to the necessity for a division of Palestine and proposed the constitution of an Arab state and a Jewish state, the report of the commission for partition presided over by Sir Woodhead in 1938, and finally the failure of the London conference of February-March, 1939 to reunite the delegates of the Jewish Agency and the representatives of the Palestinian Arabs and the Arab powers—all these stages terminated without reaching a settlement and the deadlock was announced on May 17, 1939. On the eve of the war the last *White Paper* of the mandatory power in Palestine destroyed Jewish hopes. The Jewish Agency Office and the members of the loyal opposition denounced the new British policy as a betrayal of the spirit and the letter of the mandate. In effect, the English government agreed to stop Jewish immigration from March 1940 on.

On February 28, 1940, a land rule strictly limited the right of Jews to acquire land in Palestine. What were the underlying intentions of the government? No doubt it hoped to win over Arab sympathy by closing Palestine to the immigrants. But what Arab could have refused to welcome a Jew while the Hitlerian persecutions were going on in Europe?

In 1939, nine million five hundred thousand Jews lived in Europe. In 1945 there were no more than two million seven hundred and fifty thousand. In Germany their number had dwindled from five hundred and fifty thousand in 1925 to fifteen thousand at the end of the war. Ninety-six percent of them had disappeared; most of them were murdered. The Nazi machine for the destruction of the Jews went into operation as soon as a country was invaded by the German army. The Jews of the occupied lands were to be exterminated in the gas chambers and crematories of the concentration camps. How many Jews were exterminated? Different figures have been proposed. They vary between five million and six million ninety-six thousand. If the figures are correct, 73.4 percent of the Jewish population of the countries occupied by the Germans was destroyed. One million eight hundred thousand of these victims, as you know, were children under fourteen years old. Whatever the horror of the statistics, I have seen more than fifty of my friends fall during the years of terror. My own survival is a miracle as is that of all the Jews who were with me that first day of my arrival in Israel.

My eyes could not get their fill of the countryside they contemplated on this unforgettable day. Arriving in Jerusalem, I had the feeling of stepping out on the world's balcony. I devoured the tawny colors of the hills of Judaea. From the hilltops I discovered in the distance the Mount of Moab where Moses long ago had beheld the Holy Land, inaccessible to him. I was back in this country where I was born but I seemed to discover it for the first time. I was a man of Jerusalem, attached by a long line of ancestors to the city where you too were born. I knew our country stone by stone. Yet returning after the war I seemed to be another man in another land, like the immigrants who surrounded me. You must understand that. I arrived home not as a conqueror but as a man who, having given up the temptation of the West, was returning home bringing along his brothers, all those who had decided to build the first unit of a new world. My eyes never tired of the sight before me.

How can I express the strange feeling which took hold of me as I saw the sights which I have loved since childhood? The Mount of Olives, Mount Scopus, the Valley of the Cedron, the Valley of Gehenna, the dome of the Mosque of Omar built on the ancient site of the Temple, the Church of the Holy Sepulcher, the Mosque of El-Aksa with its silver-colored dome, the ramparts of the Old City, the

Tower of David, Mount Zion, the dozens of belfries and domes which filled the city of a thousand synagogues, all that I had so often dreamt about in Europe, I rediscovered in a single glance. The starry dream of Jacob, the call of the prophets, the cry of the apostles—I saw them, I heard them in this city toward which so many prayers have poured, in the special glow of its lights and in the firmness of its stones. Such had been the place of our meeting, such was my country, the real Jerusalem of the world in flames revealed to me. A battleline divided it, and on the first day of my return, a bullet from across the way wounded me. So I shed my blood on the very first day. Beaten to the point of death by the Germans, now an Arab was after my blood. What a moment to give up my life in a conclusive baptism, my nuptials of blood with the city of David, with the city of peace, my capital of the domain of silence.

During my convalescence I learned to know our country better. The war had marked a period of appeasement in Palestine. The pressing requirements of the moment and the Hitlerian emergency had convinced the Arab High Committee, the Jewish Agency, and Great Britain to put aside their political differences in order to mobilize all their forces against Nazi Germany. The economic and political effects of the war facilitated a cooperation between the Arabs and the Jews. Everybody knew that it was possible to cooperate on the economic plane and that Jews and Arabs could easily create the conditions for a mutually profitable relationship. More than thirty thousand Israeli volunteers had joined the liberation army side by side with the allies. But the surface tranquility camouflaged what was simmering. Because the Palestinian frontiers were closed to Jewish immigrants driven from Europe, phantom ships had to wander from port to port laden with their unwanted cargo. On February 24, 1940, the *Struma* which had been denied access to Mediterranean ports sank off Istanbul. Seven hundred and sixty-eight passengers drowned. During the summer of 1947 the *Exodus* would have no doubt met the same fate had it not been for French hospitality. By every possible means my people tried to reach the promised refuge, often surmounting bloody obstacles to flee the horror of their situation in many countries of the exile. In fact, the Jewish people came out of the holocaust of the war with the inflexible will to put an end to their wandering. After the Second World War they were going to confront the British Empire to force it to leave Palestine. For the first time in history the Jewish and Arab armies were to meet in a merciless struggle. The moral justification of the Arab war against the creation of the state of Israel lay in the often repeated accusation of imperialism. You knew very well that it was necessary to find a solution to the plight of the Jews, but you didn't want it to be to the detriment of the Arab peoples. You compared the Jews coming to settle in Palestine to the French conquerors of Algeria, to the English taking possession of India, to the Italians penetrating into Ethiopia. We were colonists, conquerors, imperialists.

Were you right on this point, the state of Israel could never have been created and would have had no chance for survival. Never could the United Nations have found the necessary two-thirds majority if the new state had been the anachronistic result of a colonial adventure. The Jews would never have accepted the undertaking in principle and could never have found the moral courage and means for success. And their triumph would have had no positive outcome if the state had been founded on an essentially imperialistic encroachment.

I hear you object: "The Jews have established their state on Arab land." This Arab territory was under British mandate from 1917 to 1947. From 1517 to 1917, for four centuries, it was a neglected province of the Ottoman Empire and Turkish property.

For 550 years the Arabs had no say in Palestine. And their rights to this land, the results of a conquest, go back to the seventh century, 1200 years ago. At the end of Mohammed's life, Arab tribes from the Hejaz made several incursions into Palestine and Syria. This was the natural course of the eternal strife between the nomads and the settled people. In order to protect themselves against these invasions the Romans had fortresses built at the frontiers of the desert to keep the country safe from plunderers. The Byzantines, too, had tried to protect themselves from the nomads of the Arab desert by organizing a kind of Arab state south of Palestine comprising the territories belonging to the Nabataeans and the Palmyrians. The specific goal was to protect the Palestinians and the settled Jews from the Arab nomads. But when the Arabs decided to conquer the Holy Land, the Byzantines did not see the real danger of the undertaking. They assumed that the attacks were simply more *razzias* and not full-scale conquest. The Byzantines had succeeded the Romans. Under the reign of Heraclius (610–641) their army was weakened by defeats throughout the Empire. The Palestinian population crushed by taxes and fear was ready to accept the law of a new master.

Shortly after the death of Mohammed new raids to bring back rich booty were undertaken against the country. The Arab army responsible for Palestine had three generals at its head: Amr ben Ass was to conquer "Palestine," that is, the Hills of Judea and the coastal plain; Shurahbil ben Hassana headed for Galilee; Yazid Abu Suffian attacked Damascus. From Eilat Amr headed for Palestine. The conquest was rapidly accomplished in the ten years from 634 to 644. At the end of 636, all Syria was in the hands of the Arabs. The fortified cities, Jerusalem, Caesarea, Ashkalon, resisted for a longer time. Jerusalem fell into Arab hands in 637 or 638 after the Byzantine government deserted, relinquishing power to Bishop Sofronius who negotiated the surrender of the city to the Caliphe Omar. The Arab conquest of Palestine had a decisive importance in universal history. It opened the gates of the West to the sons of the desert and put them in direct contact with Jewish and Christian culture.

The Arabs held Palestine for three centuries exactly, from 633 to 969. The ninth century marked the fall of the Abassid Caliphate. Turkish Emirs cut up possessions which they managed autonomously. In 868 Ahmed Ibn Tolon founded an independent kingdom in Egypt. A few years later he conquered Palestine and Syria, removing them from Arab domination until the leader's death.

In the second half of the tenth century, the Fatimid Dynasty which founded Cairo continued Ibn Tolon's policy and after 969 undertook the systematic conquest of the Holy Land. They clashed with the tenacious resistance of the

Bedouins. War and anarchy prevailed in endemic states. The struggles were constant between the Egyptians and the Bedouins in Palestine. In 1024 the Bedouins succeeded in driving out their enemies but their triumph lasted only five years. In 1029 the Fatimids beat them again in the battles which took place in Galilee near Lake Tiberias.

The Turkish monarchs of the Seldjucid Dynasty took advantage of this anarchy to try to get a foothold in Palestine. Their victory put a definitive end to Arab and Egyptian domination. The war between the Fatimids and the Seldjucids lasted until the ninth century. The Egyptians held a coastal position and reconquered Jerusalem in 1096, taking it from the Seldjucids who had ruled over the city from 1071.

Then there was the dramatic parenthesis of the Latin kingdom of Jerusalem. The Crusaders took three years to reach the Holy Land. In May 1099 they landed on the shores of Lebanon and set out for Jerusalem. The seige of the city lasted from June 7 to July 15, 1099. Its conquest was accompanied by a general massacre of the population. Some twenty-five thousand Jews who were living in the city fought valiantly. Defeated, they were slaughtered or sold as slaves in Italy. The rare ones who escaped found refuge in Ashkalon and in Egypt. Godefroy de Bouillon, Raymond de Toulouse, and Tancred ruled over the greater part of the Holy Land. In 1110 the principal cities of the country were all under the control of the Crusaders supported by the fleets of Venice, Genoa, and Pisa. The first kingdom of Jerusalem lasted in the Holy Land from 1099 to 1187. Saladin, whose action was aimed at uniting Egypt, Iraq, and Syria reconquered Jerusalem and a part of the Holy Land; finally the last Christian conquerors were expelled in 1291.

The return to complete Moslem domination caused the country to lose its international importance for centuries. The Mameluks, militiamen of Turco-Egyptian origin, were its masters. For 250 years they administered the country which then enjoyed relative peace. The Turks, who had had designs on the country since the thirteenth century, finally conquered it in the sixteenth century and remained its masters until the end of the First World War in 1917.

The Romans, the Byzantines, the Arabs (from the seventh

to the tenth century only), the Egyptians, the Crusaders, the Mameluks, the Turks, and the English were the successive rulers of Palestine between the fall of the Jewish State in the second century of the Christian era and its restoration in 1948.

Each of the rulers conquered the country by fire and sword. The Arabs were also conquerors and were chased out, not by the Jews, but by the Egyptians, the Mameluks, and the Turks. And when we are accused of imperialism, it must be remembered that the Jewish nation was broken up by Roman imperialism whose triumph in the land of Israel marked the beginning of the wandering and suffering of the Jews. The day that this point becomes as clear to the world as it is to us, the Israeli-Arab conflict will be easier to solve. The Jews who returned to the Holy Land did not introduce a new colonial problem, but made amends for one of the greatest crimes of imperialism, the destruction of the State of Israel by the Roman Empire. Their struggle is part of everyone's struggle for freedom. It rectifies one of the aftereffects of Western imperialism.

During the two thousand years that the Romans, the Byzantines, the Arabs, the Egyptians, the Crusaders, the Mameluks, the Turks, and the English succeeded each other at the helm, the Jews remained present, praying, as they did everywhere in their exile, for the restoration of Zion and the reestablishment of Jerusalem. It seems to me that the Arab claim ought to be distinguished from the rest. I know that ultimately it is based on a principle of Moslem law by virtue of which a land belonging to Islam for a single day must remain so until the end of the world. In this way Spain and southern France are in principle integral parts of the house of Islam. So be it. But will the Arab Christians and those who have freed themselves from such a rigid theocratic perspective accept this principle? Even the most intransigent Moslem could have a more positive attitude toward the principle, at least, of the existence of the State of Israel. The Moslem city has always allowed the existence of a Jewish community in its midst. It so happens that more than fifty percent of the present citizens of the State of Israel are from Arab and Moslem countries. The young generation of Israelis of African and Asian origins reaches seventy percent. Is this fact not sufficient for Moslem thought to begin to justify by law the existence of a state which otherwise is a cause of scandal. Why could Moslem theologians not adapt the Omar Charter in a new spirit to permit the cooperation of the Moslem nations with the Christian states and the State of Israel?

If Arabism is no longer to be understood in its restricted sense, but more broadly as comprising everything which concerns the nations which have adopted the Arab language and culture, then the majority of the Jews living in Israel are an integral part of the Arab world. For twelve centuries my ancestors, as yours, have spoken Arabic. My case, as you know, is that of all the Jews who have come to settle in Israel from Morocco, Algeria, Tunisia, Libya, Egypt, Lebanon, Syria, Yemen, Iraq, and other Moslem countries. Today the Easterners are in the majority in Israel. Why refuse to recognize it?

My sorrow was the sign of a deep conflict. I knew the Arab world very well and had grown up with my Arab friends. I loved Arab culture and history and admired the spiritual values which the Arab world transmitted to the nations. I knew of our common past and deep friendship which has always brought the Arabs and the Jews closer together throughout Dar-el-Islam for centuries. I knew to what degree Herzl's dream of salvation for the African and Asian peoples depended today on the friendship and reconciliation of Israel and Ishmael for its accomplishment. I knew for certain how much Judeo-Arab friendship was necessary to the well-being of the Near East and perhaps the world. I also felt more sensitively the conflict which tortured us in all its horror and absurdity.

Ein breira—we had no choice—at its birth Israel had to undergo the trial of blood and fire. The Jews of Palestine in revolt against the mandatory power had an additional problem. From November 29, 1947 on, they had to face repeated attacks of the Arab troops recruited in Palestine or from the neighboring states. From May 15, 1948 on, it was invasion by the regular armies of five states each of which if taken separately seemed to be militarily more powerful than Israel.

King Farouk reigned in Cairo then. The Arab League

which had been founded in Egypt's capital on March 22, 1945, directed a violent campaign of threats, provocation, and propaganda against the very principle of the creation of the State of Israel. For the first time in centuries the entire Arab world shook with a new polemic—the holy war was preached and actively prepared from one end of the neighboring Arab territories to the other. The Jews were going to have to pay for their audacity in wanting to be free in a territory which was theirs. The Arab leaders promised them complete extermination. *El-khorban*, the extermination—such was the future which the charitable souls of the feudal Arabs were preparing for us. This hate, often vocal, was preached by the potentates and the feudal lords who then ruled in the Near East. Recruiting offices had been opened in all the Arab capitals. Training centers had been set up under the control of the "Committee for the Defense of Palestine" with the support of all the governments of the Arab League. Direct acts of aggression took place while the British still controlled the country. Under their benevolent tutelage the troops recruited in Syria, Lebanon, Jordan, Egypt, and Iraq, reinforced by some mercenaries and a few Palestinian groups, led an action of harassment against the Jewish colonies.

From November 30, 1947, to February 1, 1948, the attacks were aimed primarily against the villages of northern Palestine. The aggression by the units under the control of the Arab League, notably in the vicinity of Jerusalem or Hebron, and the isolated actions of indigenous Arabs or Arab infiltrators caused thousands of victims on either side. From February 6, 1948 on, the Arab High Committee confirmed its resolution to oppose the creation of the State of Israel in every way. And, in fact, from the end of January 1948 on numerous armed groups belonging to the Arab Liberation Army infiltrated into Palestine with the tacit agreement of the mandatory power and sometimes with the help of some native elements. With the cooperation of England the feudal lords scattered in the framework of the Arab League wanted to prevent the establishment of a Jewish state in Palestine. They wanted to make Palestine a united and independent Arab state without considering the decision of the

United Nations or the existence of Jewish colonists who were threatened with total extermination if they resisted. The plan was clear. The banner of Arab nationalism was being waved to prevent a democratic and socialist Jewish state (the contribution of the pioneers of Israel) from being set up in the Near East. The independent state of Palestine would have been a feudal state dominated by the anachronistic monarchs who were at the head of most of the Arab states of the Middle East.

How did the clever plan so completely fail?

From February 1948 on there were several thousand soldiers, Syrians, Lebanese, Transjordanians and Iraquis settled in Palestine under the command of Fawzi el-Kawukji. These troops camped in the vicinity of Nazareth, Safed, Djennin, Nablus and in the mountainous region south of Jerusalem. Their objective was to assure the relief of the British whose departure had been announced for May 15. The military action of the Arabs was to put pressure on the United Nations in order to force it to return to the decision of November 29, 1947, if possible. Should the Jews persist in their will to create a Jewish state, the Arabs would prove their military superiority and win the final say over land, sea, and air thanks to the Arab armies commanded by the Iraqui generals, Ismaël Sarwad and Taha Sacha el Hachimi.

The entire world was alerted. Numerous Jews, including some ranking Zionists, trembled as H-hour approached. It was feared that Hitler's extermination of the European Jews might be followed by that of the Jews settled in Palestine as all the voices of Arab propaganda announced and everything seemed to indicate. Some charitable souls had even predicted the opening of concentration camps in Greece for refugees of the massacres in Palestine which the feudal Arabs promised. This country was besieged on all sides by armies stationed on its frontiers. The powerful Arab Legion of Transjordan under the control of British officers was also getting ready to intervene in the final settlement. It occupied Jericho on April 29, 1948, attacked the colony of Gecher, and then on May 4 attacked the colony of Kfar Etsion. As Great Britain evacuated its troops, the Arab Legion moved in and took possession of the military camps and munition depots. From the first days of May, King Farouk and King Abdallah, torn by conflicting feelings, along with the military, civil and religious authorities of all the Arab countries, multiplied their aggressive declarations, which were widely picked up by the world press. Faced with this apparently widespread upheaval and in fear of terrible threats magnified by the thousand voices of Arab propaganda, the most ardent partisans of the Jewish state began to fear the worst. A sizeable portion of world Jewish opinion also advised prudence, patience.

The die was cast. From May 14 on, the day when David Ben Gurion proclaimed the Jewish state, the Jewish colonies underwent a general assault. Successive waves of planes bombed Tel-Aviv as a motorized column of the Egyptian army attacked Nirim and invaded the Negev. Abdallah of Transjordan informed the United Nations that his armies had been forced to enter Palestine to protect the unarmed Arabs against possible massacres. Syrian, Lebanese, and Iraqui troops crossed the northern frontiers. Unidentified planes, probably Iraq's, attacked the colonies to the east and to the south of Lake Tiberias. An Iraqui motorized column entered the country to the east of the Jordan and spread out on the banks of Lake Tiberias, shelling the colonies of Shaar Hagolan, Achdod, and Afikim. The Arab Legion occupied the headquarters of the Palestine Electric Corporation at the junction of the Jordan and the Yarmouk and turned its troops toward Jerusalem and Beersheva. Five nations totalling more than thirty-five million inhabitants, according to the untiring theme taken up by the Arab propaganda, so attacked our little state to prevent its birth. It was comprised of five hundred fifty-five thousand souls who lacked food, ammunition, and everything else except the will to live and therefore to win.

Therein lies the basic issue. Israel has no choice. It has to win or disappear. The Arab assault was impressive. The Jewish resistance surprised the whole world and especially the feudal Arabs themselves who had believed in the power of their own speeches to rally their people. But the latter neither identified with their leaders nor with their new war. Some troops had been mobilized, they were paid in gold, but their heart was not in it. At the top the leaders were quarreling. In the lower ranks the troops did not understand the goals of this battle nor the reasons for their sacrifice. What is more, instead of the immediate collapse of Israel which Arab propaganda predicted and in which the Arabs had ended up believing, they were faced with the entire Jewish people standing up to the invader, scarcely wavering under the initial assaults, and soon taking the initiative in the fight, regaining almost all the positions which had been lost during the early hours of the invasion, occupying the vital regions of the country and capturing the major part of the Egyptian army at Faluja—one of the Egyptian officers wounded and taken prisoner was named Nasser. The Arab Legion in Jerusalem was beaten while the Jewish troops drove the Lebanese back to the other side of the border and discouraged the Syrians and Iraquis from ever coming down the side of Lake Tiberias again. From that point on the press correspondents could readily evoke the struggle of David and Goliath and talk of a miracle. Jewish humor, which has a knack for hitting upon the essential, was probably closer to the truth in attributing the victory to two causes: one, a *natural* cause, was the help given by God to the people; the other was *supernatural*, the heroism of the Jewish soldiers who fought like lions.

The Arabs planned a flash war with the complete destruction of Israel in ten days at the end of which King Abdallah was to make his entry into Jerusalem on May 1. So much optimism was ultimately counterproductive because the Arabs made the mistake of underestimating two important factors: the *Hagana* and the inflexible will of a population of only five hundred fifty-five thousand resolute in its will to win or to die.

An Arab, Abdel Razak Abdel Kader, and a Frenchman, Jean-Pierre Alem, who knew the Near East well have described the distressing episodes of the Judeo-Arab conflict. I will pass over this war. It is heartbreaking to think of the absurdity of the conflict which has pitted us against each other. I will leave it at this point, telling you how much I hope that you will know the truth about that absurd war—not the war of the Arabs against the Jews or of the Jews against the Arabs, but the confrontation of a desperate group of feudal lords who intended to use Israel to strengthen their hold over the nearby Arab states. The victory of Israel, as Abdel Kader has clearly stated, brought the era of the liberation of the Arab people closer. It put an end to the sovereign power of the Arab feudal lords. Israel's victory sounded the knell for King Farouk and his feudal regime. The example of Israel, we will see, woke up the nearby Arab countries and incited them to rise up against the subjugated condition of the preceding decade. The Moslem elites formed by Western culture found the necessary courage to oppose the ancient regimes from Israel's example. The creation of the State of Israel accelerated an unprecedented economic revival in Lebanon and inspired certain initiatives in Jordan which ultimately have worked for the benefit of the Arab peoples—this in spite of the would-be hate, this in spite of the huge sums of money spent everywhere, but especially in Egypt, Syria, and Iraq to prepare for the war which for certain Arab leaders must still lead to the extermination of Israel.

The State of Israel is the first one in history which was created by a decision of a majority of the countries of the world. That decision would have remained academic if a desperate energy had not animated us to get it out of the tribunals and make it history.

A subtle observer of Islam, the historian Gauthier, once wrote that the history of the Moslem peoples is that of a fertility which does not come to fruition. In the same spirit, Gauthier, who understood the Jewish realities could have recalled the words of the poet Heinrich Heine: "Judasim is not a religion, it is a misfortune." So the Arabs, at the cruelest hour of their history, when they were dominated by foreign powers, and the Jews, who in Hitler's time had reached the worst distress in their history, one which threatened to exceed any known horror, found themselves together on the threshold of a new liberation.

Yes, the creation of the State of Israel gave a fatal blow to Farouk's regime. For a moment one could have hoped that the armistice agreement signed at Rhodes in February 1949 between Egypt and Israel would be a prelude to peace.

After all, every war, even the most terrible, ends with a peace treaty. This time the Near East was going to be in a stalemate, a situation which was neither peace nor war. In order to rule, God apparently needs the secret flaw which Satan introduced into the order of his creation. So it is with monarchs and dictators. For the felicity of their reign they need a devil whom they can wave at their whim. The 1948 defeat marked the definitive awakening of the hostility of the masses against Farouk. Egypt had been occupied by the British since 1882, the time when France was establishing itself in Tunisia. The treaty of 1936 by which the British recognized in principle the independence of Egypt had changed nothing of the country's structure. The end of the British mandate over Palestine and the crushing of the Egyptian armies in Israel could hardly be without repercussions for King Farouk and his dynasty. He did not have the courage to see through all the consequences of his defeat in his domestic and foreign policy. For three years Farouk wavered between peace and war. As internal opposition mounted he took a harder line against Israel. In September 1951 the Security Council condemned Egypt which was preventing ships whose destination was Israel from using the Suez Canal. In vain! The domestic crisis won out.

In July 1952 a group of young officers led by Neguib and Nasser force Farouk to abdicate. Egypt becomes a republic leaning toward socialism. Shortly afterward King Abdallah is assassinated in Jerusalem and on May 2, 1953, King Hussein succeeds him. The king of Arabia, Ibn Saud, dies in 1953. The Near East is transformed. In 1954 a young colonel named Gamel Abd el Nasser becomes Egypt's charismatic dictator.

Nasser has built his political power by defining in his *Philosophy of Revolution* the three famous circles where he means to establish his influence: the Arab world, the Moslem world, and the African and Asian third world. He arrives at this conclusion as a result of his effort to discover himself and, through him, Egypt's deepest mission. Nasser's progress is interesting to follow. The man suffers visibly from Egypt's internal situation. The 1948 defeat leaves him in Faluja, wounded and a prisoner of Israel. This jolt, what he learns about Zionism, gives him the will to act—not to waste his life in hopeless exaltations, but to use it to build his country, to free it from its tyrant and to dedicate it to a double revolution, social and political. In his projects Nasser clashes with his friends' egocentricity:

> *The word "I" was on every tongue. It was the magic solution of every difficulty and the effective cure for every malady. (new paragraph) Often did I meet men, referred to in the press as "great men," of various tendencies and colours, from whom I sought the solution of a difficult problem. I could hear nothing from them save the word "I."* (Philosophy of Revolution,* p. 34)

This egocentricity is coupled with a will to kill:

> *Every leader we came to wanted to assassinate his rival. Every idea we found aimed at the destruction of another. If we were to carry out all that we heard, then there would not be one leader left alive. Not one idea would remain intact. We would cease to have a mission save to remain among the smashed bodies and the broken debris lamenting our misfortune and reproaching our ill-fate.* (Philosophy of Revolution, p. 33)

For an instant Nasser believes in the efficacy of political murder and tells the astonishing story of one such attempt in which he was involved—the assassination of a political opponent. The coup perpetrated, he is haunted by the cries of the women and children who had rushed to the victim's aid. He spends a sleepless night questioning himself on the usefulness of political murder (*Philosophy of Revolution*, p. 47).

The analysis which Nasser gives is interesting for the light it sheds on his policy in general. The selfishness that he reproaches the Egyptians for becomes the cardinal principle of his thought and he projects it over all of Egypt, situated in the center of the Arab world, in the center of the Moslem world, at the center of every undertaking and every thought. When a problem is presented to Nasser, he does not answer

* Buffalo, New York: Smith, Keynes, and Marshall, 1959.

124

"I," but more subtly "Egypt." And his momentary desire for political murder which he regrets in his friends, becomes central to the policy of his country—not the murder of an individual, but that of a nation, Israel. The assassination of Israel will solve all the problems of Egypt, the Arab world, and the universe.

The realization of his dreams seems to depend on this murder of a nation. In his mind the annihilation of Zionism, by who knows what magic operation, would allow the unity of the Arab world with the additional integration of two hundred million Africans. (Is Egypt not African?) Once that is accomplished, it will be possible to erect the huge empire of Islam, transformed into a political power backed by the Arab world in the Near East and in the Magreb, and by the hundreds of millions of Moslems of the Magreb, the Near East, Indonesia, China, Siam, Burma, Pakistan, the Soviet Union, and other countries of the five continents. Here we have it. Nasser, who criticized the egocentricity of his compatriots ends his book not on the "I" which as we know is hateful, but on the "we," the obviously majestic plural. Nasser says nothing about the real contemporary problems in his book, nothing about Christianity, the West, Asia, or communism. For everything to be right, it is sufficient that having destroyed Israel, he erect his Afro-Arab empire and solidify the unity of the Moslem world.

Nasser's thought is so impoverished that it hardly merits refutation. The facts have constantly been doing this in the most bitter way for sixteen years. The pitiful victim of this tragicomedy is Egypt, enslaved by a savage dictatorship which has destroyed for a long time any chances for recovery. All the living forces of the nation have been crushed—the aristocracy, the feudal class, the bourgeoisie, the intellectuals, the French, Italians, Greeks, Jews and, since 1967, the army buried in the sands of Sinai. Nasser's record is the most catastrophic in history and few minds have had the courage to measure its consequences for Egypt and for the Arab world. It is the record of a bloody defeat which a pitiless dictatorship allows to become even more aggravated by leaving at the head of Egypt a tyrant next to whom King Farouk seems like an operetta villain. Nasser lasts thanks to his police and to the legendary passivity of a people who are tragically the prey of misery, and in whose hearts any possibility, any will, for resistance has been destroyed at its roots.

What is remarkable is that Nasser appears to be the paragon of socialism to the leftist intellectuals.

Two paths were open to him. One was that of peace with Israel and the reconstruction of the Near East based on liberty and progress. The other was war. He preferred the latter.

Under Nasser's pushing the conflict which opposed Israel and the nearby Arab states became more serious each day. The acts of terrorism committed by the suicide units, the *fedayim*, multiplied along several hundred miles of the Israeli border. On the sea, Nasser, having successfully defied international law at Suez, reinforced the Aqaba blockade. During this period I was often summoned to our different frontiers by the sad facts of this state of war—Jewish peasants and tourists murdered, *fedayim* shot, houses destroyed in our villages and our *kibbutzim*. The Voice of Cairo which was interpreting Nasser's thought proclaimed on the radio, "there is no reason for the *fedayim* who hate their enemies not to thrust into Israel, making it a hell on earth for its people."

We who had escaped the Hitlerian hell heard these daily threats with growing anxiety. The worsening of French and English relations with Egypt was to furnish the spark which would set off the powder keg. For the second time the Arab world and Israel were to fight each other.

The agreement reached between Czechoslovakia and Egypt in September 1955 furnished Nasser with the military power which made him the acknowledged and admired leader of the Arab world. In a few months Egypt's air and armored forces became four times stronger than Israel's. On October 19, 1955, a single high command was created for Egypt and Syria. When a year later Jordan joined this alliance, Israel was surrounded on all sides by armies, south, east and north, which under a single command intended to wipe the State of Israel off the face of the earth. At that time I was part of Ben Gurion's entourage. The "old chap," as we used to call him, reflected the anguish of all our people faced with this threat. Everybody hated the war. On the roads which I continually travelled in all directions, I could feel the pulse of our youth. Their solution was not free of an overriding sadness—why kill and perhaps be killed? Was it absolutely impossible to live together as brothers?

The most serious economic crisis shook the country. Immigration came to a halt, and departures multiplied. Anyone in a position of responsibility in the state was aware of the seriousness of the situation. They were trapped in their positions of authority. Arab propaganda became more belligerent as Czech and Russian arms flowed into Egypt. We understood Nasser's game very well. In his mind crushing Israel was the condition for the consecration of his dictatorship over the Arab world. Once Israel was beaten, he would extend his domination over Jordan, Lebanon, Syria, Iraq, and the entire Arab peninsula almost without firing a shot. Once he became master of the Arab East, it would be child's play to extend his rule to the Maghreb. The Kingdom of Libya, independent since 1951, Tunisia, and Morocco would soon be at his feet. With Egypt's support Algeria had been struggling against France for at least two years. Was not Ben Bella, from the beginning of his career, a beloved disciple of Nasser? Everything seems to smile on the young and attractive heir of the Pharoahs. In his euphoria he has thrown together a book which he dares to call *Philosophy of Revolution*. Neguib is put under house arrest and sundry domestic opponents are checked. The Moslem brothers, the left wing of the *Wafd*, the left wing of the free officers and the students, who on January 11, 1954, jeered at the name of Nasser in the streets of Cairo, are crushed. From April 1954 on, Nasser is the sole master of Egypt. His dictatorship rests on his personal police who have practically unlimited powers. The dictator's charisma, his tactical successes, and the legendary passivity of his people will keep him in power in spite of the most serious failings and irremediable defeats.

Sure of himself, Nasser feels so strong that he does not hesitate to challenge three powers at once: England, by nationalizing the Suez Canal; France, by supporting the Algerian revolt; Israel, whose blockade is reinforced and the hate of which is dispensed to the people just as are bread and dates. Nasser does not think of the consequences of his undertakings for a second. He waves his threats and, what is more, he denounces, arrests, and kills. Internal opposition leads to no other recourse than that of assassination attempts, and opposition from foreign powers—war.

Nasser operates with boldness and skill on all fronts. Russians, Americans, Czechoslovakians, and Palestinians are enmeshed in his labyrinthine tactics. With regard to the tragic background of the cold war between the United States and the Soviet Union, Russian interference in the Middle East takes on an importance which exceeds the gravity of the nationalization of the Canal or the existence of Israel. Everybody knows it, especially Ben Gurion, Guy Mollet, and Anthony Eden—who do not know how to approach the matter without risking the worst from the hornet's nest in which Nasser has cleverly caught them.

Things come to a head during the summer of 1956. On July 21 Nasser decides to seize the Canal. He proclaims it to the world on July 24 in a violently nationalistic speech which wins him popular acclaim.

I will not remind you of the details of this crisis which we followed from the headquarters of two camps that were to confront each other, you on the general staff of the Arab League, and I with Ben Gurion.

The tumult of the cold war, the Algerian conflict, and the interests of the Suez Company seemed far away from Israel. What mattered for us was Nasser's will to destroy us, the incessant raids of the *fedayim* from Gaza who killed our women and children and destroyed our farms and harvests. What disturbed us most was the blockade of our shores and borders and the mobilization of the Arab armies far better equipped with Russian materiel. What tortured us was that eleven years after the end of the Hitlerian nightmare, eight years after we had found our anchorhold, Israel, we had to start all over again to protect not only our lives but our right to exist.

From September 1954 to the time when the Israeli *Bat-Galim* was confiscated by Egypt in September 1956, tension had reached its peak in Israel. During these two years the Israeli government put off the confrontation which Nasser's intransigence made inevitable. Ben Gurion at his retreat at Sde Boker was recalled first to the national ministry of defense and then, on November 2, 1955, to the presidency of the Council to face the problem.

Again time lost its meaning. Since the end of October we had stopped talking about the matter which worried us all in Jerusalem. Silence was the fortress in which the Jews took refuge when they felt their existence threatened once more. Mobilization emptied the countryside.

Ben Gurion, who since October 15 had given indication of an impending Israeli offensive, takes military measures from October 25 on which will result in the attack of October 29. In Cairo Nasser and his ministers are thunderstruck. In six days, from the evening of October 29 to November 5, the Israeli armies will have broken through the Egyptian frontier in Sinai and occupied Sharm el Sheikh and the banks of the Suez Canal. The Egyptian army is in retreat. Four thousand prisoners are in the hands of the Israelis, contrasted to less than twenty Israelis taken by the Egyptians. The Jews have 172 dead, 817 wounded. The Egyptians, besides the countless dead, lose a destroyer, a radar station, thousands of light arms, hundreds of heavy arms, hundreds of tanks, thousands of vehicles, tens of millions of shells, bombs, grenades, bullets, four Mig-15's, three Vampires, one Meteor—all that in less than a week.

But no one rejoiced in Israel. We were mourning our victims. The situation, complicated by Franco-British intervention and Russian threats, dismayed us. The future after this quick victory seemed as uncertain as before the campaign. As we soon were to see, this war had solved nothing basic and had complicated the matter. Both sides could rightfully claim victory and proclaim the defeat of the enemy, both could rightfully be scandalized by the claims and intentions of the other.

Moscow was exultant: with a single threatening telegram Bulganin silenced the Israelis, the English, and the French.

The Americans headed by Dulles bask in the lucidity of their policy. Their interests had been protected in the crisis. Eden and Mollet are not the last to celebrate Israel's victory and the blow which Nasser has just felt. Ben Gurion is so pleased that with just enough time allowed to be coaxed a little, he is ready to lead his troops to the ancient borders of Israel. As for Nasser, he succeeds in convincing Egypt that it has won the greatest victory in its history by having defeated in one fell swoop, not only Israel, but even England and France. In fact Nasser remains in power, strengthens his dictatorship, and preserves all the advantages that he intends to draw from his audacity. His army has been beaten, he says, not by Israel but by two world powers. But he remains the absolute master of the Canal, strengthens his ties with Russia, demands a higher price for his friendship with the Americans, and becomes the strong man for the Arab world and the third world—the champion of the third world standing up against Western imperialism whose valet is Israel.

Moshe Dayan and the principal participants have given their versions of these awesome events. Analysts such as Henri Azeau and Jean-Pierre Alem have determined the responsibilities and the effects. The sure advantage which Israel drew from the operation were neutralized by a doubling of Arab hostilities. Nasser remained in power, overcome by a spirit of revenge. It took him eleven years to convince himself that he was ready to risk a new war against Israel.

In the meantime a revolution takes place in Iraq in 1958 and the Republic is proclaimed. From 1958 to 1961 Egypt and Syria form a Republic whose unity will be short-lived. In 1961 Kuwait, at the end of a ruthless war in Yemen, opens a new savage chapter in the history of Nasser's Egypt. In 1963 revolutions break out in Syria and Iraq, and in Algeria Ben Bella's dictatorship is replaced by that of Boumedienne. In Israel Levi Eskol has replaced Ben Gurion at the head of the Israeli government. Only Nasser has stayed in power, and he maintains the intransigence which will continue to aggravate relations between the Jews and the Arabs.

The era, 1917–1967: fifty years of hostility were to culminate on June 5, 1967, in the Six-Day War which turned the world upside down and made us take stock of ourselves.

Here again I would like to remind you of how I lived

through these events in Jerusalem where once more time
had no relevance.

Peace in the Near East was no more than relative after
1956. Jerusalem remained divided and on its several miles
of urban frontier incidents were frequent both with the
Jordanian legion and the Syrians to the north. Only the
Egyptian border remained relatively quiet thanks to the
Blue Hats stationed there by the United Nations. The serious incidents in Samoa, and in Jordan, and the reprisal raids
of the Israeli air force over the suburbs of Damascus during
which six Syrian Migs were shot down seemed to have
shifted the scene of tension away from Egypt and toward
Jordan and Syria. It would be understanding Nasser poorly
to imagine that he could give up the limelight to anyone.
The best way to draw attention back to himself was to present himself as the steadfast defender of the Arab world. On
May 13, 1967, Nasser took into account information he received from Syria and Lebanon, confirmed by Russia, which
held that Israel was concentrating its troops at the Syrian
border and preparing for new aggression. At this moment I
was in Jerusalem in constant contact with the government.
Nobody was thinking about war. The domestic political situation had reached a very critical point and was complicated
by the most serious economic and moral crisis. Unemploy-
ment and the strangulation of investments and immigration
had cast a veil of gloom over the country.

At the beginning of the month, on Mount Herzl in Jerusalem, the government had decorated the former *maquisards*
and all those who had fought against Hitler in Europe and
throughout the world. Thousands of Israelis had to rum-
mage through their minds and their papers to find again the
memories and the documents which they were to deposit in
the nation's archives. Inadvertently the great file of misery
was reopened. On the day set for the awards I again saw the
crowds of those who had escaped from the death camps.
Each had a scarred soul and often a scarred body—a court
of miracles with its cripples, its blind and its paralytic. The
guard for maintaining order was soon run over by a crowd
five times larger than the one expected. The sun was scorch-

ing and there was no shade on the huge esplanade. Suddenly one woman's nerves cracked. Confusion and hysteria ensued. That day Levi Eshkol had difficulty reading his ceremonial speech. May was starting out poorly. The celebration of the nineteenth anniversary of the creation of the State of Israel was to take place on May 14 and 15, 1967. For the first time the dates coincided with the solar calendar of the Church and the luni-solar calendar of the Synagogue. The nineteen-year cycle had been sealed. The sun and stars were in the same position as they were nineteen years previously when Jewish and Arab armies met in the war for Israeli independence. Today Nasser's voice replaced Farouk's to curse and to threaten us. On May 14 the Egyptian troops got into motion and took their position in the Sinai.

That night Jerusalem tried to celebrate the solemnity in the finest way. The Mayor of the city, Teddy Kollek, put everything to work for the beauty of the holiday. After all, our fellow citizens had the right to a carefree day of relaxation and, again, no one was thinking of the war then, Moshe Dayan less than anyone else. The sounds of the tanks in the Sinai, the inflamatory speeches on the Arab radio?—you see, in twenty years we had finally gotten used to this atmosphere. The only ones to suffer from it were those who knew the Arabs and loved them. We knew that the image which this raving propaganda presented was false. We knew the virtues, the gentleness, and the art of living of the Arab peoples. And our sorrow was deep to be aware of nothing of that in Israel—only the barking of the enraged radio, the noise of the cannons, and the fire of the machine guns. The Jews from the West who had never lived among the Arabs, the *Sabarim* born in Israel after 1948, had taken a stand and believed that the Arabs were really identical to the image which they persisted in giving of themselves on our side of the border. My son, at the age when you and I were growing up together fraternally united by the friendship of our families, had never seen an Arab and the only manifestation which he has known of the Arabs was on the border where our new house was going up. He heard the noise of the shots which the Jordanian soldiers sometimes fired at us. The mothers would run out to the balconies to cry out "come in, they're shooting, take cover." Sometimes a child did not come in. A bullet had mowed him down. It would take up three lines in the newspaper to announce his death. The Israelis know nothing else of the Arab world except hate, threats, and death.

We were not unduly disturbed by the new outbreak of hysteria on the part of the dictators who were our neighbors. Most of the time their worst attacks corresponded to some internal crisis which they solved by waving the Israeli bugbear. We got used to this unfortunate state of affairs and even stopped trying to explain the causes. When Nasser shouted, it meant that he was trying to make his domestic and foreign opposition back off or perhaps trying to hasten the conclusion of an agreement with the Americans or the Russians. In any case it was good for him to raise his voice. It always paid off.

On the morning of May 16, Jerusalem woke up from its holiday. The streets were still strewn with bunting. Garlands of multicolored lights, flags, and banners still told of the joy of the anniversary we had just celebrated. The war? —no one thought about it. Do you understand? No one!

On May 18 the news of the withdrawal of the Blue Hats and of the mobilization of troops in Egypt and Syria stunned us. How was U-Thant able to yield to Nasser's request in seconds? This still remains a mystery.

Simultaneously we learned that France, which had gathered together its ambassadors to the Middle East, had announced unilaterally in Beirut its guarantee of the borders of our country. Thant declared to the Security Council "that the situation in the Middle East was more threatening than at any time since 1956." It was only then that our government took its first steps in alerting the army.

On may 21 the Egyptian forces replace the Blue Hats in Sharm el Sheikh. At dawn on May 22 Nasser follows through his advantage and from an air base on Sinai announces the closing of the Tiran straits to ships bearing the Israeli flag and to any others carrying essential products destined for Israel. Those of us who still dreamed of peace and reconciliation are shocked. The Israeli government refuses, nonetheless, to draw any inferences from Nasser's challenge.

The blockade of the straits meant a return to the situation in 1956, as Nasser predicted, before the war had wiped out Egypt's 1948 defeat. Eshkol proposes a troop reduction on either side of the Israeli-Egyptian border where Nasser has already concentrated 80,000 men.

Alarmed by the consequences of his blind act, U-Thant goes to see Nasser in Cairo. He refuses Jerusalem the honor of a visit. Did we count so little in his opinion! We feel confidence, friendship, and our self-respect slip away. The Arabs and their friends are triumphing. The whole world has heard and read their enthusiastic speeches. Choukeiri had gone beyond the limits of indecency and stupidity by his hysterical threats. The Arabs promised themselves not only to destroy the State of Israel but further to exterminate its inhabitants. We heard all that with our teeth clenched. Jerusalem made hasty improvisations for the worst—bags of sand in windows, water and food reserves stored away. Everybody hastily begins to dig trenches and prepare a cemetery to bury our dead which the radios of Cairo, Amman, Damascus, Baghdad, and Beirut are already announcing.

While Abba Eban travels the Western capitals in search of an illusory diplomatic settlement, King Hussein signs a defense agreement with Nasser on May 30 in Cairo which in the event of war puts the Jordanian army under Egyptian command. This mistake made, he reconciles himself with Choukeiri whom he brings back to Jerusalem in his private plane. In 1956 the alliance of Egypt and Jordan had already completed the encirclement of Israel and sealed the fate of the war.

For us there was no room for hope. It was clear that every act of appeasement on our part would lead to another and that every Arab gain would lead to another until we were totally destroyed.

It was then that Israel was witness to an event for which I know no precedent. Overnight our weakness vanished and once more time took on another meaning. We were no longer fainthearted—an absolute determination took hold of us. One absolute person revealed himself in our midst. We had ceased being a people of two and a half million individuals. All social barriers disappeared. There were no

longer rich or poor, young or old, men or women, Easterners or Westerners. The political parties presented a common front. The Christians among us joined in too. Instead
of a broken and divided people there arose a new person,
that of the new Israel once more facing its cruel destiny.
Each individual was acting, speaking, and thinking in the
name of everybody. We had become what you might call
a man-people. The people was only one man in the exercise
of a liberty whose joy I had never experienced so intensely.
The area which separates the unconscious from the conscious had been crossed. We soon found out that no frontier
separates life from death in the plenitude of the spirit which
we freely revealed. We were truly seized by a transcendence
which restored us to the implacable severity of our true
vocation.

From the fifth to the eighth of June I neither slept nor
ate. On the morning of June 5 Hussein, deceived by Nasser's
illusions, plunged into the war. Thinking he would save his
throne, he gave the Arab Legion the order to attack Israel.
When the first shells—by the thousands, it is true—began to
rain on Jerusalem, we did not believe our eyes. For a while
we hoped that it was only a *baroud* (combat) for honor,
the chance for Hussein to prove that he, too, was part of his
war. The shock of seeing the Jordanian artillery and tanks
thrown into the attack on Jerusalem showed us how wrong
we were.

Someday we may know Hussein's real motivations. The
fear of Nasser and the extremists around him, perhaps the
conviction that Israel would be crushed, and the appetite
for conquest must have played a role in the young king's
thinking. Actually these feelings meant nothing once the
command of the Jordanian army had been given to a leader
of the Egyptian general staff.

Shells, bombs, machine-gun bullets—for sixty hours, Jerusalem burned in its new tribulation. I walked under fire for
hours to transport wounded Jews and Arabs. I heard the
whistle of rockets and shells burst in my ears. I was among
the first to enter the Eastern part of the city strewn with
corpses. I felt the vibrations of the Mirages and the Fouga-
Magister which came to the aid of our soldiers and our tanks.

For the entire night I saw the roof of the Dormition burning, set on fire by a Jordanian shell.

And then silence returned. The border had disappeared. To the north we had reached the plains, to the south, the banks of the Jordan, to the west, the Suez Canal. The whole world—the Arabs foremost—was stunned by the lightning victory of Israeli's armies. I could finally come back under the splendid dome of the Mosque of Omar for meditation. I was quietly praying for peace when you appeared before me the same as I had left you twenty years earlier. A war had separated us. Now a war was bringing us together again. We silently embraced. I pretended not to notice the tears in your eyes.

5 Along the Way

THE SIX DAY WAR has been over for years. Books, articles, films, and special reports about this astonishing campaign have been piling up. In Israel we still have the feeling of having been through a transhistoric event, one of those meteoric happenings which change the course of human destiny. An old rabbi expressed this general conviction on the eve of the war by saying "We will be able to win in either of two ways: by miracle or by natural means.
—What would the natural means be?
—To win by a miracle.
—And what would the miracle be?
—To win by natural means.
Humor is our lot. But once again no one in Israel was jubilant. We were relieved, even liberated, but without being triumphant. We knew that the war would still not result in peace. We wept over our dead and wounded. We were sad about the unfortunate Arab victims of this futile war unleased by the Arab leaders. Nasser had concentrated more than 100,000 Egyptian soldiers in Sinai. No one will ever know how many survived. The Arab Legion did hold its ground. Without mentioning Syria's dead, nor the civilians who fell on both sides, one must add to the total of tens of thousands dead and hundreds of thousands orphaned the enormous spoils of war which we seized in the Sinai region, Cisjordan, and Syria. For fifteen years the Arabs had invested more than ten billion dollars in their armies. In six days nothing was left of it but a junk pile. The war materiel was either destroyed or in Israeli hands. Half the money passed to the Russians, the other half to the English and Americans. What the Arabs retained from this fantastic sum was blood, tears and shame. A group of Arab intellectuals had projected what they could have built with the huge

amounts invested in this ridiculous war. Their study has
been published in *Jeune Afrique*. Here is what the Arab
governments could have given their people instead of illusions and atrocities: one hundred industrial complexes employing 100,000 people; 100 model farms constituting the
infrastructure necessary to revitalize Arab agriculture; 1,000
new schools with room for an additional million Arab children; 50 luxury hotels which would have attracted one or
two million tourists to the Arab countries; a million Arabs
could have had decent housing and employment; 20 modern
universities could have been built for 100,000 Arab students.
All of these investments accomplished, there could have
been money still left to build enough housing units to shelter
100,000 Arabs and to build 20 big modern 1000 bed hos-
pitals.

Since Israel has also been forced to put relatively equiva-
lent amounts into its army, the waste resulting from the
Israeli-Arab conflict becomes apparent as does the benefit
to the people and to the world which might have ensued if
peace returned. This inventory is all the more tragic for the
Arabs since their standard of living was lower to start with.
The military waste by the dictators of Egypt, Iraq, Jordan,
and Syria did not ruin the Arab peoples—they were just
starting out. It smiply killed the chances of reform or the
possibility of renaissance.

The road travelled is strewn with death, destruction, and
indescribable humiliations. You have to pardon my frank-
ness. It adds to your suffering, but nothing would hurt you
more than to be fed illusions. The Arab radio has shown
singular verbal irresponsibility. During the Six Day War
while the Voice of Israel imposed moderation on itself, Arab
radio did a war dance around Israel's cadaver. On Monday
afternoon, June 5, Cairo announced that 130 Israeli planes
had been destroyed. At that time Nasser was not aware that
he no longer had an air force. Nobody in his entourage had
the courage to inform him. In the streets of Cairo the crowds
were delirious over the triumphant radio broadcasts. The
people, jumping for joy, embraced each other, applauded,
and danced, shouting: "We are with you Nasser. Israel has
to be done away with, Nasser, Nasser. . . ." while Arab

blood was flowing on all borders. Yes, nothing is more deadly for a people than the opium of illusions.

In opposing Israel, Arab obstinancy systematically reached results contrary to those to which it aspired. For fifty years each attempt at a solution to the Israeli-Arab conflict had provoked the refusal and often armed opposition of the Arabs. The Balfour Declaration proposed the creation of a national home which the Arabs refused. Twenty years later, on July 7, 1937, the Royal Commission for Inquiry in Palestine proposed the partitioning of the country and the establishment of a Jewish state with an area of five thousand square kilometers—the size of some French cantons. It would have died a natural death if the Arabs had been smart enough to accept it. Once again the Arab refusal saved the Jewish interest. Again, if the Arab states had accepted the United Nations partition plan in 1947 and the creation of a tiny Palestinian state, and an international zone in Jerusalem, the problem would have been solved. The little Jewish state would have lived more or less well, worn away by its internal problems, without ever having had the possibility of true greatness opened up to it. It is strange: conflict strengthens Israel, forces it to gird its loins and outdo itself in every direction. If the frontiers had not been closed for twenty years, Israel would probably never have succeeded in building up its agriculture, nor in building an industry competitive not only in the Asian and African markets but in the stronger industrial and commercial centers of Europe and America as well. Moreover, the Israeli army has served as the backbone of unification for immigrants coming from 102 countries of the world. The wars of 1948, 1956, and 1967 have done more to solidify the nation of Israel than the efforts of the government and of the Jews the world over for the twenty years of the state's existence. The Six day War (long in preparation by the Arabs, started on May 22, 1967 with Nasser's decree of the Aqaba blockade, and on June 5 with Hussein's attack on Jerusalem) gave the Jews more advantages than they ever would have dreamed of: military glory and safer frontiers. Never before had the Arab peoples been plunged into such an impasse. Of course, it is still possible for them to dream of destruction. When

139

Podgorny, preceded by Soviet chief of Staff Mirchal Zakharov, arrived in Cairo on June 21, 1967, some Egyptians thought that the conflict was going to start again, that Nasser would put the Jews out of Sinai with Russia's help and fulfill the old dream of Israel's annihilation. Be that as it may, from the Arab point of view, the war which was senseless in June 1967 would be mad today taking into account the new frontiers where the armies of Israel are located. We Jews are cornered into mastering our victory so that you Arabs may also dominate your retreat.

In fact, our inability to establish peaceful relations only proves our lack of political maturity. The present situation which is neither peace nor war only underlines the seriousness of the political and spiritual crises on both sides of the border.

The crisis which permeates the Arab world is obvious. It is beginning to emerge from a state of subjection and immeasurable poverty to approach a new state of autonomy. It is leaving behind the feudal structures on which it has been based for centuries and is trying to adapt itself as best it can to the structures of the technological and democratic society. On the whole the problems which the Arab world has to face on the political and social planes are the same as those we have to solve in Israel. The difference perhaps is that the Arab world is obliged to develop its economy, while we are forced to build from scratch. Not only are we in a period of transition, but we are forced to make over everything upon which the existence of a nation is based. We not only have to create systems of agriculture, industry, and business, but also a people and even a language—all out of nothing.

What seems most fundamental in Judeo-Arab relations is the assessment of our religious situation. I would like to try to describe to you the seriousness of the spiritual crisis which spreads over Israel in spite of its victory. I do this with the acute awareness that our malaise is that of all humanity. Our experience is perhaps exemplary because it concentrates on a single point of the globe problems which are facing the entire human family.

Propaganda easily gives way to sensationalism. We have

not always known how to escape this. For centuries our ancestors have been satisfied with their humiliated condition, with their attachment to abjection in the hope of a messianic salvation offered to humanity. In modern times we have suddenly had to find in our greatness the justification for our being. This has not always had the happiest result. The struggle for the political emancipation of the Jews in Europe inspired a whole literature which preached Judaism without taking into account that these values have been in the public domain for two thousand years. The Christians and the Moslems share with us all the values of the Bible which they have sometimes put into practice as successfully as we. Our greatness, insofar as it exists, lies elsewhere. But we were unable to say that, cornered as we were, defending our very existence. For some the truth was that they had lost the secret of our greatness. It had slipped through their fingers. They had been released to our cruel destiny, that of Israel in exile, without knowing why they had to remain faithful to the tradition of Israel.

European Judaism, whose destiny was cruel, had to make the worst sacrifices so as to preserve the fragile chance for its historic continuity for the thousand years which preceded the creation of the State of Israel. The Jews of Europe were expelled from most countries, sometimes by the cruelest methods such as in Spain during the Inquisition. They had to face the scorn and sometimes hate of their compatriots in most of the countries where they had found refuge.

The discovery of the new world in 1492, the very year of the expulsion of the Jews from Spain, the spreading popularity of the printing press, the rebirth of learning and of the humanities often nourished with Hebraic belles lettres, the upheaval introduced to Christianity by the Reformation and the economic and political revolutions, progressively open up to the Jew a social and cultural milieu in which, for the first time, he does not feel irrevocably foreign. To the contrary, for the Jew modern society such as it begins to be defined during the Renaissance exerts an undeniable attraction.

The ghetto wall had been cracked: France was the first to sanction the emancipation of the Jews. The age of the enlightenment, the impassioned appeals of Voltaire, Rousseau, and the Encyclopedists exerted an irresistible influence over the ghettos of Europe. The French Revolution consecrates this movement on September 28, 1791, granting the rights of man and of the citizen to some fifty thousand Jews of Alsace and southern France. So begins a new era of history for the Jews.

During the nineteenth century the Jews of Europe struggled with all their strength for the confirmation of their political rights. These battles, while strengthening the Jews on social and economic planes, unquestionably weakened them on the spiritual plane. In modern times a true spiritual upheaval of the Jewish communities of Europe takes place. The reality of Jewish life no longer is expressed in the synagogues and traditional prayers, but rather in the struggle for political emancipation. In all of Europe the struggle is long, and success is bitterly achieved: Germany in 1848, England in 1858, Austria-Hungary in 1867, Italy in 1870, and finally Russia in 1917, followed to varying degrees the example given in 1791 by the French revolutionaries.

This victory was costly. The political victories of the European Jews favored the transformation of the anti-Judaism of the Christian Middle Ages into an atheistic anti-Semitism whose consequences were even more disastrous. The end of the nineteenth century and the beginning of the twentieth were marked with bloody pogroms in Rumania and Russia. In Germany the anti-Semite party is organized in 1860, triumphs in 1930, and from 1940 on extends the limits of horror by Hitler's orders.

On the spiritual plane the sacrifice made by the Jews on the altar of freedom was not any less. It forced a total revolution in their manner of being, thinking, and believing. They had to change their dress, language, first names, trades, ideas, and hopes, and had to leave their ghetto and enter into the technological era. Often without their realizing it, the upheaval caused by their passage into Christian society was as radical as the one the Jews had experienced for almost two thousand years in a separate world on the margins of history. Their universe was that of the revelation of Sinai, and the motivation of their patience was an unbelievable hope in the coming of the triumphant Messiah and their restoration to the Holy Land.

You have known the Jews of the Exile during our youth in Jerusalem. Their soul, nourished by the Pentateuch, the Psalms, and Biblical, Talmudic and Cabalistic traditions, lived in the world of faith. They existed, it would seem, beyond time and its contingencies at the very sources of revelation. The rabbis, backed by the unanimous consent of the people, knew that the ark of the exile was made to lead Israel beyond history, to an eternity of life. In the isolation of the ghetto the spiritual exercises and contemplative virtues rested on the existence of a sociologically and ethnically defined body. The Jews, principally in Eastern Europe, had an entire civilization which expressed itself in many ways, notably through the medium of the Yiddish dialect, a treasure house which had been the vehicle of the laws, customs, manners, folklore, and spiritual wealth of the Judaism of the Exile for so many centuries.

The system which had triumphed over centuries and empires, persecutions and massacres, broke down everywhere when all the nations began to open themselves to the presence of Israel. The unrealistic hope of an unreserved adoption by Christian society tended to make the closed system, where the Jew continued to pray for the rebirth of Jerusalem, burst from the inside. It is then that new religious habits arose in the heart of Judaism while the new phenomenon of the economic and political promotion of the Jews took place in Europe. The unbroken unity of Judaism of the Exile was done for. The Jewish community split into two camps: the reformed in one, the orthodox in the other. Let me tell you at the outset that a third group, perhaps the most important, is not mentioned—those who joined neither of the two camps and who simply disappeared from the Jewish community either by explicit adherence to Christianity or by assimilation into the religious indifference of the great masses.

The crisis was initiated in Germany by Moses Mendelsohn; the son of a simple copyists of Torah scrolls, he was born in 1728. In addition to the Talmud he learned German, French, Latin, mathematics, and philosophy. In Berlin at that time, this education was enough for him to begin the revolution of which his translation and commentaries on the Pentateuch were the vehicle in Germany. His *Jerusalem* reinterpreted Judaism in light of the new ideas—no longer the harsh religion born in the deserts of life, dedicated to the cult of the revealed Word, but an obligatory legislation which in the mood of the times left to each individual his freedom of conscience and action.

Meanwhile the Jewish reformation movement spread to the salons of Berlin. In France Napoleon gave it a consecration, as solemn as it was unexpected, by calling together in 1807 as assembly of notables and rabbis whom he endowed with the title of Grand Sanhedrin. He encouraged declarations from them which defined the new statutes of emancipated Judaism. Napoleon was really one of the greatest visionaries of contemporary Judaism. He predicted the resurrection of the state of Israel, and favored the emancipation of the Jews and their admission into the family of nations. He acknowledged the demise of the Jewish nation and favored the repudiation of what, in the Torah of Moses, might contradict civil law. To a man Western Jews began to swear lasting fidelity to their country. The men of the ghetto began at this time to become citizens of Israelite persuasion directed by consistories charged with administering religious affairs with respect to the laws of the state. In this way the fantastic adventure of Biblical revelation was accomplished.

The slow disintegration of the sociological structures of the ghetto, of the secularization of Jewish thought and the organization of emancipated Judaism favored a powerful internal movement of moral and often religious assimilation among the Jews. Detached from traditional beliefs and notions, cut off from his origins, the modern Jew tended to preach a Judaism which was of the same stature as the enlightenment of the century. Would the prophets, the doctors, even our fathers, recognize themselves in this preachifying which Paul Claudel stigmatized with the name of "humanitarian wish-wash"? Be that as it may, the new tendencies created a deep conflict which never ceased tearing Judaism apart. Beyond the men and ideas, two essentially different worlds met. On the one hand there was the sacral world of the Bible, the Talmud, the Cabala, and the absolute submission of the Mitzva, the order of the revealed Word where inflexible souls followed the dream of divine redemption laid claim to by the supernatural arms of prayer, charity, and sacrifice. These believers had made up their minds to refuse everything in the world so long as it was not in agreement with divine vocation, and they were resolved to undergo humiliation and death in the inflexible expectation of the ghettos, dedicated to the Messiah of glory in the hope of the triumph of his love. In contrast to the ghetto arose the century of enlightenment, free thought, reason, and progress in all the prestige of its liberating powers whose proof the Jews themselves had just experienced. For the first time in history, the Jew had a place of his own free of shadows of persecution in the world of liberty, equality, and fraternity.

The option thus opened disturbed the peace of the ghetto as surely as a war would. Emancipation encouraged the schism of the Reformation and Counterreformation whose bitter battles disfigured the face and unity of Israel, and provoked a loss of spiritual authenticity and a neglect of essential vocations which could have been fatal to Judaism if once again the cure had not appeared simultaneously with disease.

This was the predicament of all Christian society too, torn by the Protestant Reformation and shaken by contemporary atheism. The Jews really defended themselves against Christianity but the crisis of Judaism was very similar to that which was taking hold of and weakening the Church itself.

We had our own conservatives, as the Christians did.

The devil in the flesh would not have affected traditional Judaism any more than did the German Reformation. A pitiless war broke out wherever the modern trends, more or less successfully, tried to formulate new religious definitions. In the struggle the traditionalists did not flinch from anything, not from the secret accusations of the authorities, nor the denial of burial, nor even the cruelest violence. Abraham Jaeger, a reformed Jewish thinker whose life spans most of the nineteenth century, put the evolution of history above the letter of the immortal word of the Bible. It was he who launched the attack with the cry "We must decapitate the hydra." The hydra, orthodox Judaism, defended itself bitterly. The Reformation did not succeed in becoming a popular movement in Europe and never reached the great citadels of Judaism in Poland and Russia. It corresponded too closely to the aspirations of an intellectual elite concerned with the needs of the middle class emancipated from the bounds of the ghetto. It was no longer a question of authenticity, of spiritual life, but one of fostering the political and economic integration of Judaism into European society. Everywhere traditional rabbinism maintained its initial position as vigorously as it could. But in this struggle which had been carried on with courage and against the tide, did it not lose sight of the great finalities of Israel's tradition also? The teachers of Talmudism and Hasidism were too well aware of the vanities of the century and of the world to give up the dialogue, perhaps too erudite for ordinary man's ear, which Israel continued with God. In addition the Reformation caused Jewish orthodox thought to become more inflexible. It recoiled into an almost hermetic ghetto in the sharp awareness that this isolation was a condition of survival for Judaism's traditional values.

In the conflict which opposed the revealed Word to the world, the huge majority of the rabbis, often with the most extreme sacrifices, opted for God in the supernatural expectation of his redemption. Their methods were not without danger. Obedience to the law became the last bastion to maintain the integrity of the message until the end. The spiritual life of the Jew seemed to become a purely mechanical exercise, that of the fulfillment of the Mitzvot.

Were some rabbis able to avoid succumbing to the idolatry of the Mitzva? The greatest spiritual teachers of contemporary Judaism have asked themselves this overwhelming question. For if the law is not a channel which allows going beyond the contradictions of man to draw him to the contemplation of the increate Eternal, it becomes an obstacle, a barrier between God and man. It transforms itself into an idol and as such, it becomes blameable. This is no doubt what was foreseen by Bahya Ibn Pakuda whose work and influence we have already cited. He intuited that in order to save Judaism it was necessary, in the great currents of thought of the era, to bring it back to its essential fidelity, to the struggle for justice and to the great eternal and salutary values of unity, fraternity, and love which derive from great spiritual perfection.

The Jewish thinkers of the West in the nineteenth and twentieth centuries, instead of wearing themselves out writing the apologetics of Judaism as if they had to justify their existence, would have done better to analyze the almost fatal spiritual crisis of Judaism. We have seen that during the Exile it did not produce great spiritual works. The Talmud whose sources reach deeply into the realities of the Biblical era, the Cabalistic movement, the few great works of Spanish Judaism, and the Hasidic movement in Rhénanie in the tenth century and its resurgence in Eastern Europe in the seventeenth century, more or less sum up all of Judaism's exilic creation. It must be added that the works produced during these two thousand years have not contributed much to the development of humanity's spiritual patrimony. If one considers Saadiah Gaon, Bahya Ibn Pakuda, Salomon Ibn Gabirol, Judah Halevy, and Moses Maimonides as the greatest traditional thinkers of the time of the Exile, one could easily counter with Moslems and Christians whose spiritual creation is comparable. The former gave more depth to certain basic values, but lacked the original creation which would have restored Judaism to its place and importance among nations. Instead of permanent values, there was only the permanence of a struggle to save a certain number of historico-sociological realities from extinction and to lead those realities to the end of the long dark road of Exile to that passionately awaited moment, the resurrection.

In the modern era Jewish thought allies itself with humanism, with post-Kantian idealism, or with contemporary existentialism. But it does not really answer the problem of the Jewish man nor give him the real means to quench his spiritual thirst and his hunger for truth. It is Martin Buber himself who drew attention to that default.

Indeed, Jewish thinkers do not have an easy task in modern times—how to insure the continuity of traditional Jewish thought, how to preserve its spiritual aspirations in the materialistic modern world whose logic challenges the authority of the Bible and systematically mocks the great traditions which have nourished the Jews in all countries and throughout the ages.

In spite of some honest and respectable formulations, modern Jewish thought has reached an impasse. It has not yet succeeded in encompassing the totality of the Jewish adventure in order to project it into a future which fulfills the tendencies and permanent aspirations of the Jewish people. This lack is all the more tragic since the Jews have never had greater need for true spiritual liberation. Never more than in modern times have they needed to show the spiritual courage necessary to meet the great tasks facing this generation which has witnessed the great Hitlerian massacres and the national rebirth of Israel. Perhaps one of the signs of the true greatness of this rebirth is that, deprived of any authentic spiritual direction, it has not succumbed before the challenge with which history has faced it in our generation.

The spiritual impoverishment of Judaism has never been greater than in our day. Against their will the rabbis, usually lacking spiritual authority, have become administrators of the cult. They are functionaries overworked with secondary tasks and given salaries which are often ridiculous. Once their studies are over, they become circumcisors, cantors, marriers, and buriers. Burdened with their pastoral charges they have no time either for intellectual life or for the enrichment of their spiritual patrimony. Everywhere synagogues are deserted. The percentage of Jews who pray daily and have an authentic spiritual life is a mockery. If statistics were tabulated it would be shown that everywhere in the world the curve of synagogue attendance matches closely the curve for Christian church attendance but, of course, in much smaller proportions. In some countries the synagogues have become almost deserted, at least by the young generation which sees clearly that the formerly venerable teachers in the temples no longer offer what it expects for its spiritual life and for the satisfaction of its intellectual and moral aspirations.

Moreover, the Jews of the Diaspora are by definition in a minority and therefore in a position of having to justify and explain their presence, sometimes even to defend their faith against the spiritual atmosphere which in all Eastern countries is usually Christian. This defensive attitude weakens the significance of the Judaic message even more. The Jews continue to persevere in the marathon of negation. They define themselves not in relation to the truth itself, but in relation to the historic necessities of their struggle for sociological survival. The latter requires, above all, that they stand up against the world of the Gentiles, Christians, or Moslems, as if by an automatic defense reflex.

This attitude still characterizes contemporary Jewish thought. Instead of exerting an irresistible attraction for the Jews, especially the new generation, or for the masses in the countries where the Jews have settled, it often serves a contrary function because of its fears and complexes.

"Integrism" hardens the spiritual positions of the Exile and solidifies them into a mechanical practice of the commandments and into intellectual calesthenics which aim first of all at the knowledge of the Talmud. But the great spiritual traditions—those of adoration, of the liberation and deliverance of the soul, of union with God, and of demonstrating the unity which aims at bringing a witness of life into the world—the great prophetic and messianic traditions are, it must be said, almost forgotten. The traditional grandeur of Judaism has dried up and reduced itself to superficial activities. The functional concerns are administered, the budget necessary for paying the rabbis and staff is provided for, the respect for the commandments is required. But where are the great old traditions? And what future can we foresee for a religion which in the eyes of the huge majority of its followers seems to belong to a bygone era?

Contemporary Judaism has not yet found its Yohanan Ben Zakkäi, its Shimon Bar Yokäi, its Bahya Ibn Pakuda, its Judah Halevy, nor even its Moses Maimonides. We are wandering in a spiritual desert, and the Jews the world over are often nostalgically aware of it. The treasures of Jewish generosity and intelligence are cut off from the great currents of the spiritual thought of humanity, whether because most of the thinkers of Israel detach themselves completely from the traditional tree, or to the contrary, because, enclosed in the narrow and hermetic ghetto, they are unaware of the finalities of the soul and the ways of spiritual liberation as well as the great currents of human thought.

This analysis is confirmed by the poverty of the Judaic liturgies. The inheritance of the time of the Exile is strongly felt in this domain. The religious music heard in most of the synagogues of the Western world, including Israel, is lamentably limited. It only copies the refrains heard in foreign countries during the preceding centuries. Religious synagogal music does not deserve its name. Most often there is nothing religious about it and, because it is so poor, hardly deserves to be called music. To hear the choirs of the synagogues is painful because the extent of the spiritual deviation of contemporary Judaism is serious. One can readily understand the old rabbis who continue to forbid the use of religious music and the organ in the places of prayer. At least they spare their congregations from hearing bad music.

The terrible spiritual crisis pervading contemporary Judaism has been aggravated even more by the creation of the State of Israel. The moral and spiritual impasse in which the Judaism of the Diaspora has enclosed itself in modern times, let us not deceive ourselves, has not been resolved by the creation of the State of Israel. Superficial minds might have supposed the opposite. The State of Israel was enthusiastically received by the majority of Jews the world over. They saw it as the sign of salvation. The Jewish State was ready to welcome the Jews of the Diaspora who could no longer remain in their country of exile. This was the case of the Jews of the Arab countries called upon to leave their native land as a result of the Israeli-Arab conflict. It was applied to the European Jews who escaped from the concentration camps. The Jews of the Diaspora have shown their enthusiasm more than just with words. They have contributed largely to the building of the State of Israel not only on the political plane but on the financial and industrial planes as well, constantly giving the state the means of its development. In addition, the creation of the State of Israel filled the Jews with pride. Leaving behind the frightful Hitlerian cataclysm which ravaged Europe, each escapee from the Nazi hell was eager for security and dignity. The State of Israel was created to answer this need. Its resounding success in various spheres of activity were well suited for encouraging the generosity and pride of the Jews of the Exile.

There is no Jewish community anywhere on earth which does not have a part of its heart in Israel. But it is precisely because of this that the shoe pinches and Judaism of the Exile has been hopelessly constricted.

Of course I am not referring to the difficulties of double allegiance. Before the creation of the State of Israel, the Jews of the Diaspora who had not adhered to Zionism were attracted by the problem of the conflicts contingent upon their allegiance to their country and to the State of Israel. This obstacle had once prevented Baron Edmond de Rothschild from adhering to Zionism. He was clearly favorable to the establishment of a Jewish home in Palestine, but he never knew how to resolve his reservations arising from the foreseeable dangers of double allegiance. The creation of the State of Israel risked disturbing, if not compromising, the position of the Jews of the Exile. After the creation of the State of Israel, it was shown that these fears were unfounded. The crisis of June 1967 provide it. General de Gaulle's stand contradicted the interests of Israel and the wishes of the great majority of the Jews of France, but were supported by a vast part of the French nation. Fidelity to Israel could be visceral—it did not lose itself in any way in the current of opinion which swept along a considerable fraction of France, including a goodly number of ministers.

Elsewhere, no one ever begrudged the Jews their sympathy for the State of Israel. Much of the time, governments of the free countries supported the State of Israel more efficiently and sometimes with more conviction than the Jews themselves. And if the State of Israel was born in 1947–48, it was thanks to the Russian vote and Czechoslovakian arms.

The difficulties of Judaism of the Diaspora do not originate from what nations and churches think. They are of a psychological and spiritual order inherent in Judaism itself.

Because of this, they are clearly more serious than if they were external difficulties.

They arise, first of all, from the revolution which the structures of the modern Jewish world have undergone. Suddenly the State of Israel appears. Every Jew, to the extent that he is conscious of his Judaism, supports it morally and materially. But one fact stands out—most of the Jews of the world have not felt the need to come to live in Israel. The figures are irrefutable. If most of the Jews living in the Arab countries have come to settle in Israel since its establishment, moved most of the time by external factors, the European Jews, the *achkenazim*, as we say, have not felt the need to leave the free countries where they live. There are today two million, eight hundred thousand Jews in the State of Israel, mostly from the Arab countries. About a million Western Jews live in Israel while twelve times that many remain in the Diaspora obstinately attached to the lands they inhabit. It is a rather tragic answer given by the Jews to their own faith. The declarations, the manifestations of sympathy, and the financial support that these Jews give to the State of Israel do not change the significance of their attitude. This clearly says that the huge majority of the Jewish people really does not need the State of Israel, at least they do not need to settle there.

There used to be a play on words a while back distinguishing between "palestinophiles" and those who "filed through Palestine." Since the creation of the State of Israel, it has been confirmed that those who came to settle in Palestine are a very tiny minority compared to the Zionists who have preferred to remain in New York, London, Paris, Berlin, Buenos Aires, or Johannesburg. From these places Zionists come to visit us regularly in Israel. They hold their congresses there. They understand perfectly the realities of the State of Israel and, for the most part, are sincerely dedicated to the interests of our country. But as far as putting their bodies in line with their profession of faith, they carefully do not. Each individual has his private little system to explain the fundamental contradiction concerning the persistence of a Zionist movement outside of the State of Israel after the latter's creation. One can understand Ben Gurion's hostility toward the world Zionist movement. He states that the movement had as its goal the establishment of a refuge for the Jews of the entire world—refuge, national home, or state which would be guaranteed by public law. Such was the goal of the Zionist movement as defined by Theodore Herzl at the end of the last century. Today the Zionist movement has achieved this end. "What is the significance of a movement whose goals belong to the past?" asks Ben Gurion. The Zionists have few arguments to oppose the frontal attack to which they are subjected by the old Zionist leader.

The problem is much deeper than they would like to believe. Most of the time when one attends meetings which bring together the Jews of Israel and those of the Diaspora, one can feel an underlying tension. The Jews of the Diaspora continue using an often lyrical if not wildly enthusiastic tone in speaking of the accomplishments of the young state. The Israelis, more sober, know what these accomplishments cost. This heroic generation of Israel's pioneers is in a certain sense a sacrificed generation. Any one of the Jews called to the superhuman task of the building of the country and the consolidation of the state could have had a much easier and more comfortable life in the Diaspora. At all levels of society in the countries where they could have lived or settled, the Israelis would have had a less tense and certainly less tragic life than ours today, even after the June 1967 victory. The Jews of the Diaspora see it clearly. So they choose what the Bible called Egypt's dishes of meat and onions rather than the harshness of our life. As one would expect, this situation provokes misunderstandings, tensions, and complexes. Some applaud all the more loudly the more they reproach themselves for not being present. Does the Israeli have the right to ask, "What are you waiting for to come to join us here and participate in the common effort of the renaissance you are praising?" This question is all the more pertinent because the Jews of the Diaspora are no doubt richer and more cultured. Their settling in Israel would necessarily raise the standards and security of the state. The arrival in Israel of one or two million Jews coming from countries with a high level of civilization and technology would no doubt be a great boon to Israel. But if the State of Israel needs the Jews of the Diaspora, the latter answer almost unanimously: "We do not need Israel, at least to live there." The sums of money that they give only represent a small portion of the state budget.

This answer is obviously not logical, coming from the Zionists. It is absurd when it comes from men who continue to adhere to the faith of Israel. The latter have always claimed an organic tie with the land of Israel. As you know it is very difficult to define the Jew because the phenomenon of Israel is a complex one which involves three constants which can be found in the succession of generations and permanence of doctrines. They constitute the basic elements of the Jewish faith.

The first constant is a spiritual message which is completely contained in the Bible, received, studied, and transmitted in its original language, Hebrew. With the Bible as point of departure, the Jews have for centuries developed works which all have a common character. They adhere to the knowledge and meditation of Scriptures studied in Hebrew and to their commentaries, the Mishnah, the Talmud, the Cabala, or even the works of theology, metaphysics, or philosophy, all of which intend to shed light on the Biblical patrimony—one thought that is three thousand years old.

This spiritual heritage has given rise to the second constant: the formation of a people, a Jewish ethnic group, which emanated from the amalgam of a humanity and a spiritual message. This group is not a race. It is enough to see Jews who have come from everywhere in the world gathering in the streets of Jerusalem, Tel-Aviv, or Haifa to note that there is no Jewish race. What does exist is a common destiny, what the journalists formerly called a nation. And this nation, this "collective will to live," has its roots in and draws its strength from the faith of Israel, the Jewish tradition.

The third constant, inseparable from the message and the people, is the land of Israel. From the beginning the land of Israel appears in the Bible as a living person. It is the reality promised by God to Abraham and his descendants. Only in its heart will the people of Israel be able to fulfill in its plenitude the incarnation, the accomplishment of the message of the Bible. When the country of Israel was destroyed by the Romans, when the Jews were forced to abandon their country and went to enlarge the little Jewish communities of the Exile, it was only in the hope of an imminent salvation and their return to the Holy Land. The synagogue of the Exile is built upon this dogma: the Exile is an evil, a punishment from God for the expiation of the sins of Israel. This expiation could have a redemptive value because the sufferings of Israel in the time of the Exile had as their mystical function the hastening of the coming of the Messiah, universal redemption. The economy of the kingdom of God required that the Jew suffer during the Exile in the expectation of the glorious return of a restored Jerusalem for the fulfillment of the great ideas professed by the Bible, for the triumph of peace on earth, justice over iniquity, love over hate, and unity over division.

In addition, all the synagogal liturgies are oriented and centered upon the prayer through which the faithful ask God to rebuild Zion and Jerusalem, to bring back its people from the Exile and lead it back to the promised land. This is not a concomitant result. The idea of the redemption of Israel, the rebuilding of Jerusalem, and the reconstruction of Zion, and the notion which makes the Diaspora a proof and a consequence of God's anger, form the nucleus of Israel's faith. The Jewish poets, in harmony with the Gothic sculptors, call the synagogue the blind-beauty, the widow, the scorned one, she who is deprived of her husband and home because she is rejected in the night of the exile among nations.

My friend, enter into a synagogue and listen to these Jews of Rabat, New York, London, Buenos Aires, Johannesburg, Stockholm, Rome, Madrid. Listen to them as they pray. What do they say?

At that time I will assure your return and gather you together: yes, I will assure your praise and glory among all the peoples of the earth, when you shall return from your captivity.

This text is one of the first which the pious Jew recites

each day at the dawn service as soon as he enters his synagogue. A while later he evokes at length the sacrifices which his ancestors offered in the temple of Jerusalem. This recollection is made in the explicit hope of the restoration of Jerusalem and the temple. When he recites the Kaddich, the famous prayer which Ravel interpreted so beautifully in music, often it is with fervor, and he expresses once again the hope of the imminent reestablishment of the kingdom of God and the reign of the Messiah. Awaiting the last judgment is obviously linked to the restoration of Israel and the resurrection of the dead, assembled and reunited in the glory of Jerusalem.

The liturgical Psalms are almost all inspired by the same thought: Jerusalem and the land of Israel have a central position in this liturgy, integrated with the principal idea which gives life to all the Hebraic liturgy, that of the coming end of the exile of the Jews. Each of its canticles expresses the hope for the return to Jerusalem.

The gift of the promised land made to Abraham, its restoration, and the reminder of the exodus from Egypt as foreshadowing the end of the exile are repeated in almost every paragraph of the morning liturgy. And before the *Shema Israel*, which is one of its high points, the faithful affirm once more the certainty that God loves Israel and will deliver it from its exile.

Continually in the morning liturgy, in its most intense and richest parts, the silent recitation of the *Shmone Esrei*, the eighteen blessings, the idea of the return of the exiled people dominates, as do the forgiveness of sins, the hope for redemption and the cure of all ills, the worst being the Exile. Here is textually what the rabbis and faithful repeat in all the synagogues of the world three times a day:

> *Sound the great horn for our freedom; lift up the ensign to gather our exiles, and gather us from the four corners of the earth. Blessed art thou, O Lord, who gatherest the banished ones of thy people Israel.*

This prayer is followed by an eloquent appeal:

> *And to Jerusalem, thy city, return in mercy, and dwell therein as thou hast spoken; rebuild it soon in our days as*

*an everlasting building, and speedily set up therein the
throne of David. Blessed art thou, who rebuildest Jerusalem.*

These Jews seem definitely convinced that it is necessary
to wish for the return of God and Israel to Jerusalem, but
still remain in Paris, London, or elsewhere in the vast world.
The answer to them lies in the sequel to this prayer which
begs God to bring back the cult and adoration to the Temple
of Jerusalem.

And let our eyes behold thy return in mercy to Zion.

So they ask for the return of God in a Jerusalem of glory
and they wish, in their prayer at least, to be there to witness
this return. Then they ought to hasten to Zion. Do they not
beseech in their daily prayers, with a conviction that Voltaire would have considered insane, that this return take
place immediately? Do they not inveigh against God, sometimes in a very touching way, for him to let it be? So they
say: if God continues to abandon Israel and leave the Jews
to the humiliation of the Exile, it must be the most evident
sign of the weakness of God himself. So the suffering of the
Diaspora must cease.

But that is not all: at three meals every day they bless the
good land of Israel which God has given us after having
delivered us from Egypt. They pray for it daily and ask that
God be gracious unto Israel, Jerusalem, and Zion.

The text states:

*Let us, O Lord our God, behold the consolation of Zion
thy city, and the rebuilding of Jerusalem thy holy city,
for thou art Lord of salvation and of consolation.*

And also:

*May our remembrance rise and come and be accepted be-
fore thee, with the remembrance of our fathers, of Messiah the son of David, thy servant, and Jerusalem thy holy
city. . . .*

And finally that plea which reappears as a leitmotif in all
the prayers of the synagogue:

*May the All-merciful break the yoke from off our neck,
and lead us upright to our land.*

What is said three times daily in all the synagogues of the
world is repeated more forcefully and fervently on the Sabbath, the Holy Days at Rosh Hoshana, Yom Kippur, and
Passover, which is the feast of freedom, par excellence, the
feast of the return from all the exiles. One could say and believe all this without budging even slightly while the country
of Israel belonged to foreign powers which practically forbade Jews access to the Holy Land. But what do these prayers mean now that the country *belongs* to the people of
Israel?

I sometimes ask the rabbis and the faithful whom I hear
praying so fervently: "You ask God to bring you back to
Israel. That is well and good. But what are you waiting for
to return there? Not only is it possible to return, but the
entire world urges you to do so. Instead of wearing your-
selves out in daily prayers, you have but to buy your plane
or boat ticket for Jerusalem at the nearest travel agency. The
State of Israel even will take care of the fare for it wants you
to come to settle there. It was established to help you realize
your prayers concretely."

Those who continue to pray for the return to Israel and
remain in the Diaspora are victims of a kind of split personality. In a sense, Ben Gurion has already said it. The Jews of
the Exile, religious or Zionists, suffer from schizophrenia.
Their very situation puts them in a state of permanent contradiction. On the one side there is the faith which cries for
Zion, on the other the man who makes his life elsewhere.
God may ask, "Jew, you who pray, whom are you deceiv-
ing? God, your neighbor, your people, or yourself?"

It is understandable that Ben Gurion in his incessant attacks against this paradoxical situation vehemently accuses
the Jews of the Exile. They insist on belonging to Israel and
its spiritual tradition and edification. Yet they carefully re-
frain from sharing our life and our struggle. Their faith en-
gages them not to remain among the nations, precisely for
the service they would render to the world by returning to
Israel as a prelude to universal salvation. Some of them, faith-

ful to their religion and conscious of their fundamental contradiction, try to formulate a good answer. The most humble recognize one fact: their religion makes it a duty to come to settle in Jerusalem to participate in the reconstruction of Zion in the expectation of the final goal of humanity and the Messianic hope for the Kingdom of God. They mention their responsibilities, their family interests, or their business. They have a thousand good reasons for not budging. But they display the hope that one day God will allow them to overcome their contradictions to finally settle in the Holy Land. Most of the time, of course, these are only pious wishes. The Jew is well established in the Diaspora where he enjoys a higher standard of living and greater conveniences than in Israel. He has no intention of leaving New York, Paris, or London.

Others, prouder and more aware of the necessities of logic, try to justify their presence in the Diaspora by a doctrine. A few months ago one of them did not hesitate to tell me, "Should Israel be destroyed, we in the Diaspora would protect the opportunity for a Zionist restoration." I cite this attitude because it is a symbol of the paradoxical situation in which God seems to have put his people!

There are others who take a middle-of-the-road position. They say that their prayers do ask the abandoning of the Diaspora and a return to the Holy Land. I will do it some day. For the moment I am satisfied to help in the building of Zion.

It is understandable that the Judaic religion of the Exile which is based on such aspirations and scarcely fulfills them would not be very attractive to the young people. If the synagogues are deserted and if the consistories in several countries are only elected by one or two percent of the Jewish inhabitants, if religious instruction is practically nonexistent in many Jewish communities, if spiritual life is in such a decline, the fundamental reason must lie in the essential contradiction of Jewish life in the Diaspora.

Georges Friedman correctly asks: "The end of the Jewish peoples?" The author of this remarkable essay has understood the weaknesses of all Judaism and expressed them powerfully by asking his question which is not as innocent as it first seems. The Zionist movement will not be a conquering movement until it has drastically modified its structures. It has to assume new goals to take on new vigor. Until it puts its own house in order, it will be destroyed by its internal illogic and domestic struggle which are a partial obstacle to the necessary reconciliation of the Jews and Arabs.

According to Friedman, Judaism of the Exile cannot survive its fundamental contradiction without a revolutionary reform. Either the Jews of the Exile realize that they must take seriously the liturgies which gather them in the synagogues and the prayers which they say with so much fervor or they must have the courage to admit the contradiction and change religions. I know that every believer praying before God expresses desires and ideas to which he is not always faithful. If absolute rectitude existed, if our expressed prayers always inspired the faithful to actions, we would all be saints. But there is a difference between wishing for purity, perfection, and sanctity, and not realizing them totally, and doing what the pious Jew does in the synagogue. He wishes for a physical act—the return to the Holy Land, a change in his objective situation—without fulfilling it.

This act which for two thousand years was not in the Jew's power now depends only on him. This is a brutal contradiction, obviously an unbearable insult to logic and truth. The pious Jew of the Exile is lying to himself just as he is lying to God and his people even if he claims that no "Jewish people" exists. When the rabbis have become aware of the basic defect, they will be ready to adapt or disappear. It is toward this second solution that the faithful are moving with frightening speed. Only Israel and its fantastic resurrection keeps them attached to their spiritual heritage whose keys they have lost.

What is the Jew who is neither religious nor Zionist? He can only call himself a Jew to the extent that he accepts the definitions of Hitler's racism. If the Jew is neither Zionist nor religious, his Judaism no longer has any significance for the essence of the message of Israel is either an aspiration toward spiritual perfection such as it is taught by the doctors of the synagogues or an action aimed at the building of Zion and Jerusalem. Other than this the Jew may recall that his father and forefathers were Jews. He has ceased being one. This is the actual situation. The Jews of the Diaspora are converting to the dominant religions and ideologies of their countries by tens of thousands. They have effectively cut themselves off from their allegiance to their ancestral Judaism.

In this sense, one can foresee that in the not-too-distant future, the present structure of Judaism and Zionism will ultimately collapse. Other structures will develop which I feel will be much more healthy. They will take Israel and its message as a pivotal point toward the final accomplishments of the promises of the Bible. The strength of the new Israel will be in the truth of its witness fulfilled in a spirit of unity and love.

If the difficulties of the Judaism of the Exile are serious, if the Jews of the Diaspora are to face up to the problems of life and death, if the choice they have to make is unavoidable, Israel has not even begun to grow up to its own spiritual reality. I am not discussing its economic and political difficulties which are obvious. These are all too normal and well known to be elaborated upon. You cannot build up a people, nor stir up a nation, nor construct a country with the precarious and limited means which are ours and under the conditions in which we are doing so without facing the worst perils. Nor am I speaking of Israel's security problems and of that basic difficulty to which I must again refer, the conflict which is still tearing us apart, myself and you whom a war has allowed me to find again. The underlying factor is the mind. On this plane, too, Israel has terrible problems to solve, for Judaism in Israel is in exactly the reverse position of Judaism of the Exile, but just as paradoxical. In the Diaspora the Jews beg God to bring them back to the Holy Land, while Israel is waiting for them and beseeches them to come. But they do not budge. In Israel, in the Holy Land, in the light of the rebuilt Jerusalem we continue to pray to God to bring us there. That is certainly illogical and shows a lack of adaptation of which only the Jews are capable. Our spiritual attitudes remain what they were in Poland, Yemen, Rumania, or Morocco. We continue to live with the forms which belonged to Judaism of the Exile for two thousand years. With our liturgy we have transported to our free and sovereign country the structures of thought and the spiritual modalities which were then ours. This contradiction between our words and our real situation does not exist simply in form. We have not had the courage yet to realize in our interior life the revolution which tore us out of the walls of the spiritual ghetto to restore us to our glorious new liberty.

For the most part the rabbis have brought with them to Israel their psychological and spiritual reactions shaped by these years of Exile. In fact they have brought the ghetto back. They continue living within it, reinforcing it with the new vigor which the return to our land gives. We feel a soil under our feet and of course that reinforces our general attitudes even more.

Developed to an excess in the age of the Diaspora, legalism continues to take its toll on Israel. The rabbis can go on for days about such and such a juridical problem raised by a line of the Talmud. But most of the time they are unaware of the great spiritual traditions which once belonged to the people of Israel. There are only a few great masters who have succeeded in escaping the temptation of canonism and legalism to pose a few of the deep problems of man's spiritual life, and who have not only preached but fulfilled the perfections and the virtues to which one must aspire to hasten the final destiny of humanity.

Though we have lived among the Christian peoples for two thousand years and among the Moslems for twelve hundred years, we have not yet uncovered nor integrated into our teaching of Judaism either the values of Islam or those of Christianity. We continue to live with our sister religions as though they did not exist, as if an uncrossable abyss separated us. In the majority of rabbinical schools throughout the world, in the *yeshivot* of Israel, not a word is spoken, not an idea taught, about the spiritual heritage of Islam or Christianity. The traditions of the ghetto are blindly perpetuated. Formerly the essential goal of the Jew was to preserve himself so as to maintain his authenticity and to save it for the time of the return. Clearly Israel was preserved to accomplish its mysterious destiny. The efforts of the Jews were first of all to prevent Judaism from disappearing by assimilation with Islam and Christianity—hence the extreme rigor of Jewish legalism of the Exile. Any contact with the Christians or Moslems whether by spiritual exchange or intermarriage was forbidden. The *Shulhan Arukh* which is the Jewish code of the sixteenth century envisaged an extremely complex legislation to establish a strong barrier between the Jews and the nations, between the Israelites and the adherents of different religions. This barrier, strengthened by accretions in the course of ages, became a real, almost insurmountable wall. It is within the walls of this spiritual ghetto that Judaism continues to live even in Israel.

The young and the alert see the contradictions between praying for the return to Israel when we are already there, and maintaining certain principles of segregation with men belonging to other religions while aspiring, to the contrary, to a universal order of unity and love. Facing these contradictions almost all Jewish youth is detaching itself from the traditional prayers and practices. An immense void results. The young people are literally steeped in Biblical teaching without understanding its spiritual significance. For a great number of Israelis so uprooted the absence of spiritual guides is painfully felt. On the religious plane the country is split in two. There is a heroic minority which forces itself to maintain the positions of Judaism of the Exile and even Judaism of Israel. It is not easy. More than ever the religious are going in a direction opposite to that of history, are swimming countercurrent and so obliged to be stubborn. The psychological rigidity results in a severity which makes their mission and their vocation even more difficult. The religious camp is separated from the would-be nonreligious at whose head there are some extremely active militant atheists, as militant as are our most extreme integrists. The Jews from Eastern Europe and Russia have accentuated the spiritual crisis which the German Jews had initiated with the Reformation. The Jews of Poland and Russia have introduced into Israel a militant atheism obviously foreign to our people. This atheism has forced the "religious" of Israel to organize and defend themselves. This extremely serious divorce aggravates the problem of the dialogue between the Jews, the

Moslems, and the Christians because those who are in contact with them are often the atheists with whom they have no language in common. And those who should carry on dialogue with the Christians and Moslems, the religious, are isolated by the walls of the spiritual ghetto from which they cannot detach themselves.

It would be easy to smile at this disaster, these contradictions, this medley of illogical stands irreconcilable with that simplicity without which there is no true spirituality. We must resign ourselves to the same transitory period of conflict that Christianity and Islam are experiencing. The whole world is changing. We are going from the traditional framework to a society without frontiers dedicated to the conquest of the cosmos and the unification of the human race. A religious metamorphosis is taking place before our eyes. For us Jews this change is more fundamental and essential because it takes us away from our Exile and transplants us into a new state of being. To our great confusion this revolutionary change has taken hold of us. We are seeking new ways to escape from our closed condition and to open up the limitless horizons we aspire to for a pacified and reconciled humanity. Our first duty is to rediscover the purity of our spiritual sources. The impressive figure of our common father, the Patriarch Abraham, still beckons us as from our beginning, to the ultimate encounter which is being fulfilled before us.

The wall of hate and crises which for so many centuries has separated the Jews, Christians, and Moslems is really foreign to the essence of Judaism, Christianity, and Islam. We all claim to be sons of Abraham. To my knowledge the father of all believers never said "Jewish, Christian, or Moslem." He adored the Most High, practiced justice, and lived in the love of his neighbor. His religion which is ours extols the virtues which our common history has misunderstood in our often mutually harmful relations. Religion has separated us more than it has united us. Perhaps the religious history of mankind, especially the monotheists, constitutes a sin against the spirit by the horrible wars it has provoked. The three major religions profess faith in the same God, have the same spiritual sources, identical hopes, the same Scriptures,

164

and a similar vocabulary. Yet for centuries the history of their relations has been a long series of misunderstandings, mutual ignorance, violence, and war which have built up more hate than hell can contain.

"You will certainly find that those who are the closest to loving the Moslems are those who say, 'In truth, we are Christians.' That is because there are among the Christians priests and monks and because they are not proud." (Koran, S5, Verse 85). These sentences express the Christian sympathies constantly proclaimed by Mohammed. From the beginning of his preaching he proposes as a model to his followers the Christian martyrs of the early centuries and those who more recently met their death for the demonstration of their faith in Yemen. He praises the monks and priests whose virtues he had appreciated throughout his life. Mohammed did not come to replace or suppress Christ's witness. Following Moses, the prophets of Israel, Jesus, and the apostles, his mission is to "seal the prophecy."

When he loses hope of converting the people of the book, *Ahl-el-Kitab*, the family of Scripture, Mohammed breaks with the Jews but continues to deal with the Christians. He gives his faithful permission to marry Christians and Jews and to share their food. His preaching is directly inspired by Christian dogma. The end of the world, the resurrection of the dead, and the last judgement are central to his doctrine. His terminology is borrowed directly from Christian theologians and from them he takes most of the stories concerning the mission of Noah, Abraham, Moses, and the prophets, of Christ and the belief in the Anti-Christ, guardian angels, heaven, and hell. Often he allusively refers to the dogma of the Incarnation, the Redemption, and the Immaculate Conception. On an essential point he formally admits to the Messianic vocation of Jesus, his miraculous birth of a Virgin, his mission, miracles, and ascension. He even makes a positive reference to the Eucharist in the *sourat*—"the set table" so full of contradictions regarding relations between Jews, Christians, and Moslem. Mohammed concedes that Mary and Jesus are the only two beings exempt from original sin. He, Mohammed, was cleansed of this sin by the angel. His vocation gave him a new purified heart. So the Koran sees Jesus as the manifestation of the Word of God descended into Mary. He states that one must not consider Jesus simply as a man.

In Mohammed's time Arabia was the meeting-ground for heresies. The Sabellians, Rakusiens, Basilidians, Valentinians, Carpocratians, Marcionites, Gnostics, Judeo-Christians, Nasoreans, Ebionites, the Docetes for whom the body of Christ was an appearance without human reality, the Aryens who denied his divinity, the Monophysites, Jacobites, Eutychians, and Nestorians who attributed a double personality to him, the Marianites and Lollards who adored the Virgin Mary, thus opposing the Anti-Dicomarianites who denied her perpetual virginity, battled and kept constant watch over each other.

Mohammed was unaware of true Christian orthodoxy. It is absolutely certain that he never saw the Gospel texts or Holy Scripture. When he makes his frontal attack on the Christian faith, it is directed toward the sects, their divergencies, and their errors which oppose each other not only on the intellectual and dogmatic plane but on the temporal. He observed the disputes and persecutions which their war provoked as the members of the sects imprisoned, exiled, and even killed each other. With this reservation, it can be said that the general attitude of the Prophet of Islam toward the New Testament was eminently positive.

It is conceivable that faced with such a situation, the Prophet intended to place himself above all these conflicts, in this marginal situation far from the Christians and the Jews, to preach his own religion and announce his God. In every case, nothing in the early teaching of Islam about the Church foresaw the development of relations between Christians and Moslems. Since Rudolph de Ludheim most Christian authors from the seventh century to the nineteenth century—Nicolas de Cuse, Hotinger, Bibbander, Prideau, to cite a few—unanimously present Mohammed as an impostor, and Islam as a collection of heresies, the very works of Satan. According to them the Moslems are the brutes of the Koran, a web of absurdities. From the beginning Christian polemicists heap their scorn on Islam without even bothering to study it. The "trouveres" attack and oppose the Saracens by the most vulgar and crude calumny. Fables circulate in Christendom about Mohammed presented as an impostor, a sorcerer, a débauché, even an idol greedy for human sacrifice. The Koran was translated into Latin in the twelfth century on the initiative of Peter the Venerable who wrote the first Christian treatise against Islam. The relatively objective translation was to serve as the basis for an appreciable number of commentaries on the Koran written by Christian theologians. Instead of presenting the civilization of Islam and its important analogies to Christianity, they put all their talents to denying or minimizing the resemblances while exaggerating the real or apparent differences to conclude unanimously on the invalidity of Islam.

The Moslems paid them back in the same coin. During the golden age of Moslem history its thinkers turned toward Christianity with good will and objectivity. In times of misfortune and decline they too become slanderous. They condemned not the eminence of the Christian religion but its shadows and contradictions. We who have grown up in a country where Islam and Christianity have met know how impassioned the critics of these two religions have been. Old habits and traditions inherited from times of hate and war unfortunately have been perpetuated up to our own time. I think it is necessary to condemn them because these errors jeopardize the one chance for a new dialogue which may bring together nations and churches by putting them at the service of the values they profess and whose triumph they desire.

The conflicts between Islam and Christendom have their origins not in pure knowledge but in political conflicts and interests emerging from an equal will for power. Islam's triumph must have seemed scandalous to the Christians. For them, Jesus, God-made-man, had put the final touch on the religious development of humanity. The destiny of the nations is clear. The Church's mission was to convert the whole world to the faith and law of Christ. From this perspective Mohammed could only be an impostor. At all costs it was necessary to oppose his disciples who had set out on the successful conquest of the world.

The fantastic and triumphal raid of your ancestors, the

Arabs, made all of Europe tremble. When they were defeated at Poitiers, they were already at the head of one of the greatest and richest empires that world history has ever known, one that has made a vast contribution to the development of world civilization. The Moslem escapade for the conquest of Europe is answered by the Christian war against the Arabs during the Crusades.

Conquerors of the Holy Places, the Crusaders opened up far wider objectives so that there is constant interference between the religious history and the political history of the Christian and Moslem peoples. Conflicts spread and become more serious. In the fifteenth century Spain succeeds in ousting the Moslems from the country and completely restructuring the unity of Europe from then on under the sign of the Cross.

Rare are the historians who clearly place the explanation for the rise of the West and the decline of the East on the bases of the economic revolution which the discovery of America stimulated in world trade. They delight in explanations of a political or even a spiritual nature. Often the analysts hold Islam responsible for the decline of the Moslem peoples, and the Eastern religions for the collapse of the Eastern peoples, while Christianity is given exclusive credit for the growth and enrichment of the Western peoples. This would be the limit for Christianity, the religion of poverty whose God is a laborer deprived of everything and crucified: to find its principal claim to glory in the fact that it made possible the upsurge of the American and European economies. The spiritual explanation does not seem enough to me. Until the fifteenth century the countries of Islam and the Far East were the center of world civilization, industry, and technology. Europe recognizes that learning and wealth come from the East. The Christian churches of the East share, just as the Eastern Jewish communities do, in the general prosperity of the countries where they are established and often participate in a privileged way in the common creative effort. That is especially striking about the Jewish world. The prophets, the rabbis of the Mishna and the Talmud, the great theologians, from the beginning to the sixteenth century are almost always Easterners who live in Asia or North Africa. The Western Jews, such as the Rhenish mystics of the tenth century, Rashi for instance, recognize themselves specifically as tributaries of the Eastern Jewish communities which were not only at the lead in intellectual progress but who nearly had a monopoly on it. To be convinced of this, one need only refer to any history of Jewish thought (Guttman's beautiful history of Jewish philosophy, for example) to see that from the beginning to the sixteenth century, it is essentially the creation of Asiatic or North-African authors, the majority of whom lived in Islam under the sign of the Crescent. As if by a stroke of magic the situation is reversed. From the sixteenth century on the European Jews take the lead over Eastern Judaism which goes into a serious decline. The reason for this is very clear. In the meantime the technical revolution has transformed the commercial and economic realities of the ancient world. This transformation has resulted in the irrevocable ruin of the Mediterranean and Far-Eastern peoples.

Modern colonialism has poisoned relations between Moslems and Jews. In colonial countries the Church often appears as the guarantee and the accomplice of the regimes generally hated by the conquered peoples. In the colonial villages, the subprefect, the captain of the police, and the priest form a trio difficult for the natives to distinguish between. In fact Christendom intervenes in many of the colonized countries at the time of the triumph of the colonial regimes and tends to disappear with them. This has not encouraged dialogue between men of different faiths. They have had to wait for a new era, the one which allows us to move from an Atlantic economy to a global type of economy to erase a number of prejudices and allows the possibility of a new dialogue between Christians and Moslems. Louis Massignon and Louis Gardet have proved that the undertaking, difficult as it may have been, was not hopeless.

To be successful, this dialogue will have to go back to the beginning, the time when in Mecca or Medina Mohammed defined Christendom. The Christians today would no doubt subscribe to most of the criticism the Koran makes of the Christian heresies spread throughout Arabia such as Monophysitism, Eutychianism, and Lollardism which devoted a cult to Mary adored as Virgin and Goddess. The Christians would also subscribe to the attacks which Mohammed makes on the dogma of the Trinity as some Christians construed it at that time: a union of God, Jesus, and Mary. So, too, when Mohammed declares that God has no son or companion, he attacks not the Catholic dogma as it was finally formulated, but a pagan belief adopted by the Arabs who believed in Mohammed's time that the goddesses El-Lat, El-'Ozza, and Manat were daughters of God. After all, the affirmation of the unity of God as the founder of Islam conceived it is not absolutely incompatible with the dogma of the Trinity. When he affirm that Allah has not fathered nor been fathered, that he has no equal in anything, he is speaking of the divine substance in the very terms of the Lateran Council, or the doctrines of Joachim de Flore. Louis Massignon, his disciple Louis Gardet, and Father Anawatti have undertaken the clearing of the troubled atmosphere of Islamic-Christian relations. Their work cannot minimize the fundamental differences which oppose Christianity and Islam, notably in the conception of Jesus as the Son of God and the Incarnate Word, mediator and savior of humanity. The refusal of the mediation of Christ is linked to the absolute transcendentalism of the faith of Islam. But in the pure silence of contemplation will Moslems, Jews, and Christians ever be able to return together to the sources of revelation and commune in the constancy of faith?

6 Waiting in Jerusalem

From the beginning, the theologians of the three religions have always agreed on at least one thing: man is a creature made in the image and likeness of the Creator and finds his true finality in the mystery of creation. This Biblical idea became dogma for Judaism, Christianity, and Islam. In the three religions man is in the center of the universe, the end of all creation: "A single human being is equal to all creation." Any offense against man strikes God himself. The principle proclaimed by Moses in Leviticus—"You will love your neighbor as yourself"—is basically identical to the other main commandment of the Bible:

You will love the Lord your God with all your heart, with all your soul, with all your strength.

These two principles authorize the following axiom cited in the Talmud and adopted by Islam as well as by Christianity which bases its vision of salvation on it.

He who destroys one soul destroys the entire universe.
He who saves one soul has saved the entire universe.

These elementary principles have been misunderstood in the relations of Christians and Moslems, and more tragically, if that is possible, in the treatment which the nations reserved for the Jews of the Diaspora.

At least Islam recognizes the legitimacy of the existence of the Jews in its city. It guarantees them the right to life and property. The Christian city was based on the principle of absolute theocracy: whoever did not participate in the intercession of Christ could not have full citizenship in the Christian city. Neither his life, nor his goods, nor any of his rights or liberties were fully guaranteed. The Moslems disappeared very rapidly from the Christian city leaving the

Jews in a painful tête-à-tête with the Christians for centuries. The history of the Jews in Christendom for two thousand years is one of the most humiliating and astonishing chapters in universal history.

The history of the Jews in Europe consists of an overwhelming series of expulsions, exactions, rapes, murders, and massacres. One notes a pattern of historical evolution, especially during the second millenium of the Exile. The Jews are very welcome in the Christian nations during their development, but following that they are tolerated in the precariousness of an uncertain state. Ultimately they are persecuted, even definitively eliminated in times of crisis.

Strict discriminatory legislation encouraged unlimited arbitrary treatment of the Jews. Rigorous sanctions were decreed against Jewish proselytysing. The Jews were forbidden to repair or restore the synagogues and generally were excluded from public functions. They were not allowed to possess Christian slaves—the corollary to practical exclusion from industry and agriculture which required employing slaves. Nor were they allowed to do business with the Christians. During periods of crisis these rules were applied mercilessly and inspired in the masses murderous reflexes whose use has not been totally forgotten in our generation.

The worst behavior the Jews were victim of began in the fourth century when the Roman Empire began to change under the law of Christ. When Mohammed is preparing for his great mission, the Jews are expelled from Spain by Sisebut in 613, and from France by Dagobert in 629. Nonetheless, it is at the end of the first millenium that the Jewish trial begins. To tell you a few of the outstanding facts, I need only mention the massacres perpetrated against the Jews by the Crusaders on their way to Jerusalem. Any of the constant accusations of ritualistic murder and the profanation of the Host led to plundering and massacres of the innocent. There were partial expulsions from the provinces and countries which the Jews had inhabited sometimes for centuries, definitive banishment from England in 1290, from France in 1324, and then the most terrible and disastrous, from Spain in 1492. Pontiffs, kings, and princes made an effort to humanize the laws.

Nonetheless, the war was waged not only against their bodies and their gold, but against their soul and culture. The tendency of the Christians was to burn the Talmudist with the Talmud. From 1215 on, the Christians rigged the Jews in a badge and a pointed hat which singled them out for the scorn and hate of the masses. The institution of the ghetto originated from this hate and from the Jews' indomitable will to survive. From the sixteenth century on, the reserved areas where the Jews had voluntarily taken refuge or even been forcibly penned up, took on the name of ghettos. On the economic plane their position was no less precarious. In order to subsist the Jews had no other choice but to become small merchants, colporteurs, or craftsmen. The business of money, forbidden to the Christian, became their temptation. When they gave in to it, their weakness had disastrous consequences. The anti-Semitic tradition took a strong hold on all the Christian people. Jules Isaac has shown how atheistic anti-Semitism has perpetrated one of the tragic acts of universal history by permitting the massacre of several million Jews in Germany—killed simply because they were Jews.

The history of human societies has never been idyllic anywhere. Yet the history of the monotheistic peoples represents a staggering paradox. If the relations between Christians and Moslems and between Moslems and Jews were never ideal, the history of the Jews in the Christian countries has reached a rare degree of cruelty all the more painful because of its absurdity. For further understanding one must look upon the situation as the drama of a family torn by hate.

The early Church had received everything from Israel: Scriptures, patriarchs, alliances, law, cult, prophets, the Virgin, Christ, and the Apostles. Primitive Christianity was itself Jewish by its membership and its localization on the hills of Judea. Not far from us one can visit the Cenacle where the birth of the Church took place in the splendid and wild setting of tawny colors and glimmering rocks on the hills of Judea in Jerusalem. Jesus and his Apostles never break the tie with their people and its spirituality. Saint Paul is proud to be a Pharisee. After having made his way to Damascus, Saul of Tarsus does not renounce any of the fundamental ideas and doctrines of the Pharisees. To the contrary, he transmits them in the very form that he received them from the lips of his master, Rabban Gamaliel, to the new Church which takes them as the basis for its dogma. Even Christian monachism finds its antecedents in the Jewish monachism of the Essenes, better known since the discovery of the Dead Sea Scrolls.

"Salvation comes from the Jews," announced Jesus. The Church knew it so well that it proclaimed itself the heir of the Synagogue, the new Israel. Yet, one can say without contradiction that the resemblance and sometimes fundamental identicalness of the Church and the Synagogue, both dedicated to the adoration of the same God and the same hope for the triumph of love all over the earth, fostered and led to an irreconcilable hate between them.

If the Church set itself up as heir of the Synagogue, then it inherited from one deceased. Though Israel did seem destined to disappear after the unfortunate war against Rome, a contrary destiny somehow prevailed. The armies of Titus had certainly destroyed Jerusalem and the Temple. If one is to believe Tacitus, some six hundred thousand Jews had been crucified on the roads of Judea and Galilee. The Jews had lost their homeland, their Temple, and their national cohesion. There remained only a handful of survivors who crept over the ruins of their Temple and their country. Some mystery intervened to prevent them from disappearing.

In the course of its already long history Israel had confronted Egypt, Babylonia, the Philistines, the peoples neighboring the Holy Land, the Assyrians, and the Persians. The Jews had struggled bitterly against the Seleucids and had conquered them. At this prophetic hour the tiny monotheistic people, having measured up to the principal ancient pagans, had to fight against the Romans who were then at the height of their military power. In spite of their weakness, their very limited resources, and their serious internal divisions the Jews had entered into open warfare against Rome in A.D. 66. They were not definitively crushed until the year

135 after the last uprising commanded by Bar Kochba. It was then that the Church of Christ took a great step forward. The war of the Jews, which one witness, Flavius Joseph, describes as "the most important of all which have ever broken out between cities and nations," spoiled Nero's plans for universal conquest and blocked Rome's way to the Orient. The repression was terrible, as you know. Devastated by gibbets and crosses, Judea soon ceased being the homeland of the Jews.

The loss of Israel's only sanctuary, the Temple of Jerusalem, deprived the Jews of the center of their national unity and religion. Their defeat was serious on the religious, political, and social planes, but reached the dimensions of a real tragedy in the spiritual order. The Temple alone was the place of the Divine Presence, the home of the God of Israel, the only place where it was possible to utter the name of the Lord and offer Him the worship which He had required of his people in the Torah of Moses. The destroyed altar drained Israel's sacred sources of inspiration and ritualistic purity. Its disappearance undermined the spiritual life of the Jews which was cut off from its ultimate sacrificial fulfillment. So the worldly trial of Israel was the reflection of a deeper and more irremediable cosmic mystery, that of God's Exile. The rabbis accepted it as such and taught that it was to last until the day designated by God for his return and for his triumph.

The survivors of Israel had only one idea—to assure the permanence and survival of the Jewish people. The earthly country lost, the watchword issued by the leaders of Judaism—followed by the people with a ferocious determination, often under pain of martyrdom—was to save the spiritual patrimony of the conquered people. It was composed of the monuments which bore witness to the visitation of the Word: The Bible, oral tradition, the teachings of the schools, and the doctors who succeeded to Moses' chair. The people of God could certainly have been conquered by the Roman armies. In the eyes of most of the elders it was only justice since Israel had been unfaithful to its vocation. It had succumbed because of its own sins rather than the weight of enemy armies.

But if the Jews were conquered, Israel must live. After Rome's ravages, each man in Israel had become more precious than the Temple itself. Schools were founded in Galilee, Judea, and Babylonia which assured the survival of Judaism. The rabbis—understanding to what point internal division had been fatal—tried to give new and monolithic structures to Judaism. Israel had been welded to the eternal Word in absolute subordination to the God to whom it had given its faith. It was to remain at God's feet in loving submission to his will and in the hope of the Kingdom. In this expectation it was to have the spiritual strength to turn its back on the material world and transform the places of exile into bastions of the mind where every talent and every shortcoming was to be dedicated to safeguarding the ancient patrimony and, when possible, its spiritual enrichment. The destruction of the Temple marks the beginning of one of the most astonishing human adventures.

While the Christians adored a Man-God nailed to a cross with the fear and hate of a few men—Jews or Romans—and were concerned with establishing and consolidating the Christian Church, the whole Jewish people were placed, by their will not to die, in the position of the suffering Messiah of the rabbinical sermons. The Jew identified with the man of sorrows of the vision of Isaiah and the Psalms, not only because henceforth he had become a man of prayer, disarmed and delivered to the mercy of the nations and bearing the weight of their scorn and hate, but because the consolation of the sacrifice was denied to him.

The rabbis taught that the destruction of the Temple and the Exile were necessary expiation. God could chastise the Jews. It was a sign of his fidelity and not proof of desertion. The Exile is equated with expiation, but it also has a redemptive virtue. The suffering endured was a sacrifice of love, necessary in the measures of eternity to make ready the fulfillment of humanity and the reign of glory announced by the Christians and hoped for by the Moslems.

My friend, how I wish that every Christian, every Moslem, and all of you, Arab brothers, would understand it. The people of the Exile who have paid dearly with suffering, humiliation, and blood to preserve the conditions of their survival, did it not for their own glory, but to serve an absent God in the night of sorrows. Israel has fulfilled the condition of an absolute Exile. It was absent from its land, its country, and its people, dispersed throughout the world without any organ of communication, deprived of its language, and even of its God. Its suffering represented its most eminent dignity. Its humiliation, its abjection, its calvary were its true claim to glory. Later, Judah Halevy was to give a definitive form to the traditional rabbinical teaching which so realistically expressed the tragic condition of the Jews of the Diaspora. Israel was like a body without its head and heart, a heap of dried-out bones, half-dead, half-alive, defenselessly exposed to the blows of nations. But in this it willingly substituted itself for the sacrificial Lamb of which it had been deprived. Its suffering and oblation were to earn the grace of God and prepare the hour of His return.

As Israel sank into exile, it became more introverted, a fact which became the *sine qua non* of its survival. The Jew who exposed himself to the philosophy of the Greeks or Romans or the one who converted to Christianity or Islam —there were numerous cases—disappeared as a Jew. The challenge of the Exile which the Jews gallantly met, was to resist everything, to say no to everything, so that the hour of Return would come. So condemned to live on the defensive, the Synagogue had the natural tendency to define itself by opposition to the movements which could threaten its existence such as Christianity, Islam, and for other reasons, Hellenism and paganism. Facing such adversaries, one can understand why the rabbis cut the links with the outside world: so that Israel could devote itself to its own works and insure, be it at the price of a real impoverishment, the protection of its internal sources.

By vocation the Church itself was dedicated to the spiritual conquest of the world. Its empire and glory were to extend to the ends of the universe. Yet, the obstinacy of the Jews, the people of Jesus, and the prophets stood in the way of its missionary will. For almost two millennia Judeo-Christian relations developed on the basis of an enormous misunderstanding in a conflict which is the crux of the tragedy.

By their stubborn refusal of the Cross, the Jews place

themselves not only in a misunderstood position, but in one persecuted by Christians. Their dispersed, miniscule communities were incomprehensible to the Christians who considered them as foreigners impossible to assimilate and a cause for scandal. How could they react to these bearded Jews, depositories of the Sacred Texts, speaking coded languages and remaining desperately and absurdly faithful to incomprehensible practices and gibberish? How could they react to these wearers of phylacteries, to these men who did not accept any of the customs of Christianity and who prayed night and day over the very texts which Christ had sung? Did a certain Christian theology (which Jules Isaac has called the teaching of scorn) provoke persecution of the Jews, or did it arise to explain the cruel fate of my people? There is no simple answer to this question. There was no doubt interaction between a given situation (laden with all possible persecutions, taking into account the moral and spiritual state of medieval Europe) and the doctrinal and theological justification of this state.

For the Christian masses there were very clear reasons for the humiliated fate of the Jews. They were expiating for their denial of the Savior and the infamous crime of having crucified him. "Our religion is made to purge vices. Yet it fosters, nourishes, and encourages them," Montaigne used to say.

In fact the Jews' continued presence in the midst of the Christian city has sometimes led to an alienation of Christian thought. The fact that the Jews had been accused almost unanimously of deicide by the doctors of the Church is an unbelievable paradox, the sign of a real aberration, because this accusation is based on two principles opposed by all morality and thought: collective responsibility and *hereditary* collective responsibility. No theologian, no Christian moralist, no matter of what era or tendency, could remain faithful to Christ and spread such monstrosities. In the time of Ezechial the Jews had already defined, once and for all, the principle of individual responsibility. "If the father has eaten green grapes, the son will not taste their bitterness." The teaching of scorn permitted by the Church was founded entirely on two monstrous and untenable ideas, the collective and hereditary responsibility of the Jewish people for a crime which might have been committed by only a few Jews, not without Roman help either, two thousand years ago. It is amazing that the doctors of the Church—even the greatest—were not able to resist this falsification of history and thought whose consequences were overwhelming for the Jews and dishonorable for Christendom. While the Jews suffered from this calumny, did not certain doctors of the Church, presenting a mode of thought that some cannibal tribes would have been evil enough to proffer, commit a true sin against the spirit? The council of Vatican II, has, of course, condemned this stand, but has the Christian world really become aware of the proportions of its guilt, not before Israel, which after all had chosen its fate, but before Christ?

Judeo-Christian relations are dominated, of course, by the person and the history of Christ. Even today numerous Christians view Christ's passion rather summarily. For them Christ appears and delivers his message. The Jews band against him and the Christians recognize him as God. On the one hand, shadow and darkness, on the other, light. Christ is not only repelled, but crucified by the powers of darkness —the Jews. Because of their sins they are the outcasts of humanity and expiate their crime of deicide in the harshness of the Exile. Thus, the Christians become the instruments of God's vengeance when they provoke, authorize, or allow the persecution of the Jews. It is normal that "justice" prevail. This caricatural view of things does not stand up before any serious historic analysis. Too many Christians forget that Jesus was a Jew, that he lived among the Jews, and that he never broke the bridges which united him to the Jewish people and to their spiritual tradition. They forget that Mary, the Apostles, and the first Christians were all Jews.

At the foot of the Cross, next to the Roman soldiers charged with administering the Roman punishment of the crucifixion, the witnesses of Jesus' passion were all Jews. The tendency is to forget the historic context in which Christ's trial unfolded. Israel was occupied by the Roman armies. The Jewish people were unanimously pitted against the occupying forces. For the Jews not only did Rome represent an enemy foreign power, but it personified paganism, and in this respect, represented the supreme evil for the entire Jewish people. Every imperial power finds collaborators in the country it conquers. Rome found them in Jerusalem, in the Holy Land. The phenomenon is inevitable. Since the Romans were there, since their armies occupied the country, the Jews had to be in contact with them, and the authorities had to find a *modus vivendi* to diminish the hardship of the pagan occupation of the Holy Land. In the eyes of the Jewish collaborators, in the eyes of all prudent and wise men, the teaching of Jesus was as dangerous as it was successful. Seditious moments had stained Palestine with blood. Since it had been occupied by the Romans, several attempts at revolt had been brutally crushed. The Romans would let sedition develop to a point, then suddenly would unleash their cruel, bloody, and pitiless repression. One did not take imperial Rome lightly nor dare defy its legions. The soldier's heel knew how to crush any attempt at revolution.

In these circumstances the teachings of Jesus could only appear seditious to the Romans. Jesus, obviously, took precautions. He wanted to avoid misinterpretation concerning his mission and his doctrine. He said: "Render unto Caesar what is Caesar's, and to God what is God's."

He was speaking of the kingdom of God and its imminent triumph. He preached unity, justice, love, and peace. But how was this divine message concretely heard by the Jews and the Romans? Whether Jesus wanted it so or not, his teaching could only inflame the Jewish energies against the pagans. The occupier was a pagan in everyone's eyes, and it is exactly for this that the Jews reproached him. The kingdom of God for all of Jesus' contemporaries in Palestine was first and above all else the end of pagan Rome's occupation, the liberation of the country. Jesus taught in the open, and the oratorical precautions which he took to avoid confusion and misunderstanding of his message could only aggravate the misunderstanding. There are cases where strength of conviction worked to the contrary. The Jews could not help but see in Jesus a leader all the more loved because he expressed everybody's feelings when he exalted Israel which was being crushed by the cruellest of occupations. For the Romans and for their collaborators Jesus represented danger of a political order. To the extent that the people followed, heard, and acclaimed him, Jesus, against his will, shook the foundation of the Roman presence in Israel. Caiaphas and the experienced men who surrounded him understood what direction things could take. As Jesus had more resounding success among the crowds, he represented an increasingly serious threat. The Romans let him alone, but only up to a point. Then pitiless repression would follow in a familiar and frightening manner. Jesus would be executed with several hundred, several thousand, perhaps, of his disciples, in whom Rome would not see the partisans of a Christian sect, but Jews who threatened the *Pax Romana*. What Caiaphas fears above all, for the love of his people, is Roman repression. He does everything necessary to prevent the worst. A judge at the Supreme Court of Israel, Haim Cohen, maintains that the Sanhedrin did everything in its power to save Jesus. His thesis is based on a deep knowledge of the milieu and the Jewish laws. But in the eyes of the Roman pagans was it possible to save Jesus? And could Jesus resign himself to the prudence that Caiaphas desired? If it were impossible to keep the affair quiet, the conclusion could only lead to the crucifixion of Jesus, or to an even more serious catastrophe, the death of Jesus and the extermination of all his disciples. Caiaphas stated it clearly: "It is better that one man alone, Jesus, die, than the whole people perish."

The people means the nascent Christian Church, the immediate disciples of Jesus. Since the death of Jesus is decided upon, since a straight out execution is loathed and a trial is necessary, a pretext will be found. How to accuse and damn this just man among the just? He says that he is the Messiah. For this they can take him. And it is all the easier since Jesus presents himself as such. Once the pretext has been found, the trial takes place in the manner we know.

But one cannot know the Jews and still think that Jesus was put to death only for his spiritual teaching, his pretense at being the Messiah, and the claim to divinity. I know at least three Jews who claim to be the Messiah. One of them publicly states that he is God.* No one has ever been offended by his pretentions in my presence. Jewish history is filled with examples of doctors, rabbis, and ordinary faithful who have pretended to be the Messiah. Sometimes their adventure has ended tragically, but always by the intervention of foreigners among whom the Jews lived. In troubled times such as Jesus lives in, Messianic dreams are contagious. The Romans know it and know how to break the claims the Jews live by.

Messianic hope, nurtured by meditation on the Scriptures, was exacerbated by the harsh conditions of the Roman occupation. Israel's torment began in the year 63 B.C. when Pompey conquered Palestine. That was the end of Jewish independence, the beginning of the suffering of the Exile and the anxious expectation of the kingdom of God. For the Jews it was not a question of abstract ideas or doctrinal debate, but of flesh and blood. God's Person, the honor of Israel, and its place in the history of humanity were their real concern. Their teaching aimed rather at rendering live in the heart of each Jew a relevant faith which permits survival. As for the Messiah, the Jews have always taught his eternity and his transcendance: "When the world was created, the Messiah king was already born because he preexists the creation of the world." The Messiah is the spirit which soars from all eternity over the waters before the world was created. He is the mind of God, the son of David chosen to become the light of the world and its savior. He is sometimes represented as a leper burdened with the sins of the world and pierced with sorrows. A mysterious text declares that the Messiah, son of Joseph, has already come and has been put to death (Zacharias 12:10, Soukkat, 52a). Saint Paul announces that Jesus was the Messiah. Others attribute this dignity to other saints and heroes. Rabbi Akiba proclaims Bar Kochba the Messiah of Israel, thus bringing up an im-

---

* "You may doubt that I am God," he argued one day "but, men of little faith, how can you deny that I am the man who says that he is God."

passioned but calm contradiction (Taanit 68b). It will be the Romans, not the Jews, who will kill Bar Kochba—and Rabbi Akiba, one of the most noble figures of Israel.

The fundamental error of the Christian theologians and historians who have given the interpretation we know for Christ's passion consists in seeing Palestine at the time of Christ as a monolithic world. They picture the Judaism of the era as a monolithic faith with a single response to every question about God, the Torah, the Messiah, and life and its problems. Such is the source of confusion which has clouded the relations of Judaism and Christianity and contributed to their violence throughout the ages.

It is certain that in the extraordinary variety of opinions and practices which reign in Palestine when Jesus begins his public life, nothing in his person or in his teaching could exclude him from the community of Israel, not even the Messianic claim. In the very nucleus of the Pharisee party, the differences of opinion between Hillel, and Hamai, Rabbi Akiba and Rabbi Yohanan Ben Tohta are at least as great as between the young Church and the community of Israel from which it did not distinguish itself. At the time of Jesus when the Sanhedrin of Jerusalem is charged with rooting out heresy and even imposing the death penalty on the guilty, there was in Palestine an extraordinary outgrowth of contradictory doctrines and dissident sects. Let us say simply that on almost all points of thought and doctrines, the Sadducees who controlled the Sanhedrin violently opposed the Pharisees. The Sadducees denied the validity of oral law, the reality of the world to come, and the resurrection of the dead. The contradictions were even greater between Judaism of the Holy Land and Judaism of the Diaspora, notably Hellenistic Judaism. In Palestine itself, numerous different and divergent, if not enemy sects, had their own body of doctrines and teachings. Disdaining in turn the authority of the Pharisees and that of the Sadducees, the Essenes lived in the deserts of Judea in monasteries where they imposed an austere discipline on themselves. But the Essene communities, very different from the other Jewish sects, were not monolithic in their mode of life, nor in their teachings. To our knowledge, they did not possess a directing organ or a center of unification for their doctrines. It is very certain that the Jewish world always has permitted the coexistence of very different and often violently opposed currents of thought everywhere. From all evidence this was the case in the time of Christ. A Pharisee such as Hillel was certainly closer to Jesus than to some of his Sadducean colleagues. So by numerous aspects of his thought Philon of Alexandria is without any doubt a precursor of Saint Paul who was so pleased to be a Pharisee and a son of a Pharisee. Did they crucify Philon because he wrote about the great priest, "I think that he had indestructible and very pure parents, God for his father, who is also the father of everything, and Sophia, wisdom, for his mother, from whom all things are born"? This sentence taken from the *de fuga et inventione* (108) obviously announces the dogma of the miraculous birth of Christ conceived of God the Father and born of the Virgin Mary. No one in Israel has ever blamed Philon for a thought which prefigures that of the subsequent Christian theologians. Quite the contrary, when the community of Alexandria decided to send a lawyer to plead its interests at the court of Rome, they turned to this philosopher.

Jesus, affirming himself as the Messiah at the time when Roman troops were occupying Palestine, could not help but attract the passionate interest of the Jewish masses. That he also provoked a violent contradiction is certain, and it was inevitable in the agitation of the Judaism of the period. Jesus awakens Jewish fears and anxieties over the Romans whose good grounds no one could contest with regard to the very future of the community, the Church, which Jesus founds.

One fact remains certain—the divorce between the Church and the Synagogue becomes wider not because of different theologies, but rather because of their historic situation, charged with the shattering war which was going to divide them.

The nascent Church has never debated the great lines of the Pharisaic dogma, the principal doctrines of which it nonetheless has adopted. The question of Jesus' Messiahship could bring up differences. Rabbi Akiba also raised a violent contradiction when he stated that Bar Kochba was Messiah.

These differences were not enough to break the unity of the community of Israel which could withstand these deep contradictions. Those which pitted the Sadducees against the Pharisees, or the latter against the Essenes or the Zealots, for example, were not less important. The Crucifixion of Jesus, instead of dividing the nascent Christian Church from the other Jewish sects, must have brought them closer in their common horror of the reign of violence wielded in the Holy Land by the pagans who came from Rome.

But Saint Paul has said it: it was necessary that the "fall" of Israel serve divine plans and concomitantly integrate many peoples to Christian unity. The Jews, excluded from Christian society, served as a base for the apologetics of the Church to build upon. Saint Augustine, Saint John Chrysostom, and Saint Thomas Aquinas understood that the survival of the Jews in their humiliated situation could serve to prove the excellence of the Church. They could have said with equal truth that the disarmed Jews who showed so much fidelity to their God, in the remembrance of passed glories and the hope of final accomplishments, proved the existence of God and the omnipotence of the Word as well. The apologetics could be made with as much efficacy in the positive sense of love as it could by denigration. The Church was too busy with its superhuman task of evangelizing the world, while Israel buttressed itself with the sole aim of avoiding the extinction which could have been its normal lot.

The spectacle which the Jews and the Christians presented to the world would have been comical had it not been so bloody. There were two groups who both claimed, one in Latin, the other in Hebrew, to adore the God of Abraham, Isaac, and Jacob—men who in their cities and their ghettos, their synagogues or their churches, recited the same prayers with the same hopes, recognized the same scale of values, worshipped the same past, recognized the same ancestors, and aspired to the same ideal and the establishment of the kingdom of God. These men dreamed of justice, unity, and love, accepted the strictest penances and most extreme sacrifices for the love of their God, faithfully prostrated themselves for two millennia to the service of the same God in the same land, and lived in the same countries, cities, and villages without making the slightest effort to try to know each other. The Christians who adored the God of Abraham, Isaac, and Jacob, who had adopted their Holy Scripture, who had rejected their gods and idols, and burned their pagan past renounced their own spiritual realities to become Semites spiritually, according to the words of Pius XI. They had Jewish communities in their midst, and almost never tried to know their past. The Judeo-Christian polemic represents a vast tapestry of misunderstanding, calumnies, and sometimes hateful accusations. A whole folklore of hate grows like a cancer in the religion of love. The Jew is represented under different avatars of the devil. He is Satan, the man with cloven foot, responsible for the agonies of the kingdom of this world.

As we have seen, for reasons of survival the Jews lived in the Christian world for two millennia without feeling the slightest need to know Christian theology in any real depth. They rejected as a whole, and without examination, Greek, Christian, and later, Islamic thought. It is astounding to think that for two millennia up to the eve of modern times a Jewish thinker can hardly be found who overcomes the complexes and prejudices inherited from a disastrous historic situation in order to read the Gospels as one of the immortal masterpieces of Israel's thought, to unseal the spiritual and religious values of patrology, to recognize in Saint Thomas Aquinas one of the greatest thinkers of humanity, and to recognize in Saint Theresa of Avila and Saint John of the Cross God's inspired cantors, heirs of the Psalmists of Israel.

For two thousand years the Jews have had no contact with Christian thought except for peevish polemics. Everything which was Christian was energetically censured. It was forbidden to utter the name of Jesus. They called him "that man," *oto ha ich.* The anti-Jewish legislation of the Church provoked strict Jewish regulations which forbade all contact with Christians, their liturgy, their worship, and their places of worship. Every church was declared impure, and soiled the Jew who might venture there. The religious thinking of Judaism and Christianity worked together to build an insurmountable barrier between Jews and Christians. They only met to curse each other. One unfortunately can recall the Judeo-Christian controversy, and notably the controversy of Tortosa. A Christian prince, a bishop, and an archbishop eager to show his zeal for the faith, called together the rabbis who were opposed to the Christian theologians. For the Christian it was a matter of convincing the Jew of the excellence of the faith of Christ. The Jew had only to defend himself and render an account of his refusal of Christ's religion. Sometimes, as was the case at the court of the Count of Toulouse, the last word lay in the sword of the prince who ended the dispute by putting an end to the rabbi's life.

On a larger scale the anti-Semitism of the Christian peoples has doubtlessly allowed, if not initiated, the great movements of contemporary anti-Semitism. The relations between Jews and Christians remain subservient to this detestable past. A long period of reciprocal purification will be necessary before the Jews and Christians can look each other in the face, eye to eye, without a shadow to spoil the purity of their new relations.

History had carved an abyss. The hardening of thought, sometimes its very sclerosis, did the rest. But the stone on which Judeo-Christian relations are broken remains the person of Jesus Christ. Here I have to go back to some of the meanings of the Messiahship of Israel.

Meshiah: anointed of the Lord, the prince, bearer of graces and power, through whom the frontier between the increate eternal and creation is abolished, the man in whom is absolved the disparity between day and night, light and darkness, and who restitutes the glory of the real order of the world. The most ancient tradition of Israel puts the Messiah at the beginning and at the end of the creative act.

And the spirit of the Lord moved over the waters.

"Which is the spirit of the Lord? The Messiah King is the spirit of the Lord who moved over the waters on the first day of creation." The text from *Bereshit Rabbah* reveals better than any other, perhaps, the knowledge that the rabbis had of the Son of Man, of the one whom the psalmist recognized as the *Bechor*, the elder son, anterior to the act of creation but also the finality of creation. The angels, according to the tradition of Israel, had opposed the creation of man. Why was the Omnipotent going to compromise the peace of the kingdom by this striking mistake whose sin was to break the harmony of the edifice? The Omniscient has no answer for the cohorts of angels, but takes advantage of one of their inattentive moments, the eve of the Sabbath, to mold Adam and Eve out of the sod. "Why have you done this?—For the love of the Messiah for whom I have created the world." So the Creator accepts the suffering of the world for the love and triumph of the Son of Man.

First and last, *alpha* and *omega*, but the Messiah is also intimately present in the heart of man's life and thought. From its first verses the Bible reveals the structures of the world: the creative act draws the Non-Being from his eternity and inserts multiplicity. The first day, the only day, says the Bible, imposes the confrontation of the skies and earth, of the *tohu-bohu* (formlessness) of the earth, of the darkness on the face of the abyss, and of the spirit of God on the waters. The free act of God in his eternal Word starts the drama by letting lights shine in the darkness: *Yehi Or*— let there be light. The first day is announced as the succession of a twilight and a dawn, of a night and a light: a single day, *Yom Ehad*, the day of unity, as the Biblical expression may also be translated. From then on the alliance is inscribed in the nature of things. The commentators of the ancient text pointed out that the word alliance, *Berit*, had the same etymology as the verb to create, *Bara*. Today's grammarians have other explanations. It is no less true that a unique link exists between the Creator and the creature and that this link is the base of the alliance. In starting the liturgy of creation, the Creator was responsible jointly with the "work of his hands": putting creation at the beginning of its chapters, the Bible is already the book of the alliance.

The rabbis describe the hierarchies of the alliance, identical to those of the days of creation, like a pyramid. The base is the widest, all creation having as its ally the Lord who permits its work. Genesis is silent about the Adamitic alliance, but it surges from the text with an implacable power as later commentators will persistently note. The law of this alliance is the law of life: *peru u'rbu*, increase and multiply. All reality is the sign of this alliance, of this law anterior to death, at the sources of being and life.

The second stage of the alliance—this one explicit—is the alliance with Noah. The fall of Adam and his expulsion from Eden consummate the work of death. It is fitting after the Flood to redeem the rest and to revive it by integrating it to the harmony of an alliance which unites it to the living. All humanity is involved; every man participates in the sacrifice offered by Noah and can see in the rainbow the sign of his redemption in the supernatural order of unity and love. And the law that pledges this alliance, which the rabbis will articulate in seven principles of natural law, already prefigures a more decisive restoration of the original harmonies.

Third stage: Abraham. Love operates as if it wished to triumph more jealously over rebellious man and impose the plenitude of its passion to the sole elect, the alliance being the meeting point of the Lover and the loved one he possesses. The later Prophets and the singer of the Song of Songs will express it as a marriage. Abraham involves all his descendency in his sacrifice: Ishmael and Edom—the Jews, the Moslems, the Christians, all those who refer to the God Most High whom he is the first to proclaim and serve. The alliance of Abraham is endowed with a sign, the circumcision, and a more explicit and restrictive law. The Kingdom of God progresses in history to the day when, leaving his idols behind, Abraham sets out for the Holy Land.

Fourth stage: God acquires a people the day Moses concludes the alliance on Sinai which makes Israel the theophoric people: no longer all creation or humanity, nor the assembly of the heirs of Abraham's monotheistic ethic—but a people set up in a religious order dedicated to the promotion of the Kingdom of God in the history of man. The sign of the alliance (it is always concluded by a sacrifice) is now the Sabbath, symbol of the rest at the end of the days. Its law is the Torah.

Fifth stage: the base of the alliance is still too broad. The Levites will be selected, a tribe of Israel whose entire existence will be exclusively dedicated to the service of the

Lord. The only authority of their priests is God. They have broken all earthly attachment and, having no part in the temporal heritage of their people, they are the mediators between the increate eternal and creation. By sacrificial offering, they make the expression and functioning of the alliance possible. They are the intermediaries of the Lord's grace, *Hessed*, which passes through them to the body of the people dedicated to God and thus assures the union of all creation to the Will which manifests it. The priestly alliance is the supernatural alliance par excellence, an alliance of salt: *berit melah*.

The sixth stage of the pyramid of the alliance only concerns one family and one man—the royal family and its leader, the king of Israel, of whom David was to embody the most perfect figure.

At each step a law secures the alliance. The law becomes stricter and more constraining as it goes up the hierarchies—the goal of the law of sanctity is to separate man from the natural order so that he may rise in the light of the order of God, the *Mitsva*, and so that he may manifest its pure perfection within the world whose salvation he must insure. The structures of the alliance so defined assure Biblical revelation an absolute autonomy and originality by comparison to the non-Biblical traditions and philosophies. The message is inseparable from the man and the people. The mission is to reconquer the whole earth for redemption. The alliance, by putting some men in accord with the Will of the Lord, draws the earth away from its original *tohu-bohu* and breaks the closed system of its darkness to give a sense and a direction to the history of man. The pyramid of the alliance is crowned with an arrow which designates the Messianic ends of creation.

In Israel the Messiah is thus the immediate truth of the conscience. Maimonides, summing up the doctrine, could guarantee that not to believe in the Messiah as a *person* and not to aspire to his coming and his *personal* triumph was apostasy for the Jew. In fact, the Jew who stops believing in the Messiah has already denied his spiritual heritage and has separated himself from the people whose every hope is for the appearance and triumph of the Son of Man.

The Son of Man! Here the Christian will be troubled not to find in Israel a Messianology comparable to the Christology which defines everything a Christian must know about his God. It is a fact that in the vast array of Hebraic literature not a single treatise of theology exists which is devoted to the Messiah.* To analyze the reasons for this would mean retracing the entire history of Judaism. A few statements will help us put the question into better perspective. Theology in Israel has never succeeded in becoming an autonomous science. We have seen that the meeting of Biblico-Talmudic thought with Islam and Christianity on the one hand, with Platonism and Aristotelianism on the other, was necessary before the first attempts at the elaboration of a dogmatic theology of Judaism might arise (from the ninth century on Isaac Israeli, Saadin ben Yosseph de Fayyoum). Whatever the success of the elaboration of the most famous theologians of the Synagogue (for example, Salomon Ibn Gabirol, Bahya Ibn Pakuda, Judah Halevy, and Maimonides), their works never are at the vital center of the religious problematics of Israel. For the Jews the river of life continued to flow in the Holy Scriptures, in the Torah, in the Prophets and the Hagiographers in which they had recognized the revelation of the eternal Word and which they consistently accepted as the prime if not unique source of all human knowledge, enlightened by the oral teaching given in the Talmud. For the Semitic mind written revelation supported by oral tradition possesses a profound cohesion and internal unity whose harmonies endlessly illuminate and delight whoever knows how to uncover them. It is still necessary to pass through the strait gate of sacred knowledge and humbly to pay the price which allows one to participate in the banquet of the angels. It is better to turn your head and shake the dust from your feet before the barbarians who, for lack of knowledge and preparation, devastate the garden it would have been better for them never to have

* A few modern essays by the Jews dedicated to the Messiah of Israel have a historical and not theological perspective. Their concern is to know what was said or thought about the Messiah and not, as in Israel's ancient tradition, who the Messiah was.

191

entered. Here knowledge surpasses what concepts and words can express for those who have not crossed the threshold where the eye of the heart can open up and be satisfied with its vision.

Instead of beautifully constructing dogmatic theology, the man eager to achieve the knowledge that the rabbis had of the Messiah of Israel will first of all have to identify an enormous mass of widely dispersed and sometimes contradictory traditions. That is the lot of the seeker who wants to penetrate a religion which perhaps more than any other can only be known internally. But an additional problem comes up. It is true that the Messiah is the culmination of all the tradition of Israel and it is also true that Christianity builds from this tradition which it claims to accept without reservations proclaiming the divinity of Jesus Christ. The conflict between the Christ triumphant and the Synagogue forced to turn inward for survival, obliges the doctors of Israel to remain conservative in their thinking (or in the permitted traditional positions) on the problems of common interest. The common barrier obliges the weakest to the greatest prudence. The rabbis understood it so well that they emptied their teaching of everything which might permit them to stumble over victorious Christendom. It is necessary to raise the veil to rediscover the living tradition of Israel as far as the person of the Messiah is concerned. In the modern era another difficulty must be surmounted. Recently emancipated Western Judaism, never more susceptible to the influences of the surrounding milieu, toughens and tends to define itself no longer by its own resources, but by contrast to the doctrines of the rival churches. In this way emancipated Judaism tends to make of Israel's Messiahship a potpourri of humanitarian tendencies where the belief in prayer substitutes for the faith in the Son of Man. It is no longer a question of certain rabbinical preachings about the person of the Messiah (since the Christians spoke of this person too much), but of the Messianic era of peace and social justice. If the Messianic era is not to be denied, it is not less true that to renounce the Person of the Messiah and his triumph is an apostasy of Judaism. One should recall here the decisive statement of the eagle of the Synagogue, the very lucid Maimonides.

In fact, objectivity requires that one seek in the tradition of Israel only the indications of a possible Messianology, as if the theologians wished to render the Messiah present in the life of each Jew, but reserved for Him his personal revelation in his own time, to each of them. These indications exist already in the Bible, and the doctors of the Synagogue, even more than Christian theologians (Catholic or Protestant), have exhausted the possibility of Messianic exegesis of the Holy Scriptures. It may be said that there is not a verse of the Torah, of the Prophets, or of the Hagiographers which has not been interpreted in its full Messianic sense. This is inevitable in a tradition which insures the reservation of the plenitude of its revelation for the hour of the final Encounter at the end of time, for the triumph of light over darkness, and the Son of Man over the fallen angel. The promises made to David's heir are received personally by each child of Israel as the pledge of the triumph of the Word of God against the powers of the night, the beacon beyond the darkness which proves the tangible reality of everybody's salvation. Post-Biblical literature expands with multiple developments on the Messianic eschatology, whether historic or transcendent. And the Pharisaic tradition will give the most complete source of fragmentary traditions of Judaism which will help to restore the portrait of the Messiah of Israel.

The name *Meshiah* indicates already the special anointment which fulfills in him the perfect situation of a singular alliance with the Master of all life. This anointment makes him king and priest, the holder of the keys to the temporal and supernatural salvation of Israel and the world. The rabbis take up the terminology of Isaiah and the Psalms to announce the reign of the Prince of Peace, the admirable, the counselor, the hero, the redeemer.

The deepest intuition of Israel's tradition must be this: The Messiah preexists his historic manifestation. I have already cited the text, *Bereshit Rabbah;* let us recall this often cited *Beraitha*:

Seven things were created before the creation of the world: the Torah, Repentance, Heaven, Hell, the Throne of Glory, the Temple and the Name of the Messiah.*

This preexistence of the Messiah, constant in Hebraic tradition, has to be received with "the eye of the heart," rather than with the conceptual armature with which Greco-Latin thought has endowed dogmatic Christology. That is to say, never has a doctor of the Synagogue, by affirming that the Messiah was identical to the Spirit of God and anterior to creation, raised the problem of the double nature of the Messiah. The texts shed light on the basis of things without allowing controversy over what, in the last analysis, belonged to the Mystery of the Word. More important was the historic mission of the Son of Man who was to be ordained by the hands of the most irreducible of the children of Israel, the Prophet Elijah.

Here again the examination of the texts disarms the most inveterate prejudices. This constant theme of Christian apologetics is familiar: the Jews refuse Jesus crucified as Israel's Messiah because they await a victorious Messiah who will come to bring them victory and not abjection. Our Lenten preachers would be both surprised and delighted to learn that there exists in synagogal literature a whole line of thought which admits to the existence of a suffering and redemptive Messiah who justly replaces the sacrifices of the Temple of Jerusalem.

The theme of redemptive suffering (*Issurin shel Ahava,* the trials of love) enriched Israel's most ancient tradition with one of its flashing intuitions. The theologians of Christendom draw the idea of the world-saving sacrifices of a Messiah from Biblical sources. Meditation on this was to give rise to a current of related ideas, though they were formulated from other perspectives in Israel. A somewhat late, but nonetheless significant, text proves how far the

---

* Pesahim 54a. Only a poor notion of the expressions of Semitic thought allows one to wonder whether it is a question of a real or an ideal experience. Here the name of the Messiah is identical to his being. See Lagrange, *Le Messianisme chez les Juifs* (Paris, 1909), p. 218.

most orthodox rabbinical literature can go on this order of ideas:

> *In Heaven there is a palace which is called the Palace of Ills. The Messiah enters this palace and assumes all the illnesses, sorrows, pains, and burdens onto himself. If he had not taken on the punishment deserved by Israel, no one would have been able to withstand the suffering for his sins; and so Scripture adds: "He hath borne our infirmities" (Isaiah 53:4). So did Rabbi Eleazar during his earthly life (Baba Messiah, 85,a).*

So long as Israel inhabited the Holy Land, it was preserved from all weaknesses and sorrows by the merits of its sacrificial offerings. When man left that world, he received his punishment.*

This remarkable text admits to a celestial Messiah voluntarily suffering to expiate for the sins of Israel and the world. And his sufferings of love have the supplicatory virtue of the sacrifices formerly offered in the Temple of Jerusalem. Should one see here an influence of Christian dogmatics or Jewish theology, or rather the inevitable result in Cabalistic literature of a deepening of the known texts of Isaiah, the Psalms, or Daniel? The fact is that the most ancient texts of the Talmuds of Babylonia and Jerusalem give evidence of a mysterious Messiah, son of Joseph, whose vocation is to be killed, while the son of David has to come to lead Israel from its Exile and triumph over death.*

---

* Zohar, t. II, fol. 2.116, on Exodus 23:23; cf. Brierre Narbonne, *le Messie souffrant dans la littérature Rabbinque*, Paris, 1940, cf. the fine text (Pessikta Rabbati, p. 161, Friedmann edition) on the suffering Messiah, redeemer of the Jews because of his sufferings. This theme is obviously linked to the constant developments on the redemptive values of the suffering of Israel for the salvation of the world.

* Here again the theologian concerned with conceptual logic will be confounded by this apparent duality of two Messiahs within the strictest of monotheistic religions. For a single God, a single Messiah, of course! The most rudimentary meditation of the sources makes this conclusion inevitable. A double Messiah or a double coming of a same Messiah already present in his preexistence? Our aim here is only to suggest. We leave it to the individual to acquaint

More numerous are the sources which speak of the Messiah, son of David, and announce his triumph and his reign. Messianism is implicit in each page of the Bible when it is read in the traditional optic which is Israel's. It changes into a mystical current with Daniel and takes an extraordinary development in apocalyptic literature. The triumph of the Son of Light against the forces of darkness is announced in the preaching of the rabbis with a vehemence which becomes more pronounced as the abyss which separates present history from its eschatological accomplishments appears more insurmountable. The triumph of the Son of David is henceforth linked to the denouement of a universal and cosmic drama and has to reestablish creation in the harmony of an order anterior to Adam's fall. The descriptions of the Messianic era identify the terrestrial Jerusalem and the heavenly Jerusalem since the Messiah is the one who restores real unity to the earthly darkness. Master of peace, he locks up the pit of eternal turpitude forever, saves the just from the hands of the unjust, and reestablishes the victory of light over darkness, justice over enslavement, peace over war, love over hate. Because of all of this the Messiah, the restorer of unity, introduces the triumph of the Kingdom of God. He acts in the name of the Lord and through the strength of his Word. His action is conceived on the temporal plane —it has to abolish the resistance which matter opposes to the spirit and to assure the victory of the Word.

It was a question of the material certitude—one might say, of a promise—which involved the very being of Israel with the entire redemption of mankind. We have seen why the Messianic hope of the Jews takes on an otherwise singular dimension *after* the destruction of the Temple and the exile of the survivors of the wars of the Jews against Rome.

The structures of Jewish history change at the very moment when the Roman legions, 9 Ab of the year 70, destroy the sanctuary which assured the spiritual unity of Israel. The Temple was the unique place for the meeting of the

---

himself with the problem and with the sources in order to put into perspective the historical and theological arguments which arise from the comparison of the texts.

God of Abraham and his people. Through sacrifice (only possible on the altar of Jerusalem) the Jews had access to the sacramental ways of penance, pardon, redemption, and communion.

Israel suddenly found itself enclosed in an age of its history which reached in its very principle the outer limits of the tragedy. It identified itself with the drama of the Absence and the Hope. A Christian could easily understand Israel's spiritual situation after the destruction of the Temple by imagining the state of Christendom deprived of its Pope (Israel no longer had a Temple or high priest), deprived of its cardinals (the Sanhedrin existed only embryonically and ephemerally after the destruction of the Temple), deprived of its bishops (*Semikha*, ordination, no longer had the same significance and no longer conferred the same powers), and deprived of priests. The sources of sacramental life drained in Israel, the Jews had to settle in this abyss of their temporal and spiritual exile in the memory of destroyed glories and the hope of their restoration. The glory of the Jews in their first age was their acceptance of God and his Word, and their welcome of the witness of the Prophets whose message they identified with and preserved by protecting it with life itself, if necessary. Their merit is no less great for having accepted the situation of the Exile and the paradox which it was to inscribe in the history of man, without weakening.

Since then the Messiah was awaited with a more immediate fervor. His role before the destruction of the Temple was generally conceived as that of the hero who would bring back to the borders of the earth the message of God, whose triumph among nations he was to assure. Driven from its land, deprived of its Temple and the fulfillment of its sacramental life, subjected among nations to exceptional treatment whose savagery would mark its agony from century to century, Israel would survive all expeditions against it, from the time of Constantine to the reign of Adolf Hitler. In the shadow and confinement of the ghettos Israel would expect of this Messiah both a more human and a more divine mission.

The Messiah would put an end to the Exile of Israel—certainly the temporal Exile which permitted the suffering

197

masses to wander between hostile frontiers, in order to bring them back to the land of Israel, but more importantly, the spiritual Exile. He was to bring back the Jews from this land of Egypt which was more harsh than that of the Pharoah, where they wandered deprived of the help and comfort of sacrifice since Titus had ravaged the altar of the Temple, this unique place of the meeting of the increate Eternal and the created. And this expectation was in no way a sentimental revery. A transhistoric and supernatural intervention had given Israel revelation, alliances, priesthood, and sacrifices. From man to man and generation to generation, since Moses and Aaron they transmitted the knowledge and the powers inherited from Sinai, like a golden thread. In one blow the destruction of the Temple broke the traditional continuity. Though knowledge (henceforth deprived of its greatest possibilities of fulfillment) was to continue to be transmitted during the Exile to maintain the memory of former glories and the hope of their restoration, power was not.

Yes, Israel could very well say: "Look and see if there is any sorrow like my sorrow." In the frontier of the Exile there was only one way to survive in the shadow of the ghettos—to abandon oneself to the will of the Lord, purification, submission to the *Mitsva*, and hourly prayer for the coming of salvation and the appearance of the liberator. The latter, the "Messiah of our justification" was awaited, is still awaited with an impatience which continues and is renewed each day in those Jewish milieux which have not lost their faith. A dozen times a day in its liturgy Israel asks the Lord to "send the Messiah near," "to restore in Jerusalem the throne of David, the Lord's servant," "to let David's posterity flourish and to raise his trumpet in salvation," "to give us the privilege of the days of the Messiah and the life of the world to come." These prayers are repeated everywhere from moment to moment where destiny has abandoned the Jews, for millennia upon millennia, forging the souls of a people and weaving in the thread of history the certitude and the conditions of its preservation and resurrection. Israel's life in exile was completely oriented toward the appearance of the Messiah and preserved by the certitude of his victory. The fathers recited these prayers every day, the mothers tirelessly repeated them to their children and dreamed of them each night.

The Messiah was to be the bearer of the keys which would open the gates of the Exile, the one who would gather the exiled, bring back the Judges and the Judgment to Israel, pass sentence over the wicked and do justice to the just, bring back the real presence *(Shekinah)* of the Lord to his rebuilt city Jerusalem, let the trumpet of salvation sound there again, bring back the adoration and fires of Israel to the heart of the rebuilt Sanctuary, to the glorious return of the mercies of the Lord and the reestablishment of his Presence in Sion, for the victory of every peace.*

Was the intervention of the Messiah to be absolutely transhistoric and were the Jews to expect everything from the decrees of Heaven? Yes, such was the traditional attitude of the doctors and faithful—to sustain themselves in the all-powerful passivity of prayer until the Lord deigned to revive his mercies. In the specifically spiritual order, however, an attempt was at least made to hasten the coming of the days of the Messiah. After the expulsion of the Jews from Spain in 1492, the victims of the monstrous decree went in great numbers to settle in the Holy Land. The souls burning with mystic fervor expected the judgment of God after their tribulation. By their preaching the mystics of Safed, the doctors of the Cabala, maintained the living hope for the end of time. Since the assemblage of the exiled in Sion seemed to have been fulfilled, would it not be possible to take one further step and reestablish the ordination which would give to its members-elect complete jurisdictional powers whose transmission, we have seen, had been abolished since the destruction of the Temple? Rabbi Berab (†1541) from Spain, settled in the Arab Kingdom of Tlemcen and, was a refugee after 1534 in Safed under Turkish domination, where his erudition and sanctity won him a great deal of authority among his colleagues. Referring to a thesis of Maimonides,

* These attributes of the Messiah are summarized in the key liturgical prayer of Israel, the eighteen blessings *(Shemon Esre)* which the Jews repeat three times a day, and which review the universal trek, from Abraham to the triumphal days of the Messiah.

he upholds that the unanimity of the doctors of the Holy
Land reunited in council could reestablish ordination by the
laying of hands *(Semikah)*. Berab considered that the reestablishment of the Sanhedrin was to precede and prepare
the coming of the Messiah. Implacable, but faithful to the
deepest meanings, Levy Ibn Habib, Great Rabbi of Jerusalem, made the attempt fail by recalling that the Messiah
alone, priest and king, had the powers and keys that Israel
awaited. The coming of the Messiah was to precede the
reconstitution of the Sanhedrin and the reconstruction of the
Temple. Berab's desperate enterprise failed, but the problem
which it raised and which it intended to resolve, contains one
of the keys of the spiritual Exile of the Jews in Israel and
throughout the world.

If it were necessary to retrace the schematas of the Messianic incarnation through Israel's history, one would only
have to follow the very unfolding of that history and the
"mystery" (the word is Saint Paul's) that it inscribes in the
history of men.

The genesis of Israel is that of a people who gathers at
the call of its prophets to receive the message of the Living
God, assume its burden, and promote its order. Theophoric
people—Israel is incomparably that during the first part of
its history from the time of Abraham to the destruction of
the Temple in the year 70, *bearer of God*, which sees in Him
the sole master worthy of being served throughout Israel,
henceforth the guardian responsible for the promotion of
His reign. Sinner, of course, but who is not? Who else has
given birth and reception to the line of prophets who define
forever the law of all humanity at this crossroad of the lands
and traditions which Israel represents? It is the bearer of
God until the final hours of its existence as a living people
because the nations see arisen in its midst a Crucified One
whom the Christians go on adoring as God.

A singular people: the second act of the mystery of Israel
is no less significant with respect to the Messianic fulfillment
(of the incarnation, if you will) in the history of men. The
people of the Bible remains faithful to its profound vocation,
its inescapable and absolute dereliction in the trials and trib-
ulations of the Exile. The doctors of the Synagogue, faithful

to the prophetic teachings, see the reason for the defeat of the Jewish nation not in the superiorities of the Roman armies, but in Israel's infidelity to its vocation as a theophoric people. The Jews are uprooted from their land, deprived of their Temple, torn from their preeminence and driven out among the nations of the earth where they are to expiate for their sins, disfigured, defiled, and unrecognizable. By their suffering they are to beseech God and wait for their redemption—the ultimate Passover of all creation—the true and holy passage from the *Golah* (Exile) to the *Gu'ullah* (Redemption). So Judaism appears less like a religion than the particular incarnation of a revelation assumed by a people who manifests its presence in the continuity of a historically lived experience.

Two thousand years to receive the Message—two thousand years to bear its burden in exile and darkness. And now? Now here we are at the threshold of the third age of a history whose true problems and exact dimensions the world, above all the Arab world, must perceive, since in a certain sense its future involves those peoples—Christians and Moslems—who have inherited from the spiritual patrimony and Biblical sources of Israel as well.

The third age is that of the return of Israel. The Jews, threatened with total extermination by Hitler, bled white in concentration camps and crematories after the most difficult trial of their history, have the exact opposite reaction to the one expected of a normal people. They again challenge the impossible and launch against winds and tides into the reconquest of the Holy Land which becomes again the Land of Israel such a short time after the fires of the crematories have been put out. The Jews prove to the surprised world that they are not only a people of soldiers, but that they can fight ten to one; not only a people of farmers, but they can make the desert itself fertile and make forests out of rocky hills which have been barren for two thousand years; not only detached from money, but they prove it by engaging all their resources and capital in the apparently most quixotic undertaking of the century, and define a style of life in the *kibbutzim* where man can finally be delivered from the servitude to Mammon. And further, they, whose culture was heteroclite, revive the language and the culture of the Bible. This historically unprecedented linguistic revolution seems to be the most decisive for the future of Israel's resurgence. Its consequences are incalculable for all those who claim the heritage of the Bible. In May 1970 Israel celebrates its twenty-second anniversary, but already it is possible to foresee in this Biblical land the fulfillment of a destiny which is not unworthy of four thousand years of history of which the Jews, with the Christians and the Moslems, are heirs.

Our true struggle is that of the necessary reconquest of spiritual unity for the entire world. The creation of the State of Israel puts an end, in a certain sense, to the earthly wandering and temporal exile of the Jews. But it makes the depth of the spiritual exile even more clearly apparent. And the masters of Jewish spirituality emphasize that this exile, more unbearable when it continues in the heart of Jerusalem, will end only with the transhistoric and supernatural intervention of the Messiah. The schema defined by the ancient prayer of the eighteen blessings will then assume its full meaning—the gathering together of the exiled, Messianic intervention, restoration of the Sanhedrin, return of the presence (*Shekinah*) in Sion, fulfillment of the Messianic promises, and the final vocation of Jerusalem, first and last crossroad of the increate Eternal and creation. In this way the coming of the Messiah is traditionally linked to the last ends of humanity and its fulfillment in the last judgment and the resurrection of the dead.

Our Christian friends may be surprised that one can speak of the Messiah of Israel without even mentioning the name of Jesus of Nazareth. In fact it would be possible to deal with Jewish Messianism without saying a word about Christianity, though not vice versa. But it would be lacking in objectivity to disregard the meeting of the Church and the Synagogue with respects to him who is to abolish their conflicts and allow their reunion. For the Master of Unity, the Messiah, has no other mission than to let unity reign on earth as in heaven. And Jesus, though he may separate the Christians and the Jews, is also their true bond. It is clear that to the extent that Christendom learns about Israel, the latter will recognize the true stature of Jesus Christ.

Let us admit it. It is a tremendous paradox that the Synagogue is divorced from one of its children whom entire peoples hail not only as a priest, prophet, or king, but as a God, the leader of all Christendom. It would be deluding oneself to place the reason for the separation of the Church and the Synagogue on the plane of dogma and doctrine. Let us say that though ecclesiastics and rabbis fed their war on arguments drawn partially from dogma, the conflict had deeper and more valid causes.

The Temple destroyed, the Jews crushed by Rome could either disappear or refuse to accept defeat and turn all their energies to survival in order to rise up again. Even before saving their own skin, to last, for them, meant to preserve the Holy Scriptures which they alone could read in their authentic text, and to maintain intact the spiritual tradition which made them since Sinai the theophoric people. To survive without land, State, or weapon, solely by the strength of the spirit at the cost of every disparagement and mutilation of the body—these were to be the risks in the certitude of the triumph of the promise made to the Father. Israel itself could fail; but He, God, could not lie. It is the certitude of the vision which has permitted the miracle of Israel's survival during two thousand years of exile—a survival achieved by a willing mutilation of the soul and body. In order to maintain its personality in the struggle, Israel has no choice except to refuse confrontation with religions and philosophies foreign to its unique destiny. This refusal could only be accompanied by the diminishing and impoverishment of its being. But this aspect of the abjections of the Exile did not disturb the life of the soul, determined in its contemplation and desire of the Lord eternally present in the Torah.

Driven from its land because of fidelity to its God, Israel would assume the function of pariah among nations, the man without arms, in Europe as well as in the East—would accept, barehanded, the fight against the powers determined to destroy it. A people of conscientious objectors? More than that—a people condemned by its unique condition to bear witness among nations to the eternity and primacy of the spirit, a witness without pomp or empty phrases, which signed its name in blood. The ghettos were centers of the most devout prayers. In adversity the watchword was to accept death freely, with the prayer of praise on one's lips. Such was the sense and value of the election, in the humiliation of the bloody exiles.

The most authoritative thinkers of Israel see the preeminence of the people of the Exile precisely in its universal incarnation of the figure of the suffering servant. An entire people, the very one from which Christ came, had voluntarily put itself in a position to accept the calvary which was to measure the time of the nations and of their awakening to the supplications of the Word. And the Christian who thinks that there is a charm in knowing and loving Christ will recognize the price of a sacrifice which deliberately involes giving up one's own happiness. The Jews were to maintain themselves in the exercise of a violence which separated them from the earth, from men, and from God himself, by virtue of a supernatural hope which moved them toward the absolute of the meeting with the absent Prince, in the certitude of his appearance. Is there a clearer, purer lesson of humble heroism?

First and last, *alpha* and *omega*, the Christians announce him and the Jews await him; the Jews expect his arrival and the Christians expect his return. Ambiguity of words, hypocrisy of situation! The Jews were in fact crucified on this cross whose virtue they denied, and most often by the very ones who claimed to be the worshipers of a crucified Messiah.

Is not the real situation of man in relation to the Messiah rather the one that this lesson describes? We all pretend that we await the Messiah (his coming, his return, what does it matter?) so as to better excuse ourselves from the effort which would surely lead us to him. And we claim to wait for him when in reality he is dying as he waits for us in the poor, in every man who suffers from injustice and hate. Whether you are a Jew, a Christian, or you, my friend, an Arab, let us understand this well.

But in the truth of hearts, already love is on its way to reunite the children of light beyond all the frontiers which spirit and matter render bloody. A God, Creator, is necessarily beyond the frontiers which limit the creatures in the heart of the Jerusalem of the real world. It is in this center that the Messiah watches and waits for the men who will know how to hear his message, in order to fulfill it in peace, unity, and love. The expectation of the Messiah, the hope for deliverance—to answer Him one has only to be faithful to the light, to life.

But it is on this threshold that we have been crushed once more under the weight of centuries in our final departure toward our new Temple.

7 Convergences

Yesterday we met again at Mahane Yehuda after the explosion of that bomb which ruined a whole neighborhood, killing twelve persons and wounding many others. Again this time our eyes met, burning with the same anxiety. I was afraid of finding the familiar face of a women, a child, or some friend among the burnt bodies. A similar humiliation and fear disturbed both of us. The chain of violence has been set in motion as each assault provokes and accelerates the diabolical succession of repression and death. Jerusalem's population has to live in fear of what the next day may bring.

The Jews and the Arabs enjoy the new situation of a reunited city which is experiencing great prosperity without precedent in its four-thousand-year history. The city has been restored to life since the barrier dividing it has been torn down. From every corner of the globe come Jerusalem's admirers. Each one dreams of rebuilding his life and increasing the splendor of the city the Prophets called the model of beauty. Suddenly I became aware of how the tale of Sleeping Beauty could apply to a city. In a single night of blood and fire we were shaken from our lethargy and together we realized the urgency of our destiny. Beyond our personal limitations, beyond ourselves, we rediscovered the ancient epic. We had to become the heralds of Abraham's message again, movers of history, responsible for its fulfillment. For the first time the history of Jerusalem depended on us, not on the Greeks, Romans, Byzantines, or Arabs, not on the Crusaders, the Seljukians, the Turks, not on the Egyptians, Iraquis, Syrians, or Lebanese, but on us alone. We were the legitimate children of this land—you, the Palestinian deeply rooted in the soil of this city, and I, Israel, back from my wandering. Both of us were faced with the horror of outrage and caught in the same web of humiliation.

Trembling with fear and shame, we were huddled among the decomposing bodies. The lofty themes which had led up to this critical situation, such as triumphant Sion or an Arab Empire reborn to its ancient splendor, no longer existed. In the panic we dug among the ruins of the houses to find and identify the corpses. Only twice in twenty months was Jerusalem's peace so disturbed, but therein lies our anxiety and history's challenge.

Beyond the night dawn can be seen as the city rises up again and is rebuilt in every direction. It must be the richest place in the world considering the number of men coming as pilgrims and the amount of capital dedicated to the work of reconstruction. It is the land where in its most heroic dimension, the beauty of location and the beauty of man and his handiwork is displayed in its purest form—blazing rocks, breathtaking cupolas, minarets, and steeples, sloping streets built in sorrow through the ages. The city is waking up as if from the dead, but pierced with the events from all the ages of mankind.

Too much blood has flowed between Jews and Arabs— three wars in twenty years.

From the beginning there has been someone in every generation ready to exterminate the Jews. It began with the Pharaoh twenty-three centuries ago and continued throughout the Biblical history of Israel as it confronted all the powers of the ancient East until crushed by the Roman Empire's formidable war machine. In any book of Jewish history you will find a long list of successors to the Pharoah. We thought that this fate to which we had been condemned for thousands of years, this *hunting* which for three thousand years mobilized all the resources of our energy to escape threatened destruction, would end with the fall of Hitler. After the slaughter of six million people, we naively thought that we had earned our rest, that we could breathe finally, and be able to grow our flowers and raise white goats and little minks with soft fur. Decked with flowers, we could, if we liked, stretch ourselves out on a beach and breathe the salt air and warm ourselves in the sun until the end of our days.

Even when our condition was at its worst, things seemed to be improving. Six million dead, including one million four thousand children, is a great deal in any language, even in the days of push-button warfare. But the Christians finally took a stand to say that we had not all personally participated in Christ's crucifixion, that there had been extenuating circumstances, statutory limitations, and other surprising things we were pleased to hear. The Catholic Church reversed itself to declare to the world that we were no longer guilty. Past history was forgotten. The Germans, too, to ease their conscience a bit and to help us forget, began to say kind things and wanted to soothe the former prisoners of the concentration camps. They gave Israel a billion dollars (I exaggerate and round off the amount, only $862,-500,000 in fact—enough for the State of Israel to live on for less than three months).

The United Nations said that we could settle there as we wished in order to be more sure of our future, and we could even create a State of Israel if that should please us. Things went along as in a fairy tale, as in the old legends of Israel when the Sabbatim River stopped flowing on the Sabbath. We could finally think about something else!

That is when the only spot of our body which had remained intact began to erupt. We had an account to settle with almost every country in the world, expelled from one place, robbed in another, martyred in others. The only untainted places were those where we had never settled—among the Chinese, Japanese, Hindus, South Americans, and Eskimos, and among the Arabs, too. Until Islam appeared the Arabs were the only people whose wisdom the ancient Hebrews admired. Islam's appearance had certainly complicated things. God always complicates things. It was understandable that Mohammed wanted to make Moslems out of us. Our refusal was not easy for him, but he got over his disappointment quickly. Since we were unwilling to convert, he rapidly made a compromise. We were like the Christians! His theologians managed to allow us a small niche in their city, a protected place for the *dhimmis*.

It was not always very comfortable, but we got used to it. We had never had very serious incidents with the Arabs, nothing even remotely comparable to Hitlerian genocide, nothing slightly reminiscent of the Inquisition pyres or the mass expulsions from Spain, France, and England. With the Arabs things were rather safe. When everything went well for them, things went equally well for us. When things were rough, naturally, it was bad for everybody. It was bleak, it was harsh, it was bloody, but for everybody. We learned to know each other. We accepted each other as members of the same family. No earthshaking relationships or problems arose because we were basically so similar that we did not have much to say to each other. Side by side we patiently worked our furrows. There was nothing else to do but pull the plow to which we had been harnessed and help each other whenever we could. During Hitler's era—when a Jew's time or life was worth less than that of a mule wherever the Germans ruled or had influence—the Arabs would say: "Be patient. It will pass. Allah is greater." Yes, with you we felt secure. But that is when you went berserk.

We both shared the enthusiasm within Jerusalem's walls, and in the excitement of the present we looked to its past founded on Holy Scripture, in one case the Bible, in the other the Koran, whose glories had tarnished in the ghettos and the colonies. The long history of the Arabs and the Jews should be completely rewritten not only from the perspective of the incredible parallel of the two vocations and development of ideas, but also by comparing their historical and economic destiny.

For Israel the period of most intense creativity had been during the tenth century before the Christian era, at the time when David chose Jerusalem as his capital. Jewish autonomy was ended by Titus' attacks in 70 A.D.

The earliest surviving reference to the Arabs appears in the ninth century B.C. in an inscription from Shalamanasar III in 853. Various Biblical texts mention the peoples of Arabia. This long past has its true destiny opened to it in 622 A.D. when Mohammed leaves Mecca for Medina. Here the Arab epic begins with one of the most fascinating chapters in mankind's history. I have in front of me the map of this Empire which stretches from the shores of the Atlantic to the banks of the Indus—Spain, Morocco, Algeria, Tunisia,

Libya, Egypt to the edge of the Sahara, all of Arabia, Palestine, Syria, Iraq, Mesopotamia, Armenia, Persia, and Kurdistan. The world had never admired a vaster empire more rapidly established or more peacefully administered, a privileged place for the development of one of the most brilliant civilizations in history. The Arabs had the genius to involve the Persians, the Egyptians, and the Jews in their enterprise. Joined to the Christians of the Empire, together they expressed themselves in the imperial language, Arabic. The sciences, theology, philosophy, poetry, architecture, and art reach their zenith and place Arab civilization in a unique position. The Arab poets write their immortal masterpieces in the continuity of the Koran's rhythm. The theologians and philosophers, as we have seen, give new life to the religious thought of the world by rediscovering the Hellenic traditions. The doctors lay the basis for medical science in which Jews such as Maimonides can become illustrious. Algebra, geometry, trigonometry, mathematics, physics, and chemistry flourish. If the zero and Arabic numerals are not their original invention, it was the Arabs who popularized them by integrating them into general mathematical theory and transmitting them from India to Europe. Thanks to the Arabs, Europe discovers Aristotle and Plato, making its Renaissance possible. I would like to reiterate—Jewish thought owes its golden period of the Exile to the Arabs. The Arabs draw from Persian and Chinese sources, but contribute enduring works in the domain of the arabesque and architecture. The Dome of the Rock in Jerusalem represents one of its most perfect examples. Remember that on the social plane the Arab achievements are crowned by liberalism toward the Jews who enjoyed one of the rare respites of their Exile during the heyday of the Empire.

Expansion and glory continue from the seventh to the eleventh centuries. Decay begins with the decline of the Caliphate and quickly spreads over the whole Empire. In Europe the Christians drive the Arabs out of Spain and Sicily in a wave of conquests which culminate with Crusaders disembarking on the Holy Land's shores. In Africa the Berbers make up an independent empire which extends from south of Morocco to Senegal and Nigera. Tunisia, Libya, Egypt, and the East progressively break away from an empire which disintegrates as fast as it was assembled. Power, glory, and unity vanish.

It is at this time that Columbus discovers America. In 1488, Diaz had opened the sea route to India. In one stroke the European discounted the Far East as the provider of necessary goods and products. From now on Europe could consider the Far and Near East and the Moslem states of the Mediterranean as negligible and become involved in a profitable exchange with the New Indies. Europe was motivated by a very sure instinct that the newly-named America would replace India as the supplier of European markets in goods and resources, especially precious metals necessary for the growth of the European economy.

European trade with India had provided the Moslem countries with their chief source of wealth. Arabia, the Near East, Turkey, and North Africa had as their prime economic function the servicing of the overland trade routes between India and Europe. Cities such as Constantinople, Alexandria, or Venice, were the bridgeheads and became the wealthiest. Trade between Europe and India made the Mediterranean the center of world civilization for centuries. Now a technical revolution was going to cut the continental routes between them. America was going to free Europe from its Eastern supplier. When Moliere makes fun of Mamamouchi, it simply means that the West no longer needs the East and has freed itself of its dependence as a traditional and captive client. The West could rightly congratulate itself for this revolution. For the Orient it was no trifling matter. The upheaval which America's discovery brings to the world economy would precipitate its decay.

This decay, serious though it might have been, brought about a complete revolution in the world's economic and spiritual equilibrium. But above all, it was the first step in an irreversible process of change. Strengthened by the surplus which America's discovery brings, Europe will prime its industrial revolution. The genius of the white man, inhabitant of the northern hemisphere of the planet, manifests itself by the additional power which his discoveries bring him. The industrial progress of Europe will bankrupt the tottering Moslem and oriental economies. A specific example will illustrate this. When the English discover weaving, they immediately set out to produce a good grade of cloth inexpensively and, of course, no longer need the Asian and African textile artisans. This is only the first stage. As soon as the British textile industry is strong enough, British merchants bring English cloth to all the markets of North Africa, the Near East, and the Far East at prices which defy any competition. Every bolt of English cloth sold on the Palestinian, Turkish, or Moroccan market destroys the local weaver, and with him go the tailor, the spinner, the farmer who owns the sheep, and the shepherd who watches them. The Orient, whose riches Europe had always coveted and which for centuries had been the world center of civilization, soon became a ruined continent. The rapid decay of the countries of Africa and Asia ensued. Naturally, the Jewish communities shared in the general decadence. Once the process of economic failure is completed, Europe will have only to complete the ruination of the Eastern peoples by conquering them politically. Colonialism is the logical conclusion of a double process which results in the staggering enrichment of the Western peoples and the impoverishment of the Eastern peoples to the point of bankruptcy.

How can the overwhelming success of Christian civilization in comparison with the Islamic or Oriental be explained without thinking about a basic physiological flaw! This essentially racist theory had the advantage of simplicity and that of being able to soothe the conscience of the victor. If the African or the Asiatic is basically inferior, then the very principle of colonial conquest may be justified.

But, paradoxically, as we have seen, the discovery of the New World and its consequences have contributed, by the irresistible movement of thought which they presented to the world, to the awakening of the Eastern world and of the Jewish communities which insured a certain permanent presence of the East in Europe. The French Revolution, itself a product of the Reformation, played a determining role in the changes taking hold of the world. It aimed at freeing the Jews and simultaneously was the first to contribute to the awakening of the Moslem world. In another way Western sovereignty raised new needs and hopes as it introduced the values of Western culture and technology through the generosity of its leaders, teachers, and missionaries. Africa and Asia were put in close communication with Europe and America as the world began to perfect itself. By the powers and prestige of emancipation modern Europe had insured the spiritual conquest of the European Jewish communities and Eastern communities where it exerted its influence. Henceforth, it could devote itself to the political conquest of the Moslem world.

A spiritual and intellectual awakening simultaneously renewed the realities of Islam and Judaism.

Napoleon's expedition into Egypt in 1789 was aimed at England and the routes to India. It indirectly provoked Europe's intervention in the Arab countries of the Mediterranean which were prisoners of apathy and ruin. The sudden appearance of these armies in the Near Eastern states jolted Egypt, as did the technical, military, scientific, and intellectual power of Europe. Al-Jabarti, a writer who died in 1825, described the surprise of the Egyptians confronted with Napoleon's miraculous success.

France occupies Egypt from 1798 to 1801. Great Britain settles on the Arab banks of the Persian gulf in 1820 and lays the foundation for its long Eastern supremacy. In 1830 the French settle in Algeria while the British merchant marine weaves its web by establishing regular lines between India and Suez, and between the waterways of Iraq and its ports which are linked to Egypt and Syria from 1836 on. In 1839, the British occupy Aden. They close the circle of intercontinental communications by establishing a railroad line between Alexandria, Cairo, and Suez between 1851 and 1857. Diggings for the Canal begin in 1869. The English occupation of Egypt will be completed by 1882. The partitioning of the Arab Empire by the West is followed by the conquest of Tunisia in 1882 and of Morocco in 1912 by the French, and of Libya by Italy in 1911. In 1861, the Porte accepts the creation of an apparently autonomous Lebanon. The crumbling of the Ottoman Empire in 1917 was to erase all illusions by replacing Turkish domination with the mandates of France in Syria and Lebanon, and of those of England in Palestine, Transjordan and Iraq, all under the guarantee of the League of Nations.

It is very clear that the collapse of the Arab and Islamic world is linked to the loss of control of the great overland and sea routes which drained the international trade depended on by the Arabs and the peoples it had united in the same empire. The productive Arab Empire such as it radiated over the whole world in the tenth century, the Arabicized and Islamized world such as it appears after the establishment of the Ottoman Empire, is literally carved up by the West of the nineteenth and early twentieth centuries. The West can dispense with the colonized peoples as with goods, objects which it must fit into the general order of its economy, that is to say, of its domination. The tragic situation of the Arabs is universal. If the monotheistic peoples are brothers, historically the Arabs are the most poignantly disinherited in their widespread territory.

The colonial abuses discredit the West in the eyes of the Arab world, Africa, and Asia. If they benefit from the knowledge of the West, the Arab, the African, and the Asiatic suffer from a tormenting gloom. The Arab in contact with Western culture more quickly becomes aware of himself. The presence of the European monster makes him more sensitive to his subordinate status and, in some respects, his inferiority. Discriminatory practices, often sanctioned by law, consolidate and safeguard the supremacy of the white man of Christian religion or origin from the northern hemisphere. He is destined to exploit the countries which his power has allowed him to conquer. It goes without saying that the Arab, African, and Asiatic peoples will also have to serve the greatness of their masters.

Sartre and Memmi have analyzed the process of colonial alienation. We lived it in Jerusalem at the time of the mandate when everyone seemed to be a foreigner to his country and to himself. The Englishman, surely, was uncomfortable in his role as successor to the Turkish sultans. The Palestinian accustomed to the long series of successive dominations had little to say. We Jews, whose presence had been a silent one for two thousand years, appeared suddenly as ghosts from the dead—all strangers antagonizing each other in the confrontation of goals, interests, and cultures.

In the course of time, the English and the French introduce the railroad, steamship, automobile, refrigerator, radio, and television to the Arab world. These inventions transform the earth while the Arab elite, educated in Western schools and universities and moved by a humiliation which Western ideals make more unbearable, dream of the means of escaping their subjection and European domination to rediscover the liberty and glory of yesteryear. The nationalist surge organizes into clubs and then into political movements. The religious spirit and essentially socialistic aspirations are mixed in the same desire to drive the foreigners out of the house of Islam.

The undertaking was not easy. The modernization of the Arab world remained superficial. The colonial regimes had not really changed the bases of society, built on feudal-type structures. The land was dominated by foreigners and political power was entirely in the hands of the West. It was difficult for the Arab world to effect its revolution.

In 1908, the young Turks had been successful in theirs. They overthrew Islam and established a new, essentially secular regime. But with the exception of Syria, their revolution did not catch on in Iraq, Arabia, nor, surely, in any of the countries directly controlled by the French or English.

In 622 Mohammed left Mecca for Medina. One hundred years later, in 732, this miniscule city had become the capital of an Arab-Moslem Empire which stretched from the banks of the Indus to the south of Gaul. Now, nothing remained of this splendor. Nowhere was Islam master of itself. There was only humiliation and servitude. In this the fate of the Arabs and the Jews was similar.

But the identity of the two peoples shows itself on deeper and more general planes—the Jews, by writing the Bible and founding the Christian Church through Jesus and the Apostles are, with the Arabs, the only ones in the world to have created such a vast spiritual empire. Four hundred and fifty million Moslems, nine hundred million Christians owe them the knowledge of their God, the God of Abraham, Isaac, and Jacob, the Creator of heaven and earth. And here they both are reduced to an equally cruel fate—the one, dispersed and persecuted throughout the world, the other, deprived of autonomy and freedom in its own former empire. Sixty-two percent of the human race owed them their faith and culture. Not a single man, Asian, African, or European, idolater, or atheist could say: "I owe you nothing." Yet, Arabs and Jews, we were in the saddest of situations in the early twentieth century, dispossessed of our body, subject to the good will of the princes who ruled over us, our soul threatened with death.

The Jews of the Arab countries shared the fate of the Empire while the Jews of the West had to face, from the beginning, the often bloody war waged against them by a Christianity which had deemed it necessary to ruin the power and prestige of the Jew in mission lands. It took advantage of the Jew while keeping him a degraded witness of the passion of Christ for which the deicidic people were accused of being responsible. The teaching of scorn was reinforced by a legislation which organized against the Jew a pitiless system of degradation which strongly impregnated Christian sensitivity in regard to him. The Jews in the traditional Christian city had been driven back into a juridical no–man's–land where they were guaranteed neither life nor property.

We have seen how, beginning with the French revolution, political and economic evolution progressively opened up to the Jew a social and cultural milieu which was not irremediably hostile and whose attraction many experienced. This was the case in all of Europe, but these political victories were Pyrrhic in many respects. Anti-Semitism of Christian essence disappeared and gave way to a more fearsome monster, atheistic anti-Semitism, whose consequences were even more dreadful, shifting from the pogroms which took place in Rumania and Russia at the end of the nineteenth century and in the early twentieth century, to the massacre Hitler ordered. This massacre was a more blatant horror because, as the world has now realized, to a man it had done nothing to prevent the holocaust.

During this time the Arabs were going through their own

purgatory in the countries ruled by the Western powers. Arab and Jewish suffering, provoked by identical causes, was going to give rise to political and intellectual movements which were simultaneous, parallel, and even when in opposition, of a similar nature. Such is the trap in which history has caught the Jews and the Arabs. Arabism and Zionism have identical historical causes which operate in different contexts and provoke effects whose transitory confrontations prevent neither fundamental identities nor very deep interrelationships.

Staggering parallel! In contact with Western civilization and the Christian world, together we awoke from our secular sleep and sought our new language, each for his own reason. Arabic, and Hebrew more so, were two Semitic languages fallen into disuse. We had to revive them, give them new status, and relearn them so that they might become the adequate interpreters of our thought. In order to rediscover the uniqueness of our mission, we had to transform our linguistic expression. For this each of us had his immortal model—you, the Koran, myself, the Bible—from which to draw not only our words, but the images and the vision to inspire our modern renaissance. The fundamental characteristics were identical and exceptional enough in the history of mankind to deserve emphasis. Other than Hebrew and Arabic, is there another sacred language which is a living language? This linguistic renaissance put our scholars in the same situation. For while language is an instrument of horizontal communication with one's neighbor, it is vertical in relation to the spiritual sources which authorize and justify man. For the Jews and the Arabs, the easy solution would have been to give up their linguistic sources and adopt one of the great modern means of horizontal communication. In both cases they chose without hesitation the heroic effort of going back to their origins and being reborn only by the resurrection of a culture which could justify them and carry them to new heights.

Since the Babylonian exile, Hebrew had ceased being a spoken language for the Jews. For almost two and a half millennia it had been limited to pious and devotional purposes. The Arabic situation was different. It had suffered from the economic decay of the Moslem peoples. It had broken up into twenty different dialects, some of which were not recognizable compared to the splendor of the Koranic model. From the sixteenth century on, the decline of Arabic seemed irreversible. Its rank as a language had crumbled into scarcely articulate jargons throughout the Moslem empire. The grammarians, lexicographers, and linguists had to make an enormous effort to create a new language in every sector of modern human activity, taking as their base the traditional languages which had reached their zenith in bygone eras.

The thought which these languages expressed was often unbelievably similar. Islamic intellectual reform, *Al Nahda*, is contemporary to, and in many ways identical to the intellectual reform of the Jews, the *Haskala*. We can discern in the Arabs and in the Jews the same slightly condescending gratitude to the ancestors who opened the first windows of the ghetto and the *ummah* (the Islamic community) to the modern world. The location is different: the *Nahda* develops in Cairo, Beirut, and Damascus; the *Haskala* in Eastern Europe. But both, in the second half of the nineteenth century, set about encouraging an intellectual movement in the Arab and Jewish worlds which makes the awakening of the masses possible. In Israel Isaac Baer Levinsohn (1788–1860) is the promoter of a movement which is paralleled in Islam by a series of exemplary individuals: But'rus al-Bustânî, Yaziji, Jvijî Zaydan. Essayists, short story writers, novelists, and journalists make an effort to insure the awakening of the masses deadened by persecutions and humiliation of exile or colonialism.

The *Nahda* has had its pioneers, Jarmanus Farhat, a Syrian, Faris Al-Chidyac, a Lebanese, Jamal ad-din el-Afghani, an Afghan—innumerable translators and journalists who have introduced the great Western masterpieces into Arabic literature. The philologists and masters of style have given the Arabic language a new vigor and have adapted it to the needs of the modern world; the religious reformers have provoked a movement of Moslem counter-reform, and the philosophers have introduced into the Arabic language European humanism, post-Kantian idealism, German neo-Kantism or

European phenomenology, and existentialism. All this provokes a renewal of the mystical movement Sufism. Orators and political leaders fight to insure the life of their people, historians describe the event of the Moslem renaissance, and the poets sing their epic. One could name a counterpart who accomplishes a parallel and often surprisingly similar work in Hebrew to Israel's credit.

In a startling way contemporary Arab literature in Lebanon, Egypt, Iraq, Syria, the Sudan, Tunisia, Algeria, and Morocco is often comparable in theme and aspiration to the new Hebraic literature. They are parallel in the different ages of their new creation, in their founders, their classics, and their pioneers. The newspaper article, the short story, the novel, and the philosophical essay are used to sing the glories of the past both for Israel and Ishmael in order to lament their present trials and to describe the changes of a society trying to free itself from its traditional status, ghetto or tribe, and which is trying to free itself from its traditional status, ghetto or tribe, and which is trying to rid itself of the ghosts of its past, and create the social framework within which its new values may crystalize.

One must read the works of the writers who have been hammering out for a century the new Hebraic literature in Jerusalem or Tel-Aviv, and modern Arabic literature in Cairo, Damascus, Beirut, Baghdad, Tunis, Algiers, or Fez, to see at a glance remarkable similarities. They are obvious when one reads an author such as Judah Bourla, of Eastern origin, born in Israel in 1886, whose entire work skillfully exploits the rich colors of the oriental environment in his novels and tales which deal with his childhood memories or with the life of the Jews of Boukhara, Turkey, Persia, or Yemen. His writing is akin to that of many writers of Egypt, Syria, Lebanon, Iraq, or North Africa—the same florid style, the same rhythm, the same skill at presenting a fact or an idea. There is no dearth of choices to finding a parallel to his work. Analogous is that of Mohamed Abdouh, for example, who was born in Egypt in 1849 and died in 1905. At the time when Bourla was a young adolescent, Abdouh was one of the striking personalities of the Orient and greatly influenced the intellectual awakening of our time. Did

Bourla ever read Abdouh? I do not know, but it seems highly unlikely. The fact is that their works fit into the same realm of the Judeo-Arab renaissance. What is true of an Eastern storyteller such as Bourla is no less true of many a writer of European origin. Joseph Hayyim Brenner (1881-1921) is a Hebraic novelist and storyteller who describes the problems of the Jewish intellectual elite which is unsure of itself and questions everything, including its own reality. In inspiration he is not very far from Bishr Farès, born in Egypt in 1906, who also analyzes "the linguistic, cultural, and social difficulties which a modern Arab writer encounters." Bishr Farès' analysis has been repeated in Hebrew in almost identical terms, and many Hebraic poets have been able to write as he did: "I am still the shadow of yawning sleep." To insure Israeli-Arab friendship on timeless bases, it would be more useful to found in Cairo and in Jerusalem chairs of comparative Arabic and Hebraic literature rather than hold political lectures. After the Jordanian defeat and the reunification of Jerusalem, a French archeologist, Jean Perrot, asked an Arab nationalist who was visiting our country for the first time what he thought of the Israelis. His answer was spontaneous: "It is frightening how much we resemble each other." These words go to the heart of the matter and perhaps we must find the root of the Judeo-Arab confrontation in the extraordinary similarity of mission, culture, and historic totality.

Judaism and Islam are at the same time a community and a religion. In both cases the spiritual order and the temporal order blend into a global vision of reality which the classical distinction and hierarchy in Christendom do not allow. From the end of the eighteenth century on, the Jewish theologians and philosophers have to solve the problem of the often dramatic encounter of an essentially sacral traditional society with the modern world and problems. In both camps, scholars set about showing that Judaism, freed of its exilic burden, and the Koranic faith, purified of its past scoria and superstition, can renew themselves and adapt to the exigencies of the contemporary society. The reform begins almost simultaneously in Israel and Islam. It is sparked by the same causes and has to find solutions in extremely similar structures and very comparable circumstances. One has to admit that the degree of success of this perilous enterprise has been, on either side, as contested as it is contestable.

From the nineteenth century on, Jewish and Moslem reformers teach, independently, that Judaism and Islam have the dual obligation, spiritual and temporal, to insure the happiness of mankind not only in heaven but also, and especially, on earth. They have to forego everything in the traditional teachings which prevents the necessary adaptation. They have to free themselves of the old beliefs and customs, give up their ancient social framework, deny their dogmatics, and show a greater effort to adapt religion to the requirements of the world. Both sides preach the necessity of a return to their origins: for the Jews the reform is made in the name of the Prophets; the Moslems seek authority for reform in the Prophet. The Arab *Salafiya* shows both the need to return to the sources of the Ancients (*Salaf*) and the need of a reformation (*Islahiya*). It closely follows the Judaic reform which begins in Germany, as we have seen, with Moses Mendelsohn, but manifests itself perfectly simultaneously with the Arab reform from the second half of the nineteenth century. Abraham Geiger (1810–1874) and Leo Baeck (1872–1956) are the contemporaries of Jamal Al-Din al-Afghani (1839–1897), Mohamed Abduh (1848–1905), Tashid Rida († 1935), or of Allal al Fassi whose work, *Al-Nagd Al-dhati*, published in Cairo in 1954, calls for a fundamental renewal of Islam. In spite of the difference in situations, the tendencies and problematics are the same. Many of the pages written by our reformers are interchangeable and could be attributed to one or the other.

The reformers and the modernists inspire contrary but equally severe reactions in Judaism and in Islam. Both counter-reform movements are characterized by a hardening of the traditional positions, introversion of thought, and the refusal of all dialogue with the world. The Jews, who began the reformation sooner because they were nearer the cause, go further in the direction of counter-reform, not having the immediate problems in their exile communities which the *ummah* could not avoid.

If the differences are great, the similarities are overruled in the major currents of the religious thought of the Jews and the Arabs in the modern era. The widespread religious disaffection of the Arab and Jewish masses faced with the great challenge of today's world is everybody's lot. Wherever the modern world touches, it disintegrates the ancient religious structures and leaves the Jews and the Arabs, whose sole real vocation was to proclaim God to the world, without God, without faith, and often without a law. The tie which united the Jew and the Arab to his God was so strong that it required the absolute submission of the believer—such is the meaning of the word *Islam*, submission. Now, the essence of the modern world which encourages rebellion and brings about social atomization is responsible for the identical plight of the Jewish and Arab masses deprived of their traditional religions, and wandering in the contemporary desert in quest of spiritual food to satisfy their hunger.

Will the friendship which binds us, developed in the days of our youth, allow me to go further, to take one more step and to tell you that I think that Zionism and Arabism, so violently opposed to each other, also proceed from the same causes, present identical structures, are undergoing the same mutations, and have to serve the same ends? This is the crux of the matter. It will appear as a contradicition only to those who are not involved in the Israeli-Arab problems. We were reunited under the Dome of the Mosque of Omar after twenty years of separation. During all these years you, the Arab, and I, the Israeli, have served the two warring camps with all our strength. We are able to communicate immediately. In spite of the turmoil of the twenty-year struggle, at our first glimpse of each other none of the resounding conflict which had opposed us remains—an embrace, some tears, the certitude that the past is dead (*Eli fat mat*, says the Arab proverb), and that we will have to build our future together. Neither of us has a choice except to live with one another, for one another, and build the future of peace which may exalt and continue the glories of the Arab and Jewish past, fulfilling the boldest dreams.

In the nineteenth century, Arabs and Jews are in the depressed and often tragic situation that I have described. With all their strength they aspire to a liberation which is more difficult to achieve since they have no political power.

The Arabs represent the dust of the countries which are ruined and subject to colonial regimes. The Jews are scattered across the earth in a multitude of communities having no organ of common direction and often crushed by the hostility of the anti-Semites. The strong will to break out of a situation which has become unbearable for both will express itself in spiritual and political movements which appear to be different, but are identical in essence. From the second half of the ninetenth century on, the Jews in the Diaspora organize the political action destined to free them from the weakened status which the laws or social practices reserve for them where they live. In a very different context the struggle for their political emancipation in Europe is essentially the same as the struggle of the Arabs against the colonial rule which crushes them.

The Jewish will for emancipation in Europe is contemporary to the violence and murder which you know. I also am aware of the price the Arabs paid for the wars they had to wage to be freed of their yoke. Both of us had innumerable victims. The share of the Judaic sacrifice is, alas, the more significant, not relative to the greatness of our people, but in the absolute. Yes, in our common quest for liberty, we had to face the same enemy which showed itself, depending on the country and the time, under different disguises and pretexts. The word "racism" is convenient to designate the evil from which we suffer, but in most cases it is inexact, imprecise, and insufficient.

Our suffering and impoverishment is identical. We are victims of the scorn of mankind, kept in a humiliated and miserable condition, whether penned up in the ghettos of Europe or in colonial shantytowns. In the desire for deliverance, there is one key idea on both sides—that of a subjugated people who must be freed. This idea, blurred in us by centuries of exile or colonial enslavement, comes into focus again in the century of awakening nationalism. We had to initiate our first battles to convince the Israelites of the reality of the Jewish people and to convince the Arabs of the richness of their Arab nation. We both built on the community of language and culture and on a historical destiny laid claim to from the past and hoped for in the future.

In the Diaspora it was a question of obtaining the fullness of the rights of man and citizen for the Jew, but this liberation was incomplete unless accompanied by the restoration of a national Jewish home and the creation of the State of Israel. With varying success many books have described the vicissitudes of our struggle, the ideals which inspired it, the main ideas which permitted us to transform our aspirations into dearly paid-for historic realities. Not a single one has shown that the fight for the liberation of the Arabs and the Jews was the same war, led by kindred peoples, on two different fronts.

The stages of our struggle for freedom cover the same decades and were equally costly to Jews and Arabs. I have already noted the principal dates of political emancipation in the various countries. In 1894 Theodore Herzl had already verbalized the dream for the revival of our national center, Israel. Three years later the World Zionist Organization is founded and in 1917 the Government of his British majesty favors the creation of a Jewish national home. It becomes a reality in 1948 after a long war waged by the Jews against the soldiers of that same British majesty.

The Arab war for independence was as painful as it was long. Iraq essentially obtains its independence in 1932, and in 1936 Egypt signs a treaty with England which recognizes its independence in principle. The center of the fight against imperialism is in the Near East, in Syria and in Lebanon, which become independent republics in 1941. The League of Arab Nations is founded in 1945, three years before the creation of the State of Israel. In 1951, Libya becomes an independent Kingdom by a one-vote majority in the United Nations. That one vote is Israel's. In 1956 the Sudan, Tunisia, and Morocco become independent. In 1960 Mauritania, in 1961 Kuwait, and in 1962, finally, Algeria complete the historic process of the liberation of the Arab world.

In our course it was inevitable that we should clash since we both set our sights on Jerusalem. At the end of the nineteenth century both Arabism and Zionism had reason to champion the cause of their despised and persecuted peoples who shared the same will for liberation and a rich spiritual heritage based on the sacred books and on a monotheistic religion. Both desired to no longer live simply in the contemplation of historical achievements, but to create new living values. Both yearned for a flag and a land to liberate. Arabism had all these things in common with Zionism, but it lacked the main thing—a fulcrum point. Zionism found it in the rich Jewish communities of Eastern Europe. Without Edmond de Rotschild, without the generosity of the Jews of America and England, the will of Israel's pioneers would have been broken, the dream would never have become history. The educated and rich Jews of the Western countries started the drive which allowed the political, human, and social fulfillment of the State of Israel. Thanks to their efforts, it could integrate the heavy population of Jews from the poor countries of Asia and Africa, and, by a common effort, redeem the land. The dynamism of the Zionist movement resulted from the coexistence of a positive pole, the rich communities of the Western countries, and of a negative pole, the poor Jews of Eastern Europe and the Arab countries. The mystique of the refound land and the misfortunes of the century sparked the drive and the results which you know.

The Arab world was condemned to a situation which was terrible in many respects. It did not have, as the Jews, a progressive wing established solidly and dangerously in the West. It was captive, first of all, of the immense North-African and Asian poverty. Hunger, disease, and ignorance were its lot, without mentioning the political regimes, be they colony, protectorate, or mandate, to which it was enslaved. Under Nasser's impulsion it accomplished in Islam what Zionism had achieved for the Jews. His calls for liberation, human dignity, social justice, and the awakening of the Arab masses could be applied to the Judaic context of the Zionist movement just as well were it not for the inevitable differences of style and words. As for the Arab leaders, they were directly inspired by the Jews in their struggle for liberation in their organization, in their methods of attack, and often in their social and political achievements.

An even more remarkable fact is that the two movements are never more complimentary than when they vehemently oppose each other. There is the paradox: the Zionist movement progresses the more the whip of its Arab enemies strikes. The political course of the State, its economic and agricultural foundations, its military and financial power, and its international importance would have been altogether different without the Arab attacks. The canton of five thousand square kilometers that we dreamed about has become by virtue of Arab opposition thirty years later, a powerful state of one hundred thousand square kilometers. But during this time several thousand drying Egyptian cadavers are nourishing the sands of Sinai, the children of the refugees are hungry and cold, the Arab peoples are ruined by their effort to destroy a state which each of their aggressive acts —since their refusal of the partition plan proposed by the Royal Commission in 1937, until the Six Day War—has only served to strengthen. Each time that we risked becoming apathetic along the way, Arab vigilance obliged us to make the superhuman effort which allowed us to climb out of the rut and redouble our activity. The converse is also true. The Palestinian conflict cements Arab unity and contributes to the establishment of the League of Arab States in 1945. The defeat of 1947-48 unifies the group of officers around Neguib and Nasser who swear to overthrow the corrupt regime of Farouk. Abdallah, king of Jordan, is assassinated following the Zionist victory. His death closes a chapter in the history of his kingdom. His hate for Israel makes it possible for Egypt to overcome its lethargy, to rid itself of its monarchy, and to proclaim the Republic in 1953, the very year Ibn Saud dies. The unfortunate Suez campaign in 1956 helps Nasser to overcome Syrian resistance and to give reality to his old dreams of the ephemeral United Arab Republic which he founds in 1958. The Iraquis also outdo themselves in overthrowing their monarchy and declaring the Republic two years after Suez. Inspired by the desire to take revenge on Israel, Nasser adopts in 1961 what he defines as "Arab Socialism" which is to be the foundation for Ben Bella's regime (1962–1965) and for Boumedienne's. It is to provoke the revolutions of 1963 in Syria and in Iraq.

For twenty years Zionism and Arabism have been feverishly working toward the same goal, and their constant interaction hastens their consciousness and accelerates the pace of necessary accomplishments. But they each have their own peculiar problems.

Zionism has a tendency to be a victim of its own success. I shall leave for later a discussion of the difficulties which followed the Six Day War. I am referring to something much deeper and more essential which affects Israel's very destiny. There is no precedent for a revolution which has outlived its triumph. That is not surprising since a revolutionary movement rises to achieve a previously defined goal. The goal achieved, the movement has no purpose and naturally disintegrates.

For years the Jewish world has been concerned with what it calls the crisis of the Zionist movement without having precisely identified the causes of the crisis or defined the means to overcome them. The World Zionist Organization has shown an extraordinary aptitude for achieving the goals so clearly defined by the Zionist Congress at Basel in August 1897: "Zionism has as its goal the creation for the Jewish people in Palestine a refuge guaranteed by public law." But once the State was created, Zionism no longer had a purpose. To speak more precisely—until May 14, 1947, Zionism was a revolutionary movement, animated in the eyes of Jews the world over by a heroic ideal. The creation of the State makes that ideal one more historical detail. What was yesterday a revolutionary hope becomes a routine job. Heroic combat becomes an administrative task—one of managing, preserving, and administering as well as possible. And the State was in a better position. Thanks to Arab opposition, it could still draw inspiration from the epic ideal. The end of immigration and the widespread unpopularity of Zionism, a word which had become almost pejorative for the young Israelis, have both superficial and fundamental causes. On the surface operates the weariness of an administrative machinery poorly adapted to its new functions. It supposedly seeks to organize the immigration, but is really incapable of effective long–range programs. It deals with integration and colonization, paralleling the government's work, but without having the latter's power or means. Its organization is clumsy and inadequate, its bureaucracy frustrating. The empty words of some of its leaders, its excessive politicalization, and its inability to reorganize its ranks hinder rather than encourage general progress. Basically Zionism is a dead movement which nothing will be able to restore to its former status. It has fulfilled all its goals by giving birth to the State of Israel.

Arabism has not been fulfilled or effective because it lacks that organic duality which Zionism has, and without which no movement can exist. It groups, or rather it means to regroup, some extremely poor nations which share the same problems and which, unfortunately, lack the means to solve them. The idea of creating a solid block of disinherited nations is touching, but is unable to present the semblance of solution either on the intellectual plane or in political reality in spite of the proliferation of treaties, agreements, and conferences. In fact, the Arab world is poorer and more divided than ever. In its misery it cannot fill its stomach either on cannons or on the speeches of demagogues. The modern world is far away and only vaguely answers Egypt's expectation. Iran and Turkey, for example, established diplomatic and commercial relations with Israel long ago. The fact that thirteen Arab countries have gone to war, in principle at least, against Israel has not solved the internal conflicts which divide Tunisia and Egypt, or oppose the latter to Yemen, Iraq, or Jordan. Painful contradictions appear internally in every Arab country. One example is the war of the Kurds against the central government in Iraq. Another is the repressive police action in Egypt which in fifteen years has crushed varied opposition to the regime—the Muslem Brethren, the feudal lords and the aristocrats, the capitalists and big corporations, the foreigners who have almost all left the country, the Jews whose community has totally disappeared, the intellectuals who have to side with the regime, and finally the army, which at every level is the greatest current victim of the regime.

King Hussein, who launched into the war adventure with a haste which he shall forever regret, fights to protect his throne from the Iraquis, Syrians, and Palestinians. In Syria and Iraq, the regimes have to face internal crises which periodically disrupt the other Arab countries—Algeria, for example, which three years after independence was confronted with the revolution of 1964. It put Boumedienne in power and a new revolution almost drove him out in 1967 and 1968. The hijacking of an Israeli commercial plane and the confinement of its passengers—that is what satisfies Arab honor, Moslem generosity! As for the Third World, it was wishful thinking to expect it to identify with the quarrels of the Arab League. The votes in the United Nations following the Six Day War have surely proved it.

Arabism and Zionism, such as they have defined themselves in the closed universe from which they have emerged, sense that because of each other they have both reached an impasse which became clear to everybody after the June war. For fifty years the Jews and Arabs have been quarreling, brandishing their claims which they insist they have on the Holy Land. "Arab land," you say; "Hebraic land," we answer. The Jews base themselves on the Bible and age-old hopes of obtaining reparations for the misdeeds of Roman imperialism in the first century of our era. For the Moslems there is the underlying theory that a land which has belonged to Islam, no matter when, remains a land of Islam forever—"Besides, we are the heirs of the English and the Turks!"—"If there is prescription in matters of sovereignty, your rights are forfeited as you claim ours are!" Arguments proliferate and become so technical that they could be discussed to the end of time. The 991 pages of the Israeli-Arab dossier published by "Temps Modernes" in June, 1967, in spite of their length, are only a small portion of the millions of papers and billions of words published on the matter. Three hundred twenty pages of Israel's justification answer 360 pages of Arab accusations. To each Arab argument, Jewish thought counters with ten answers. To each of these a subtle mind could find one hundred definitive replies, to which one thousand reasons could be opposed, ad infinitum.

During all these years I have followed the evolution of your thought step by step in the articles you published in Arab magazines and newspapers, in what the press reported of your speeches. I recognized the keenness of your intelligence, the vigor of your style, the courage which always pushed you beyond the limits which prudence and sometimes reason could advise. I also knew the ties which bound you to Israel: Your family came from one of those villages of the hills of Judea where, as in Galilee, the population remains unchanged. You loved to boast of your genuine descendence from the people of the Bible and all evidence was on your side. As many Palestinians, you spoke Hebrew with a delightful Eastern accent. You rehabilitated our language deformed by a great number of Israelis from Europe who neglected to pronounce the gutturals the way they should be. You were nourished on Hebraic culture, steeped in the ideals of French liberalism, and carried away with the feeling of innate power which sought to emerge in your thoughts, words, and action, not to mention the emotional ties with so many Jews. In your work I looked for a trace of what I felt was your true image. Nothing remained of that part of you which so dearly united you to me, to Israel. You had erased all the Judeo-Arab past. You wanted to ignore the achievements of Israeli Zionism. For you no possibility existed for a new Israeli-Arab relationship to serve the peoples of the Mid-East and the peace of the world. You were taken with democratic ideals: Nasser's dictatorship seemed to suit your new conception of socialism.

Ultimately, I saw the monster which Arab propaganda sought to wedge between us creep into your writing—a hideous Jew, a repulsive synthesis of the caricatures proposed by the anti-Semitic hate of the Middle Ages and the German national-socialist party. Reading you, I felt my nose become hooked, my eyes push out of their sockets, my ears flap, my fingers turn into claws and my feet become cloven like the devil's. I felt ready to drink the blood of Christian children . . . Remember that sketch which depicts a horrible Jew, his nose as hooked as possible, and his neck caught in the central hexagon of Solomon's seal, while a righteous knightly Arab pulls tight the point of the two intertwined triangles. The hate of these inventions! The themes of Arab propaganda concerning Israel are not numerous but they are constantly reworked with so much conviction that they end up disturbing even the clear conscience of an honest man. Through violence, Sarah makes Abraham drive out the servant Agar and her son Ishmael into the deserts whose son he becomes. By a ruse Jacob usurps Esau's blessing from Isaac. Arab propaganda furiously tells the world: "Biblical history continues: through violence and deceit, the Jews have dispossessed us of our land, our goods, our honor, and our freedom. We will not rest until we are avenged." And in fact, the wound in the Arab soul is deep. Arab criticism denies any shadow of value in the Zionist thesis: it ingeniously strives—and for some time now, successfully—to present an image of the Jew which may resemble us but which we have difficulty recognizing. Do we have to repeat the themes of this propaganda? We are imperialists, colonists, land robbers, usurpers who have deceived not only the Arab nations but the United Nations. We are strangers in our own land to which neither the Bible, nor history, nor the decisions of the United Nations have given any right—bloodthirsty aggressors, thieves whom the Security Council has never ceased condemning, racists who condemn minorities to dispair and shame, dishonor, and misery. We are the producers and the profiteers of the refugee tragedies.

These traditional grievances have been amplified considerably since the June 1967 War, the results of which confirm for our critics the accusations they have been heaping on us for twenty years. After having done almost everything necessary to drag us into this sorry mess, they turn to the world and shout: "We told you so!" A pamphlet published by the Iraqui embassy in Paris after the Six Day War sums up this point of view: Israel is only made up of a group of men of diverse nationalities who have come from the four corners of the world to take possession of the land and goods of an entire people, to drive it out of its home. They are impelled exclusively by racism and deny the principle of majority rule and the right of self-determination. This campaign has a very obvious goal—to frighten the world. "By exerting all sorts of pressure on the information media, Zionism has succeeded in distorting uncontestable facts to its own profit and to further its objective which is the definitive spread of its domination of the world." Arab or pro-Arab writers who have poured their testimony into the Israeli-Arab dossier of *Temps Modernes* use their technique and their talent to analyze these great themes, to develop them, to embellish them with arguments based on theology, reason, law, and indeed, with regard to morality, justice, and humanity. They even make their case by defending the interests of Judaism and the Jews who should understand by themselves the extent of their wrongdoings, ask forgiveness, pack their bags, and finally make room for the Arabs before the latter exterminate them. That is what a good Christian Arab of this country told me on June 3, 1967! That is what was written by the foremost Arab or pro-Arab thinkers, philosophers, jurists, and sociologists such as Maxime Rodinson for whom Israel is only a "colonial fact." Mounthir Anabtawi is less circumspect accusing Israel of being a "colonial, chauvinistic, and militaristic movement" representing a permanent danger for freedom and world peace. Abdul Wahhab Kayyali, whom you know for his activity at the Research Center of the Organization for the Liberation of Palestine, emphasizes "the aggressive expansionist character of the State of Israel." The refugee problem is the source of the least refutable arguments of the Arab thesis, strengthened by the great pity for the Arab victims of the last war. Loufti El Kholi accuses Israel of being a ghetto and a bastion of imperialism. To support this stand, a more highly inspired Moroccan is referred to—Abdallah Laroui denies the socialist character, in the scientific sense of the term, of the State of Israel. If he considers Nasser's Egypt the perfect example of applied socialism, I feel ready to subscribe to his judgment. Another Moroccan, Tahar Benziane, concludes a long analysis rather vehemently: "If the Jews, on the contrary, refuse to integrate themselves, Palestine will have no recourse but to reject this foreign and aggressive body which will not obey the elementary laws of humanity." Luckily, he excludes me from the anathema: "The Jews native to Palestine are rightfully on their own land which is that of their Palestinian ancestors of Jewish persuasion." If I had the slightest desire to debate, I would ask Benziane what he does with the four or five thousand Jews of North Africa who in Morocco, Algeria, or Tunisia were rightfully on their own land which is that of their Mograbin ancestors of Jewish persuasion and who nonetheless had to leave, expropriated of their goods.

An admirable cry from the heart of an Egyptian, Ali Alsamman, whom you must have met in Paris where he is the correspondent for *Al Ahrem*, concludes the exposé of the Arab themes collected by *Temps Modernes*: "I hate this Zionism which separates Arab from Jew." A cry of love and a cry of hate at the same time, is there a better way to admit the impasse to which the current Arab point of view on Israel leads?

There is so much bloodshed and unimaginable suffering of the survivors, widows, orphans, and other relatives of soldiers killed at the front. There are also the unspeakable misfortunes of the refugees. Have you read that frightful account published by *le Monde* in which one of them tells how, moved by despair, he drowned his baby daughter in the Jordan?

There are the dangers of world war which the Near-Eastern conflict risks. There is the burning of billions of dollars thrown into the foreign treasuries of ammunition dealers and into Mirages. There is the loss of independence which this absurd conflict provokes by making us dependent on the great powers which use the Jews and the Arabs for their own policy on a world scale. In this perspective our conflict makes us pawns on a chess board.

But even more seriously, perhaps, twenty years of war have made us strangers—we who used to live as brothers. I seek in your face marked by the tragedy of your war and your defeat, your youthful expressions which I knew and loved in Jerusalem and later in Paris. Where is the freshness of your smile, your laughing eyes, the relaxed confidence of our close friendship? We had no secrets from each other—David and Jonathan resurrected on the hills of Judea during our pleasant walks. I see you ravaged by your personal disappointment and the unheard suffering of your people. In twenty years we had become strangers to each other and yet our studies, our plans, even our stars prepared us for the same future.

I am now involved with the affairs of a state which is not yours, and your defeat explains my survival. I grew up in Arab surroundings. My son, in Jerusalem, never saw an Arab before our reunion, and the only expression of Arabism which ever reached his ears was the rifle fire which the Arab legion sometimes aimed at our windows.

In Israel the Arab minority, victim of the conflict which tore us apart, turned inward and had almost no contact with the Jews. In Arab countries the ideal was to pretend that Israel did not exist. They removed its name from maps, from newspaper advertisements and, in some churches in Lebanon, from the Psalms which the faithful recited. The areas of contact between Arabs and Jews which twenty years ago covered the whole expanse of the Arab world had undergone the fate of the "peau de chagrin." Everywhere we burned our bridges and only interacted at the most painful and critical points.

In Arab countries the Jewish communities had been plainly liquidated, creating hundreds of thousands of refugees of whom no one speaks and no international agency has thought of taking into its charge. Jews are simply abandoned to the care of the Jewry. Throughout Islam, at each disruption caused by the Israeli-Arab conflict, the Jews leave the countries in which they had been settled for millennia and where they had often preceded the Moslem conquest. Everywhere in Asia and North Africa the triumph of nationalism is accompanied by the total or partial dissolution of the Jewish communities. All the Jews of Yemen, ninety-eight percent of the Jews of Iraq, all the Jews of Aden and Jordan, ninety percent of the Syrian Jews, ninety-six percent of the Egyptian Jews, ninety-five percent of the Libian Jews, most of the Afghan, Kurd, and Indian Jews, a significant portion of the Iranian, Turkish, and Lebanese Jews, ninety percent of the Tunisian Jews, ninety-nine percent of the Algerian Jews, almost ninety percent of the Moroccan Jews have left their country of birth since the creation of the State of Israel. Their exodus has often been dramatic and clandestine, especially where they were pursued by the police. Most often they left everything behind only to have it immediately confiscated by the Arab governments. These refugees lost their goods and savings representing generations of work and had to start their new life in Israel from zero. I prefer to gloss over the way in which the Jews living in the Moslem countries have learned about the kindness of the Syrian, Egyptian, or Moroccan police. Yes, let us move on.

The war of 1948 and the armistice agreements had transformed the State of Israel into a fortress hermetically sealed off from the Arabs. For twenty years the gap between the Arabs and the Jews widened so much that it seemed as though we were living on two different planets rather than in different sections of the same country. Contacts had become either impossible or futile. In Israel a bloody frontier separated us. Elsewhere, in North Africa, Libya, Egypt, Lebanon, Syria, Iraq, Jordan, and Yemen the Jews who outlasted the great exodus no longer had the possibility of free exchange.

The conflict poisoned relations between Arabs and Jews wherever they lived together and ruined any chance for dialogue. During this period I often had occasion to speak with Arabs. In Israel their situation was neither secure nor comfortable. Whatever their opinions on the advantages and disadvantages of our presence for them, they could not express these without exposing their complex about us. They felt tortured by the barrier which separated the Arab countries from Israel. We were so aware of this that we finally stopped talking about it. Our daily problems were enough to keep us all busy. We were dedicated to the construction of a country. For twenty years, in spite of foreign instigation, coexistence was possible even if lacking true communication. Our sorrow festered—the Arab and his war, the Jew and his search for rest. As with old family rivalries, we lived together without speaking to each other.

The Arab isolation was worse than ours in many ways. In Israel they were citizens of a state whose creation most of them had not approved of and where they were forced to take security measures difficult to accept. The State of Israel had to worry about survival first of all. Whatever its intention was as far as Arab integration was concerned, its policy forced it to take measures which the Arab population considered injurious and discriminatory. The effort made by the Israeli government in the domain of health, education, and housing did not ease the plight of the Arabs in Israel. They could enjoy the highest standard of living known in the Arab world, they could have achieved the highest level of instruction for their children, they could even see the futility and insanity of Egypt's quarrel with Israel—that did not change their internal anxiety, encouraged by the loud voices of radio Cairo, Amman, Damascus, or Baghdad. I really understood their plight which was aggravated by the consequences of the partition, the separation of families, the departure of refugees, and the confiscation or expropriation of certain land. The Hebraization of the state made their integration more difficult. The principle of equality could not function in the war economy which tore us apart.

In addition, certain Arabs had the opportunity to complain of their fate in a report addressed to the Secretary General of the United Nations in 1964. They declared themselves victims of political oppression and racial discrimination, and felt that the Israeli government pursued a policy of hate against the Arabs and stimulated hostile feelings both among the adult Jewish population and the students. More than in the realm of feelings and propaganda, the Arabs condemned the real violation of their rights. They referred to the consequences of the 1948 war, to certain land expropriations (the law on the property of absent persons of 1950, criticized in its very principle), destruction of villages, Ikret, for example, or even legal expropriations made at unacceptable prices. All Israeli legislation to facilitate the Hebraization of the state and the Judaization of Galilee was bitterly denounced as being contrary to order and to the international obligations of the state. The problem of the property of religious foundations (*Waqfs*), taken into custody by the Israeli administration in the absence of their beneficiaries, was brought up. These measures were strongly condemned.

Military authority, charged with safeguarding order and security in the Arab sections of the territory, was denounced as the work of the devil. According to this report, it only "spread dissention, fear, and terror," and could only aggravate the policy of discrimination against the Arabs of Israel in all aspects of public and private life.

This report was inspired by the claims of the group *Al Ard* which desired the end of discrimination and oppression for all the Arabs of Israel, the adoption of the partition plan

237

of 1947 for Palestine which, at the time, had been accepted by the Jews and refused by the Arabs, and the recognition of Arab socialistic and neutralistic nationalism. *Al Ard* was persuaded, especially after it was banned by a judicial decision, that the government of Israel had as its goal "to create a state of fear, dispair, and submission.* All the pressing legislation which had come in the wake of the war was denounced.

Of course, *Al Ard*'s point of view was shared by many Arabs. For them the promises from Cairo and from the other Arab capitals were real. Their situation as a minority—indeed a privileged one compared to that of their brothers of other Arab countries (on the economic plane notably)—was temporary. The day of revenge and salvation would come. 1948 and 1956 had disappointed the Arab hopes. But if two battles had been lost, the war was not over. So when the crisis of May 1967 erupted, the Arab nationalists inspired by Nasser fully expected that the day of glory had arrived. "Why do you not leave the country before the Egyptians exterminate you," one of them said to me, "you would at least save your life." Others tried to identify the houses they would occupy after their victory. Some Arab students advised their Israeli pals to buy bathing suits which, after all, could come in handy when the Egyptians, Syrians, and Jordanians threw them into the sea. This rancor and spirit of revenge was not shared, however, by a large segment of the Arab population concerned primarily with peace, nor by the Druzes who were very well integrated and aware of enjoying their full equality of rights and duties.

From May 15, 1967 on, Nasser's threats were no longer simply verbal, but were accompanied by a display of power. Nasser's armies prepared to pounce on ours in order to exterminate us. Again we were separated by an abysmal isolation. The Arab radios brought us the demented growling of the Arab dictators or their spokesmen. There was the same barrage of threats on our lives that was hurled at us in Hit-

* "Le conflit israélo-arabe," in *les Temps Modernes* (Paris, 1957), p. 792.

lerian Europe, except now it was in Arabic. It was not a matter of presenting us as we were, but as we had to be to justify the great massacres reserved for us in Cairo, Damascus, and Amman.

> *"Slaughter, slaughter, slaughter and have no pity,*
> *Slaughter, slaughter, slaughter, and toss their heads*
> *Into the desert,*
> *Slaughter, slaughter, slaughter*
> *As many as you like,*
> *Slaughter all the Zionists and you will win,"*

chanted Cairo's popular singer Umm Kulthum in Cairo and in Damascus. So that we might be slaughtered, it was necessary that in the minds of our eventual assassins we stop resembling human beings. So the colonials and the racists had developed a technique of very efficient propaganda aimed at dehumanizing the enemy—the one who must be exploited and killed—to the point of reducing him to an object and not a person. Then murder is not hampered by conscience. These formulas had proved themselves in Asia and Africa where the Westerners opposed the colonized peoples. But in this case the Arab dictators directed them against Israel.

For us the blockade of the Straits of Tiran decreed by Nasser on May 22, the incessant attacks on our territory by the Syrians, the heavy bombardment of Jerusalem by the Jordanians on the morning of June 5, 1967 were characteristic aggressive tactics. Yet the Arab leaders continue to talk about Israeli aggression. In their own way they are right because they deny our right to live. The very fact of our existence as a state introduces a problem for world order, and constitutes a permanent aggression against "their" peace. Even if we spend our days and nights singing psalms and hymns, we would not slacken our perverse aggression which could end only with our annihilation.

We were convinced that an Arab victory would fulfill the prophecies and ambitions of Choukeiri—the extermination of the survivors of Hitler's massacres. At the end of the Six Day War we candidates for martyrdom suddenly found ourselves in a position of strength, at the head of an empire vaster than our ancestors had even imagined possible. We were the occupiers and, therefore, responsible for policing the country. What a strange twist of fate—the victim became the executioner. Although relieved by our victory, we were cognizant of its burdens. We knew that our calvary was not over. Rather, we had overcome one barrier along the way. Israel had become the occupier in spite of itself, victor thanks to the obstinacy of its enemies. Suddenly the problem became terribly complicated. Formerly our situation had been relatively simple. It was a question of being or not being. We knew where we stood. We carried out the role we envisioned for ourselves, which corresponded to what the world had expected of us for four thousand years—those who had been given a reprieve. As our destiny unfolded it was possible to predict and expect a tragic end, the continuation of death's work. So long as there was one Jew alive, there would be room for him in the huge cemeteries or smoke-filled crematories of history.

Now that we were victorious, all bets were off. The little Jew of the ghetto had cheated the world by becoming the undesirable winner of a war which had no doubt represented an unbeatable masterpiece of conventional strategy. The whole world, and we too, could expect a suitable end to the trouble which Israel has constantly introduced into history since Abraham's first mad adventure—that suitable end, the collapse of the Jewish army, the Arab hordes attacking our women, our children, and our homes to complete the job Hitler had left undone.

We are at the head of an empire which stretches from the slopes of Hermon to the Suez Canal, from the Gulf of Aqaba to the banks of the Jordan. Our very self-assurance and dominant role made us guilty troublemakers who were overturning the scale of values. Nietzsche, himself, would no longer recognize the Jews—slaves suddenly promoted to the rank of master. But even in this we were surprised and hurt because we were less in search of domination than of life and liberty. Our new image which surprised the world still continues to bother us, some by revelry, others by nostalgia. The new situation has shocked the world, put the old values

into question, and undermined the most deep-rooted stereo-
types.

The weak no doubt hide behind this victory to dream of
a solution which will deliver Israel from its enemies forever
—keep all the conquered territories, maintain a position of
strength until the total collapse of Arab resistance. The
others dream of peace and of Messianic deliverance. They
physically need to see the lion and the lamb lying in peace,
and wail before their visions of tanks converted into ploughs.
Tragic and ridiculous rhetoric, Jewish rhetoric!

Within our frontiers, we Israelis are hurting ourselves
with our useless contradictions and domestic struggles as
our ancestors split hairs over the subtleties of the Talmud.
Our anguish leads to an academic debate so long as those
with whom we should be in conference remain trapped by
the fear and shame of their defeat.

As the tragedy becomes more serious, as new assaults cost
more victims and as repression sows fear, the extremists get
stronger: Nasser, the great loser of June 1967, continues to
preach the extermination of Israel. More subtle Arab propagandists try to make a distinction between genocide and
what they call politicide—it would no longer be a matter of
killing the Jews of Israel, but their state. As if the former
could survive the latter! Reacting to these threats reminiscent of some Arab voices of 1967 and those of the forties
which, in Germany, announced actual massacres, we hear
some Jewish voices trembling with anguish as they insist
that the State of Israel take radical defense measures to save
us by a violent elimination of the dangers of terrorism. On
one hand, they wish that Palestine could be entirely Arab,
while on the other, they see Israel's only chance for survival
within the framework of a Jewish State reaching from the
edges of the Hermon to the banks of the Jordan and the
Suez Canal.

It seems very clear that these extreme solutions would
contribute to the absolute negation of the only chance we
have to fulfill our historic calling. The reality of our daily
life since our reunion under the dome should encourage us
to define and realize other solutions. To do so, we should
arm ourselves not only with courage, but with imagination.

We should impassionately aim at finding, among the obstacles along the way, the narrow passage which would allow us to escape from our present impasse.

Arab impasse: the extremism of Nasserian nationalism leads to results diametrically opposed to the ends it sets up for itself. Israeli power has been proved and confirmed by the blind opposition of Arab nationalism. So the Palestinian resistance of *El Fatah* leads to the constant weakening of the Palestinian population of the Israeli occupied territories. Each terrorist assault causes a chain reaction which operates to the detriment of the very people it was intended to help. Insecurity causes the departure of the less strong. All of Israel's efforts, all the skill it uses to avoid catastrophe, are nullified by the mechanism methodically unleashed by the Palestinian resistance and its Arab, Chinese, or Russian inspirers. Contrary to the wishes of the huge majority of Israelis who sincerely desire an equitable peace which safeguards the rights and dignity of the Moslems and Christians of the country, the terrorism intensifies the uprooting and its cortege of mourning.

On the Jewish side, the injury is no less serious. Theodore Herzl, who predicted everything, had never thought about the Arab refusal and the war in which it continues to plunge the heirs of the promise made to Abraham. For more than half a century the Jews have not been able to let their defenses down because of the necessity of preserving their existence and their work, begging the Arabs to accept their existence and to make peace. And here are these supplicants, these candidates for martydom, these eternal losers, promoted to the scarcely enviable dignity of occupiers, dominators, torturers. The world is becoming accustomed to an image of Israel which contradicts both the realities of the past and the wishes of the present.

In the streets of the important capitals graffiti try to impose a new, odious equation: ✡=卐 . All the rationalizing in the world will not change the tragic realities of our conflict, so long as we do not learn how to transcend them and find a just solution for ourselves. Our dilemma consists first in choosing between the route to life and the route to death. If we can resist the temptation of nihilism and the

242

pressures of those who would like to push us into it, we will have to define the conditions of our survival simply in order to exist. The Arab refusal and the interests of some great world powers would be helpless if we decided to unite as brothers to build the new city of Israel and Ishmael on the land of Abraham. All the conditions of a perfect solution to our impossible problem would be ours if only we knew how to recognize and fulfill them. To the absolute contradictions which separate us, we have to oppose the absolute of a solution which can unite us indissolubly in the framework of a land which belongs to both of us, of a message to which we both lay claim, and of two peoples who have been created and preserved because they are reserved for the accomplishment of the same saving mission. The essential lies in our will to resist the attraction of death and to impose on ourselves and the world the feeble chance for survival, for salvation.

Since it is impossible or dangerous to eliminate one of the terms of the contradictions, we must work out their harmonious coexistence in the framework of the two cities, the one Arab, the other Israeli, managed by states united by political, economic, and cultural agreements. The problems of national defense, of international representation, and economic and social promotion could find their solution in federal-type treaties which insure the full respect for the rights and aspirations of all. Two freely elected parliaments, the parliament of Israel and that of Ishmael, would legislate the laws to govern the two allied cities. All the Arabs of Israel, wherever their residence, would be electors and eligible for the Arab parliament. All the Israelis, even those who settled in Hebron, Nablus, Gaza, or El Arish would belong to the city of Israel. Jerusalem's mission would be to serve as the spiritual and political center of a new and reconciled people. The Christian, Moslem, and Jewish holy places would enjoy the international guarantees to which the government of Israel has committed itself. The cities would enjoy extensive autonomy and their council would be elected by universal suffrage. At this level a mixed representation of Arabs and Jews would allow the best defense of local interests.

The question of borders, such as it presently exists, is a serious obstacle to finding a peaceful solution. I would like to say here that this question should in fact be secondary in the framework of a peace settlement. Essentially, the question of nationalism is independent of the geographical realities which sustain it. The Jews have lived for two thousand years without a territorial base. In the Biblical era the frontiers of the Jewish state were constantly at the mercy of political realities. Islam, itself, is unaware of the notion of national frontiers. By law a Moslem is at home everywhere, a full-fledged citizen throughout Dar-el-Islam. If the two cities of Israel and Ishmael participate in a certain transcendence, this constitutes a wealth which should help us solve our contradictions. The problem of administrative divisions is secondary to that one basic necessity—the Jews, the Christians, the Moslems must be able to feel at home throughout the land of Israel. This land has been described by the Psalms as the Land of God. Our only title, the only proof of our filiation, is found in our creation, in the evidence of our fidelity to the fraternal ideals which we both claim to teach and fulfill.

Our problem is no longer one of finding the means of eliminating each other, but rather that of healing our breach so as to present our new peace as an offering to the world— the secret of its reconciliation and its salvation. This is the challenge presented by the conflict which has bathed us in blood—to go beyond the limits of the notion of the state as Hegel defined it in the nineteenth century. Beyond the notion of states, man and we Jews and Arabs must first of all rediscover the true identity of our countries. In our new union we should be the heralds and promoters of the message of universal reconciliation.

The new society of Jews, Moslems, and Christians in Israel should never be a Near-Eastern ghetto. In order to realize its deepest vocation, it must reach out to the world. In the future Jordan, Lebanon, Syria, Iraq, and Egypt will be able to integrate with the central nucleus by essentially federative treaties. The land which today is the object of our dispute will become the keystone of our new unity. Jerusalem will realize its vocation as a spiritual center. Along with the Hebraic university, an Arab university will spread the everlasting values of the Arab language and culture across the world. The Ecumenical Institute of Bethlehem, founded by Pope Paul vi, could also be one of the important factors of our necessary convergence.

To our central nucleus around Jerusalem on the land of Abraham, would gravitate a second circle which would encompass the Arab or Arabicized world on the one side and the Jewish world on the other. The League of Arab States and the World Zionist Organization should come to terms and cooperate in the immense project of peace, in the heart of a new political, social, and cultural organism in which the Arab and Arabicized states and Israel and the Jewish communities of the world would be represented. This organism would have as its mission to help the spiritual and human development of the land of Israel and Ishmael and their peoples.

A third circle would contain all those in the universe who are linked to the Koran or the Bible—the Moslem states, the Christian states, and all men of good will who, without formally adhering to a revealed religion, share the ideals of peace, fraternity, unity, and love, and who are united in the message of the Bible, the Gospels, and the preaching of Mohammed. Together we should pool our energies to reinforce on the spiritual plane the institutions animated by an ecumenical or universal spirit. On the political plane we should cooperate to give a new substance to the United Nations so as to insure the tangible accomplishments of our spiritual ideals and moral aspirations in the temporal order.

The constitution of this vast political and spiritual organism resting on solidly established bases throughout the world, nourished by its great historic origins, would surely condition the salvation of the Near East and could become a decisive factor in the establishment of world peace.

But, you say to me, there is the war, its scars, its aftermath. Certainly, but this war, truthfully speaking, has never been wanted by either of the opponents. The Jews wanted and continue to want peace. As Rabin stated so well: we are not a belligerent nation; we have neither military traditions nor ambitions. The best aspect of our wars was their brevity and we hope that the Six Day War is the last of all wars for us. Yes, we await the seventh day, the day of rest when we lay down our arms.

There is another reason for the brevity of our wars—they have never been wanted or supported by your people. They have never felt that it was their fight, but they were always its first victims. The war was the problem of the Turkish or English occupiers, or of the Arab League (in its various contradictory manifestations), not the conflict of an entire people united and resolved to fight and die for the triumph of its cause. I do not believe in the animosity of Arabs and Jews. The cloud will pass and our people will again find each other as we ourselves did under the dome of the Mosque of Omar. The memory of our dispute will disappear as a nightmare. The Arab states will forget their dictators just as they have forgotten their Turkish and English governors and their despotic sovereigns. Nasser is only one phase of Arabism—a necessary phase, perhaps, for the development of our self-awareness and our awakening from a long sleep. The Middle East is impossible to build with men such as Nasser, Aref, and Atassi. The European situation was impossible, too, with Hitler and Mussolini. The hate, anger, and suffering accumulated by European dictatorship in the cultured, educated, and important nations infinitely surpass in horror everything the mid-Eastern conflict might have produced in bitterness since its origins. And yet in spite of the tens of millions of victims of the World War, dead, wounded, deported, in spite of unimaginable horrors and apocalyptic destruction, and the centuries-old hate among struggling nations, a developed Europe has finally emerged.

There is more. The Jews and the Germans do not have the reputation of being difficult people. The tragedy which separated us has exceeded the limits of horror, and yet the generation which has witnessed that trauma has been the same one which has been able to overcome its grief and resentment to prepare a new peace between Germany and Israel. David Ben Gurion and Nahoum Goldman are the contemporaries of Adolf Hitler. It is they who signed the

246

agreements which brought the two countries closer together.

Hate must not and cannot eternally succeed hate, for if that were the case when would hate ever come to an end? Hate must not, hate cannot succeed hate, especially when hate has no reason, no goal, and when it is more apparent than real. An Arab author, Abdel-Kader, has answered the Arab League's eight principal arguments against Israel. To his arguments, published in a prophetic little book, *Le Monde arabe à la veille d'un tournant* (Paris: Maspero éditeur, 1966), I would like to add one more: anti-Zionist hate. It deforms the face of Arabism and that of Islam. Where is the generosity and the nobility of the Arab in Nasser's diatribes? Where can you find the grandeur, magnanimity, and courage of the Arab or of the Moslem in the antics of a Choukeiri?

Yes, it is possible to become reconciled on the indestructible basis of our reunion, in justice. We can ally ourselves forever to rebuild the Arab world and Israel and restore them to their vocation of eternal greatness, in the service of the ideals of peace and progress of which they where the first heralds. Peace will save us from everything which ruins and dishonors us, from everything which hurts and kills us. The question of borders, of Arab and Jewish refugees, of discrimination against Arabs in Israel and against Jews in the Arab countries, the psychological and social conflicts caused by our war would all be wiped away in the new order of peace. We must patiently build this peace which will be a safeguard for us and will be an unimaginable blessing for the world. "The nations of the earth will be blessed in your posterity," the Bible promised Abraham. That verse which contains a promise made to our common ancestor four millennia ago, could define the formal purpose of our reconciliation and henceforth be translated into revolutionary political realities.

In their fundamental complimentarity Arabs and Jews can constitute a pole whose attraction may bring to the Near East and to the world an answer to the most urgent questions which are presented by the survival of the human race.

My long letter is coming to a close. The sun is rising and

247

illuminating Jerusalem's sky where the voice of the muezzins, the bells of the churches, and the ancient rhythms of our Hebraic chants intermingle.

Although I am addressing myself to you, my friend, beyond you I see the horde of Arab poets, novelists, philosophers, essayists, and journalists who have taken upon themselves the wholesome and saving work of the regeneration of their language and their people. I see the multitude of young Arabs throughout Dar-el-Islam, and I beg—let us combine our efforts, let us unite our wills to commit ourselves to the true battle of the new man in this cruel century.

Beyond the words, beyond the chants, the unexplored universe of silence opens up in our deserts. There we may find the spirit which inspired Moses, Jesus, and Mohammed. It is there that the true resurrection of the dead is being prepared and announced. New horizons are being created in a new land, the land of men, around your walls, Jerusalem, in the light of our reconciliation.

Postscript, 1972

A book is like a bottle cast adrift. Each one has its own story, its own destiny. Here are a few words about this one.

For a long time I have been impelled to consider the Arab world my principal concern. I was born and brought up in an Arab country, Algeria, whose day-to-day evolution made me identify with the tragic conflict which pitted it against France. Very early in life I spoke Mograbin Arabic and became extremely interested in the Islamic culture and mystic. My first book was devoted to a treatise on ascetic and mystical theology written in Arabic by a Spanish Jew in the eleventh century, *Introduction to the Lessons of the Heart* by Bahya Ibn Pakuda. More than fifteen years ago I arrived in Israel and placed myself in the epicenter of the Israeli-Arab conflict on the frontier at Jerusalem. Everything in me revolted against the war which I was to label absurd and idiotic. The end of the long incubation of this work was hastened by my election as deputy-mayor of Jerusalem, with Teddy Kollek as mayor, in 1965. My new responsibilities in the center of Israel's capital forced me into seeking a solution to the absurd conflict which was tearing us apart. One day my carpenter, Djerassi, an Arab Christian of Jerusalem, was felled in a courtyard of Nôtre Dame de France by a Jordanian soldier who was on guard duty a few yards away on the other side of the line which divided Jerusalem. Djerassi was a fine young man of about thirty. Why did he have to die?

Involved in the management of Jerusalem, I formulated my resolution when the 1967 conflict took shape. I had lived out the 1956 war in Jerusalem. From the beginning of 1967 the toughening of our positions could be felt. At that time I made contact with an important Syrian individual to beg him to transmit our wish for peace to his government. We hoped that nothing would be done to escalate the deteriorating situation. Shortly after my meeting with that Arab friend, I learned that he had been imprisoned by his government. In April 1967 things began to get worse. As for me, that mysterious time of preparation for a book was finished. I informed Teddy Kollek that I would take an Easter vacation. I went to stay in an Arab village in Galilee, Tarshiha. There, in a tiny room which looked out to the beauty of spring in Israel, I dictated into my tape recorder and rewrote the body of my *Letter to an Arab Friend*.

The work was brutally interrupted at the end of April. The deterioration of the political situation in the Middle East became obvious. I had to put aside my literary project to hurry to Jerusalem.

On May 13, in his talk at Fatima, Portugal, Pope Paul VI declared, "The world is in danger." This danger took concrete form in the Middle East two days later. We were celebrating Israel's Independence Day in Jerusalem trying to give some atmosphere to the solemn occasion. But our hearts were more aware of the dangers which threatened us than the joy of yesterday's victory. With Moshe Dayan, by a campfire near the Convent of the Holy Cross in Jerusalem, we were discussing one thing or another when the full-scale crisis erupted.

Syria accuses Israel of preparing a "new Suez." The Egyptian Army, battle ready, deploys its troops in the Sinai. Syria, Jordan, Iraq and Kuwait follow Cairo's example, forcing Israel to call up its reserve. On May 18 the United Arab Republic asks the United Nations' Forces to leave its territory. U Thant gives in to the demand. No sooner are the Blue Hats gone than Nasser decides to blockade the Tiran Straits. Nobody can doubt that we are on the brink of war. At City Hall in Jerusalem dejectedly we try to foresee the worst and rapidly prepare for it. We are overwhelmed by the perspective of a war which is imminent and by our serious lack of preparedness.

Almost nothing had been done to prepare the city for the fight which was coming. No one is a prophet in his own country. We continued to believe and say that in case of a conflict Jerusalem would be spared as in 1956. We asked the government not to leave Jerusalem in spite of its proximity to the border. We certainly thought that Hussein once more would be cautious enough to avoid engaging his troops on Jerusalem's border.

From the first of June to the evening of the fourth we visit our fellow citizens who live on the border to observe their problems and plan for their protection. In haste we dig trenches to serve as shelter if necessary. Since the men have been mobilized, it is up to the old men, women and even children to dig them. A group of youngsters are busy filling bags of sand and I surprise them at singing a Pascal hymn with contagious good humor: "We are the slaves of Pharoah."

On Sunday evening, June 4, I inspect the most vulnerable spots and by way of encouragement I say to my friends at Abu Thor that in case of an attack the border would disappear in less than three days. And I make an appointment with some friends from Herzlia, nervous about our being situated right on the border facing the Arab Legion's strongest positions, for a coffee date in the shadow of the Mosque of Omar in the Old City for the next Saturday, June 10.

At dawn on Monday, June 5, I leave for Tel-Aviv where I am supposed to be at the Sheraton. On my arrival I learn about the breaking out of hostilities between Israel and the Arab countries. While the sirens are screeching in the deserted city, I instantly make a beeline for my position in the ranks of the capital. When I arrive in Jerusalem, the city undergoes waves of bombings by the Arab Legion. From the windows of City Hall I can see our house at Abu Thor on the border serve as a target. My wife and children are there. As I go to join them under fire, my car quickly becomes a sieve.

During the sixty hours of battle in Jerusalem this book takes its definitive form in my mind. When I make my way toward the western wall of the Mosque of Omar on Wednesday, June 7, the streets are littered with corpses and the shooting continues. I still am under fire but at least I know what I will have to say to my Arab friend should I survive.

The Jerusalem government is faced with overwhelming tasks after the Six Day War and the reunification of the city.

These tasks slow down the publication of my book. Nonetheless it is published in its present form at the beginning of the spring of 1969. The Very Reverend Father Riquet, S.J., learns of its existence and requests the text. After reading it he writes: "I have read your book very carefully. It is excellent, solid and urgent. Madame Doria shares my enthusiasm and wishes to publish it as quickly as possible. This is the moment to spring your book on the public. It answers the needs of the times so precisely and bears a message which may persuade even the Arabs. I am convinced that it will be a landmark which will have lasting and worldwide reverberations" (Letter of January 25, 1969).

I give my text to the Maison Mame publishers who immediately start work on it. While it is being printed in April 1969, I am on a world tour which will take me across Europe, North and South America, to Japan, Hong Kong, Thailand and India for an extensive series of lectures for the Alliance Israelite Universelle. The proofs follow me but catch up in Jerusalem only after the book's appearance at the end of June. I return to Paris for its launching. Less than two months will elapse from the time I give my manuscript to the editor and the press conference which I hold at the Israeli Embassy in Paris on July 1, 1969, presided over by the Very Reverend Father Riquet.

The reactions are quick in coming. The July 4 issue of *Le Monde* has Eric Rouleau reporting on my press conference and presenting my propositions for the settlement of the Near Eastern conflict. He asks: "A utopia? André Chouraqui does not deny it," but he adds, "was not the State of Israel such as Theodore Herzl envisaged it also a utopia before it became a living reality?"

I had no idea that I was proposing a utopia in this book. For me it was a matter of life, of history, and an attempt at finding a rational solution to a conflict aggravated by so many different interests and pressures. Yet, it is the word utopia which recurs most often in the hundreds of reports on the work. In *L'Arche* Arnold Mendel speaks of an idealism which begs the question and of a lyrical optimism (July 26, 1969). In the Jesuit Order's *Les Etudes* Pierre Rondot writes

in the same vein: "At this juncture it is not the Utopian quality which is open to criticism. It is useful to exercise the
imagination by dreaming up utopias for peace" (February
1970). "Utopia? No doubt," writes Anne Marie Gentilly
in *La Terre Retrouvée* (Sept. 10, 1970). "But every accomplishment begins as a utopian dream, including the Jewish
State . . . Incomplete and blurred vision? Surely, as is every
poetic vision which is fulfilled only by the accomplished
fact. Messianic ideal relevant only to 'the end of time'? Certainly, but every thought, every human act, hastens or slows
down the coming of the Messianic era."

In *Le Monde* (August 30, 1969) André Fontaine is more
skeptical. Presenting my conclusions he does not speak of a
utopia, but of a dream: "You have to have a staunch faith in
God and man to believe that such a dream may ever become
a reality," he writes, "but in the land of Palestine where the
reality of mistrust and hate so tragically contradict the spiritual message which originates there, it is good for the voice
of love and friendship to be heard."

A utopia, a dream! How is that for an interpretation! The
novel-essay form that I used won as much praise as criticism.
The latter was all the more severe when the critics knew
me better. Some of them were disturbed by this Mattatias
Mizrahi who resembled André Chouraqui so well in so many
ways, in his thoughts and actions, without the two ever
actually merging. Along these lines, after having mentioned
my biography, André Fontaine writes: "Instead of using his
own experience as a point of departure and addressing a
living Arab, why did he invent this Mattatias Mizrahi, a
Jerusalem Jew . . . and the no less fictional character with
whom he corresponds? . . . He has opted for a hybrid form
which for those who are so aware of his talent and magnanimity has marred the book throughout" (*Le Monde*, July
30, 1969).

Several critics repeat this criticism in some way or other.
Why in the world is this Mattatias not clearly André Chouraqui? As for Ahmed Benghanem, does he really exist? Are
we faced with fiction or reality? This question confuses
many critics. The beginning of an answer is in an article

which appeared in Brussels in *La Libre Belgique* (August 29, 1969). "Why did André Chouraqui have an intermediary relay his message? . . . Perhaps for the sake of discretion. It is always touchy to tell one's own story to illustrate a theme, no matter how illustrious it may be. On the other hand, the contemporary history of Israel can be understood only through the personal experience of those who have made it." The author of this article signed F.M. understands that "Mattatias Mizrahi is more than an individual. He is the heart and conscience of his people. It is in this way that he can write without any presumption: 'I, Israel.' Chouraqui does not assume the right to speak in the name of the conscience of an entire people. More simply and more humanely he says: 'When I question my Israeli conscience, here is what it answers.' "

The debate went beyond my person. What was to interest the reader was an objective problem and not the vicissitudes of my private life, even though I tried to interpret my own experience with Israeli-Arab relations in this book. Did I succeed? Are Mattatias and Ahmed really the interpreters of their people and not particular cases or products of the imagination? Here again criticism was divided. Some went so far as to claim that these two characters were but "propaganda tricks." What did the Arabs and the Israelis think? And what was it really?

Elie Eliachar is an Israeli born in Jerusalem. For generations his family has lived in this country. Commenting extensively on my book in an article in *Bamaarakha*, he states: "If I had to write the chapters of my life spent in Jerusalem and describe my relations with the Arabs of my same age with whom I went to the local schools or to the universities of Beirut or of Egypt, I would not have been able to present a truer and more penetrating account than Chouraqui's. What he describes has been my experience with several families—the Husseini, the Nashashibi, the Muhatdi, the Dadjani and more. These childhood friendships were further solidified when we served together in the ranks of the Turkish Army during the First World War" (April 1970).

Indeed, there are thousands of Mattatias Mizrahis who have had solid friendships with the Arabs in Jerusalem, in

Israel, in the entire Arab world, just as I have had in Algeria. Eliachar correctly judges: "Some critics . . . have not accurately appraised the profound truth of the descriptions which Chouraqui gives of the relationship of the two friends, the Arab and the Jew, nor his faith in the possibility of a peaceful coexistence of Israel and its neighbors." Eliachar's testimony is corroborated by that of the Israeli Jews who have lived and are still living the same experience.

And what about Ahmed Benghanem? When my book was published in Paris at the time of the battle for positions on the Suez Canal and the terrorism of Palestinian organizations was at its height, he was understood in Europe as a pleasant invention by well-intentioned critics who were poorly informed about the Israeli realities. In their eyes Ahmed Benghanem was a happy find, a stylistic device which allowed me to add my say to that of the "colonial," "imperialistic," or "Zionist" propaganda. Organs such as *Le Nouvel Observateur* (November 1969), *La Vie Spirituelle* (April 1970), or even *Etudes* (February 1970), did not spare me this type of criticism.

Many Arabs feel differently. Since its publication my book has enjoyed an impressive public throughout the Arab world. All the positive reactions to my theses cannot be printed yet. Some of them should be made public, however. I have been consoled by the enthusiastic adherence to my ideas defended in this book which André Malraux considered "inspired in many respects." In a long article published by Ahmed Abassi in the Arab paper *Al-Arba* (December 5, 1969), a title was given full-page spread: "Letter to an Arab Friend: Courageous proposals for resolving the Arab-Israeli conflict." The paper stresses the mutual recognition of a Palestinian entity and a Jewish one, the juxtaposition of two Parliaments (one Jewish, the other Arab) joined by essentially federative links, and the advantages of peace for both peoples. "The problem of borders will resolve itself automatically with the formation of a federal union of the Jewish State and the Palestinian State in such a way that Jews and Arabs will all feel at home." Ahmed Abassi emphasizes the main contribution of my book which is, he writes, "to introduce a new style into the Judeo-Arab dialogue, the 'style of peace'." And if my solution surprises him, it also pleases him and leaves him with one question: When will the Israeli leaders accept my ideas?

Ahmed Abassi's spontaneous adherence to my project was to be followed by equally moving statements from everywhere in the Arab world and at all levels of awareness and responsibility. I gave a series of lectures in Israel, Europe, the United States and Canada, Latin America, and the Far East. Often there were Palestinians and Arabs of various origins in my audiences. They did not spare their criticism, notably over my violent attacks on Nasser's regime which was still at the height of its glory. But on the whole my theses inspired a very serious interest. Private conversations proved this general impression.

The impact of my book grew even stronger when it won the *Prix Sévigné* in 1970. The Parisian jury presided over by Pierre Lyautey included Hervé Bazin, Jean Follain, Madame Edgar Faure, the Count of Clermont-Tonnerre and several other literary and political personalities of France. This award initiated a new wave of articles and letters, new contacts, and a new opportunity to defend my ideas in a *Tribune libre* which *Le Monde* published with the title "A will for war" (July 8, 1970). I ended the article as follows: "The alliance of the two states founded on the land of the Covenant—the Arab one and the Israeli one—would be the decisive act which would allow the peaceful coalition and cooperation of all the peoples of the Near East. The considerable resources thus freed because of the end of hostilities, the capital which would flow in from the world over whose investment would be so appealing in a pacified Near East, the energies which such a revolution would free, mobilize or inspire, would be such that in one or two generations this part of the world would be restored to its ancient splendor and again become one of the great centers of world culture."

The tone of the reactions to my 1970 campaign was already very different from what I had heard in 1968. No longer did anyone speak of a dream or a utopia. Adopted was a more suitable note which the Very Reverend Father Riquet had struck from the very start in his editorial in *Le*

Figaro (July 5, 1969) entitled "Suggestions for peace in the Middle East." At that time, after having analyzed my arguments, Father Riquet wrote: "Theodore Herzl's dream has given way to André Chouraqui's. But may not the astonishing fulfillment of the one not assure us that the other is no less chimerical? More than one of us thinks so. Those who do not doubt that Israel and Ishmael, Jews, Christians and Moslems will one day be united and reconciled in the blessing of Abraham, their common father are the ones who believe so the most."

My book had been read by several chiefs of state, ministers, influential politicians. Its ideas had penetrated numerous chancelleries. My contacts from then on became more technical. No longer was the crux of my thesis discussed with skepticism. Rather, an attempt was made to adapt my theory to the specifics in directly applicable political terms. Conversations with informed statesmen helped me make my "lyrical meditation" (as my earliest critics used to say) more precise in terms of rights. Two letters from Pierre Mendès-France (September 4 and October 15, 1969) aided in this direction. If this eminent statesman approved of the spirit that inspired me and the avid search for a peaceful solution, he "could not picture how one could conceive of two nations, two states, two sovereign powers, living in the same territory."

I admit that I had accentuated the projective character of my proposals by beginning with the hope for a revolution in the notion of state, pleading for a new type of state which would be neither Hegelian nor Napoleonic, nor Prussian, and which would allow a diversity of peoples in the same territory. Unity in diversity has always seemed to be the basic principle for any solution to the Near Eastern conflict. It is not surprising that it would clash with the classic and traditional view by which a state must have a country, a people, an army. Mendès-France wrote: "In many domains I have been considered too daring. In this case, I am sorry that I cannot be so daring as you." In fact my "audacity" was less great than it may have seemed three years previously. The sequence of events seems to lead us to a time when yesterday's madness can become tomorrow's wisdom.

By now much water has flowed down the Jordan. The evolution of the political situation has been spectacular. Nasser has disappeared. Yesterday's disciples have purged themselves of the very memory of the man they adored. Today Sadat has harsher and more destructive words for Nasser than even I had five years ago. Israeli-Arab cooperation has spread and deepened in Jerusalem, in Transjordan and in Sinai. For almost two years the banks of the Suez have been totally quiet. The terrorist organizations have become powerless after an unusual sequence of events. Trade prospers between the two banks of the Jordan. And almost everybody is filled with dreams of peace. The Yarring mission, Rogers' suggestions, the moderation of the Soviet leaders have encouraged a new maturity which the world press reports daily. In my personal file, I note the echoes of this revolution. The "Arab friends" who answer my *Letter* have become more numerous, more affirmative, more impatient for true peace.

"The difficulty with the present situation in Palestine is that two theocracies have confronted each other and each one believes in its mission," Cardinal Tisserant wrote to me on July 20, 1969. It was my hope that one of these "theocracies" (in so far as the term may be accurate) could be convinced of the identicalness of their missions and interests. There have been Arabs who have told me that they agreed— Egyptians, Syrians, Jordanians, Palestinians, Lebanese and North Africans. One of them, an Algerian physician, Dr. Moktar Moatemry, emphatically informs me of our common points. He does not keep his stand a secret and assures me that he would have it as well known as possible.

Another Arab physician, from Jerusalem, writes: "Your thesis is captivating especially for someone like me, a native citizen of this country who has observed the varied events of six decades. The numerous points of historic and religious parallels which you so masterfully sketch make your arguments truly persuasive." A Tunisian writer who signs his manuscript with a pseudonym makes a heartfelt and urgent plea for peace among Israel and the Arab nations and chastises the warmongers who are ruining their peoples. He sends along a painting depicting the reconciliation of Israel and

Ishmael: a light shines in the darkness illuminating a minaret and the tower of a temple as well as a seven-branched candelabra decorated with the Islamic crescent. He writes: "I am sending you the illustration of my essay. Do not be too critical of it. The menorah and the crescent are the symbol of the forthcoming accord. Their shadow hides the shame of fanaticism to redeem the blood spilled by the power-hungry dictators."

Salah Elekhouan tells his story: like many his age, he was brought up hating and scorning the Jews. His awakening inspires his sensitive appeal for peace. "Know that the Arab masses are only waiting for the opportunity to proclaim their deepest wish for peace." The title of his manuscript is "Arab brothers! The name of our future is peace." Henceforth, the anguished search for peace is his obsession.

In Europe the principal objection to my book was that it addressed itself to an unknown person. The state of war between Israel and the Arab countries was held so widely that obviously it was impossible for the public to conceive not only the peace I announced, but even a friendship between an Arab and a Jew. This theme recurs as a leitmotif. Almost all the critics ask: "Does Ahmed Benghanem exist?" "And who will answer your *Letter to an Arab Friend?* When shall we see an Arab author's *Letter to a Jewish Friend?*" eagerly asks the *Informations Catholiques Internationales* (September 15, 1969). And in a more cutting way Philippe de Saint-Robert writes in a review in *L'Orient* (September 12, 1970) from Beirut, reprinted with a commentary in Algiers *El Moudjahid* (September 23, 1970): "This letter to an Arab friend no doubt may touch many Arabs, and many may even answer it, except, alas, the Palestinian Arab." So the tragedy of the Palestinians is recalled. Saint-Robert, who has never said that he was a friend of Israel, shares his certitude on this point with excellent Jewish critics. One such critic says in *L'Information juive de Paris:* "One does not really believe that these two individuals exist—a Jewish David and a Moslem Jonathon, both in love with Jerusalem. They are fictional characters in street clothes and have no psychological truth." This is what Arnold Mendel writes in a second article on my book (October 1969). In Israel David Ben Ami also shared this opinion. Happily, these prophets of doom and their negative judgments have been proven false for once.

The most moving incarnation of my "fictional character in street clothes" appeared in my home on December 31, 1969. The numerous articles printed about my book in Europe, America, and several Arab countries such as Lebanon, Algeria, and Transjordan, the radio and television broadcasts, and the public debates devoted to it ended up by creating a movement. No longer was it said as Dov Bar-Nir said in the Hebrew newspaper *Al Hamishmar* in his excellent book review: "The reader may object, 'it is a voice crying in the wilderness.' No doubt—but we live in a political wilderness where sometimes the swallow sings until deaf ears hear" (September 19, 1963).

The wilderness began to be inhabited and ears began to hear. One day Ahmed Abassi asked whether I was ready to receive a leader of Palestinian nationalism, Mohamed Abu Shilbayih, well known in the Arab world. He was born near Jaffa during the British Mandate. He attended secondary school in Jerusalem and from 1944 to 1949 studied Arab literature at King Farouk University in Cairo. Meanwhile the State of Israel had come into being. His family shared the fate of the Palestinian refugees and their homes and land were confiscated by Israel. The only thing left for Abu Shilbayih to do was to join the Palestinian Resistance.

He settles in Damascus first where he writes critically about the Arab kings who have caused the sorry plight of the Palestinian people by starting a war they have not been able to win. Driven out of Syria, he goes to Jordan and earns his living in the Normal Schools of Jerusalem and Irbid. In addition he writes newspaper articles defending the Palestinian cause which, of course, does not go over very well in Amman. The Jordanian government arrests and imprisons him several times without a trial. From 1954 to 1961 he serves more than five years in the jails of the Hashemite Kingdom. The June 1967 war catches him in Jerusalem and involves him in spite of himself in the new realities of Israel. The Israeli invasion so upsets him that he burns all his copies

of a book he had published in 1964, *I Lost My Country*. If
Hussein had thrown him into prison for five years without
even a trial because he was a Palestinian nationalist, what
could he expect from the Israeli soldiers?

Retrospectively he laughs at his fears today. Israel left him
free to do, think, and write whatever he wished. He became
editor of an Arab newspaper in Jerusalem, *El Ouds*, of
Palestinian nationalist tendencies. Now he directs an Arab
weekly in which he continues to defend his opinions. On
reading my book Mohamed Abu Shilbayih recognized himself in Ahmed Benghamen: the same origins, fate, concerns,
the same motivations, the same political involvement. Mohamed, like Ahmed, left his family circle to study away
from home, the one in Cairo, the other in Paris. On their
return the identical sad fate and battle awaited them.

I shall never forget the visit I had on December 31, 1969,
the last day of the year of publication of *Letter to an Arab
Friend*. Appearing before me without even saying hello,
Abu Shilbayih said in Arabic, "I am your Arab friend." And
from our first sentences of this meeting we both had the feeling of having known each other forever. I reminded him of
his Israeli friends with whom he had grown up in Jaffa, Tel-
Aviv or Cairo. For me he evoked the Arab friends of my
childhood in the small city of Aïn-Témouchent in Algeria,
the lycée in Oran, the University of Paris and, later in Jerusalem. The painful search for an equitable solution to the
Israeli-Arab conflict brought us even closer together. As
we exchanged opinions about this, we saw very clearly that
we agreed more than we disagreed. Before leaving Mohamed
solemnly promised to answer my *Letter*. "No one will be
able to say that you preached in the wilderness and that no
Arab, no Palestinian, answered the *Letter to an Arab Friend*
with a *Letter to a Jewish Friend*.

Mohamed Abu Shilbayih's book came out in Arabic in
Jerusalem in 1971. It is neither a letter nor a novel. It is an
essay entitled "No Peace Without the Creation of a Sovereign Palestinian State." This work whose first edition was
depleted in four days had a loud reaction in all the Arab
centers of the Near East. More than fifty articles have been
published about it in the Arab press. Since it is written in

Arabic and no French or English translation exists yet, the Western press, with few exceptions, has not recognized its true importance. The work presents the ideas that its author has been fighting for all his life. He does not want his children and the children of Israel to defend interests which are not theirs, and speaks in the name of the Palestinians who with him reach out to Israel because together, Palestinians and Jews are the victims of a fatal conflict which benefits only other great powers and societies. The Palestinians want peace, writes Abu Shilbayih. Will Israel be able to make it possible?

The first section of the book is entitled. "Two States in Palestine." It reviews the recommendation of the United Nations General Assembly on November 29, 1947, to create in the former Palestinian territory under British Mandate a Jewish State, a Palestinian State, and an international zone in Jerusalem. The Jews had willingly accepted this decision which satisfied both the vast majority of Palestinians, principally the socialists led by Samy Taha, and the communists who followed Moscow's political line, a line favorable to the creation of a State of Israel at that time. But Great Britain, intending to sabotage the partition plan, found willing instruments in the former mufti of Jerusalem and the Palestinian feudal lords whose emissaries assassinated Samy Taha in March 1948. The Palestinians who opposed the partition plan at that time represented a minority of less than ten percent of the Palestinian people. This is what unleashed, with the support of the governments and armies of five neighboring Arab countries, the endless tragedy of the Israeli-Arab conflict.

The second section, "Goats and Lambs," gives an analysis of the Hashemite Kingdom's policy with respect to the Palestinians. It brings to light the conflict which pits the majority of the Palestinian people against the Bedouin minority that supports the Hashemite dynasty and throne in Amman. The author insists that the refugee problem, instigated by the Israeli extremists and abetted by the Palestinian extremists, was solidified and perpetuated because of the joint desires of the Arab High Committee of Palestine, the

Hashemite dynasty, and the dictators who rule the Arab states neighboring Israel.

"Transjordan Given to Israel," the third section, is a penetrating analysis of the June 1967 war which, according to the author, served only to strengthen the Soviet Union's hold on Egypt and the United States' hold on Israel. Abu Shilbayih stresses King Hussein's responsibility for the war. He persistently encouraged Nasser to fight, thereby consciously or unconsciously serving as an instrument of the great powers whom this conflict suited so well.

The fourth part, entitled "Palestinian Organizations," is an indictment against the "imaginary leaders" of these movements. For the author Al Fatah's fight, that of the National Liberation Front, as well as that of other Palestinian organizations is a losing battle because these organizations in no way have the means to beat Israel and even less the great world powers (including the Soviet Union), who have a selfish interest in the existence of the State of Israel. Instead of fighting windmills the Palestinian leaders should reconsider their policy and devise more realistic goals. Here the author returns to his basic premise, the creation of an independent Palestinian State along with Israel.

"What do the Palestinians Want?" is the final section. The author answers with one word—peace. He would like elections supervised by the United Nations in Gaza, Transjordan and among the Arabs of Jerusalem to elect a Palestinian constituent assembly which itself would elect a temporary government. The latter would negotiate with the Israeli government the issues concerning Israel and the new Palestinian State. The borders would be open between the two. The refugee question would be settled on the basis of an indemnity which would permit settlement in the territory of the new state. Also taken into account would be the fate of the Jewish refugees driven out of the Arab countries following the Israeli-Arab conflict. The states would sign cooperation agreements. At the end of a ten year period, necessary for the new state's consolidation, it would be possible to join the States of Israel and Palestine in a federation destined to be the center of a vast confederation of the Near

Eastern countries which initially could be linked in the framework of a Near Eastern common market. One should note that Abu Shilbayih's conclusions coincide not only with the wishes of the majority of Palestinians but, beyond that, with the thinking of a growing number of Israeli leaders. An example of this thinking is Shimon Peres's fine book, *David's Sling: The Arming of Israel*. Its conclusion, "Israel and the Arab world," leads, through different paths, to the same wish for peace and for the establishment of an essentially federative union of the Arab states of the Near East.

In recent years these ideas have received much attention. On several occasions numerous Palestinian and Israeli leaders have adopted them and advocated them publicly. A collection of the speeches, articles, and books expressing this tendency would reach considerable proportions, without including all the private talks and secret meetings in Jerusalem, Amman, Beirut, Cairo, Paris, New York, London, Geneva and elsewhere which have prepared the road to peace.

King Hussein officially consecrated the cause for peace on March 15, 1972. In a message to the nation read before five hundred people from both banks of the Jordan, he declared his intention to divide his kingdom into two federal provinces: Jordan and Palestine. Amman would be the capital of the united kingdom. Jerusalem would serve a dual function (the king subsequently clarified this point): capital of Israel and administrative center of the Palestinian province of the kingdom. The king would be head of state with chief executive power, assisted by a council of ministers having authority over the entire realm. Legislative power would be delegated to a national assembly. The king would be commander-in-chief of the unified military forces. However, each of the two provinces would have its own executive power, a regional council of ministers headed by a governor-general native to the province.

This speech soon had important reverberations in the capitals the world over. For once not only were people discussing peace, but they were proposing suggestions for ending the Israeli-Arab conflict. But what was the actual situation? Radio Amman pointed out that the king's speech was of historical importance in three respects: it presented peace in the Middle East as unquestionably desirable; it recognized the Palestinian personality and provided an autonomous political framework for it; and finally, it admitted, by specifying the coexistence of distinct national communities, the principle of an essentially federative organization whose broad outlines it sketched. Such a revolution in thought and action is not without consequence. In Iraq, Lebanon, Cairo, Damascus, Libya and in every capital the motives and the significance of the royal speech were appraised. Everywhere the constant rumors since October 5, 1967 of secret Jordano-Israeli meetings were recalled: meetings between Levi Eshkol and the Jordanian king's emissaries; alleged meetings of King Hussein and Abba Ebban (September 1968), with Ygal Allon, vice-president of the Israeli Council (November 1970); negotiations between Golda Meir and Anouar Nousseiban, former Jordanian defense minister and the king's confidential agent (March 1972). Everywhere it was emphasized that Hussein's project had been prepared by a long evolution of thoughts and of the facts of local and international policy.

If this is the true situation, why Golda Meir's categorical refusal of the king's proposals?

It has been said that a woman of the world who says yes immediately to any proposal is no longer a woman of the world. But not only is Golda Meir a woman of the world, she is a head of state.

Had she said yes right away, she would have jeopardized any chances for success for Hussein's project. She would have solidified against him the Holy Alliance of his internal opposition, that of the Gahal nationalists and the external opposition of his enemies.

Why say "yes" when "no" was preferable?

But a fifty-year-old conflict has resulted in some odious habits. Distrust is the prevalent mood proving that nobody says what he thinks and does what he says. If an observer wants to keep things straight, he has to *guess* what is thought and not said, what is said and not thought, and what will be done that is not said or what will not be done of what is said. The most clever can be lost in this labyrinthine game, as was Nasser in June 1967 when he lost control of his words and his actions. This is the first hurdle which was crossed during the Six Day War, the one which separated the delirium of words from the harsh realities of war.

"Whom is he addressing?" is the first question asked whenever any leader in the Near East speaks. Almost every one of them says something different depending on whether he is talking to the enemy, Russia, the United States, his internal opposition, his political party, his army; and the tune changes as elections approach or after a coup d'état has taken place. In this turmoil that no computer yet developed can unravel, the prudent keep silent, or when they do speak, make sure that they say one thing and imply the opposite. So it has been with Hussein's plan. It is apparent that it presupposes a preliminary and solid agreement with Israel in order to have the slightest chance of execution. But a portion of the speech which was not disseminated abroad deals with Arab hostility toward Israel, usurper of Palestinian territories that must be liberated, and agent of Zionist imperialism. In her answer before the Israeli Parliament on March 16, 1972, Golda Meir scornfully rejected Hussein's plan, but added that if this proposal were accompanied by an agreement with Israel, it would be considered perfectly legitimate and as an internal matter of the United Kingdom of Jordan, would be a matter against which Israel would have no say. Nothing is easy in these questions, and the devil himself must occasionally be confounded by them.

The worst aspect of all this lies in the war psychosis which still prevails in countries which have not known peace for more than half a century. Mention peace to certain military men and they will laugh in your face. For them war is a constant in Israel's condition. And everyone should know better than to dream of peace for it will not be achieved for several generations, no more so than the perfect fusion of the Eastern and Western communities of the country.

It is this defeatist attitude that my book aims at primarily. The Near East is not destined for war. Those who believe that it is demonstrate a pitiful lack of imagination, a complete lack of magnanimity and faith, unless they are poorly informed, as is often the case, or unless they are protecting selfish interests, as is also the case at times. Not only is peace possible, but it is necessary and desirable for the great majority of people who have been involved in this dispute against their will. The belief in a war destiny prolongs hostilities endlessly just as the belief in the perenniality of the abyss which separates the Easterners from the Westerners of Israel maintains and deepens that division. If the founders of the State of Israel had believed in the permanence of the exile, we would never have witnessed the creation of the State and the homecoming of the wanderers, the reclamation of the desert, nor anything else that our country has accomplished in spite of fate.

If a secret formula for peace exists, it is this: We must hope for peace with the same energy and courage, with the same openness and determination that we have hoped for everything else. Unfortunately, this kind of singleness of purpose is not as widespread as one might like among the heirs of the prophets and the pioneers so that we might be free of any worries about the future. Israel has to fight for peace with the same faith, courage and selflessness that it has fought to guarantee its survival. This time it must do so hand in hand with its friends, more numerous than one might suppose, among the Arabs. But to hope for peace, the Jews and the Arabs must have the heroism to conquer their disheartening and paralyzing fear. The first victim of Israel's march to new greatness must be its own fear and lack of confidence.

Several Israeli ministers have expressed in their own particular way their support for a peace settlement based on the same fundamental principles as Hussein's. Abba Ebban, Ygal Allon, Israel Galili, and Shimon Peres (who was kind enough to write the preface to the third French edition of my *Letter to an Arab Friend*, when he was Minister of Arab Affairs at the center of Israel's government) seem to have accepted the two fundamental principles which appear to be the crux of any peaceful solution: the recognition of the Palestinian personality and the adoption of a federal system of organization for the national powers of the different communities of the country and of the Near East.

There is still some quibbling over borders and the Jerusalem problem. As far as the borders between Israel and its Palestino-Jordanian neighbors are concerned. Ygal Allon opposes the plan bearing his name to Hussein's proposal. Actually, the question of borders has no theoretical importance except within a framework of war. If the question is raised within the context of peace, it is evident that the entire Near East is called upon to become an economic and political federal entity which can only assure its liberty and prosperity by following a policy of open borders. In the interim politicians should seek to demystify the idea of borders by making a clear distinction between borders for national defense, territorial and administrative borders of states, and finally, community and national borders. These three types of borders need not necessarily coincide.

I can very well see the distinction between frontiers for defense and national frontiers. In some ways the frontiers for the defense of the United States coincide with those of NATO and are different from the geographical ones of the United States of America. Military agreements between Israel and the Arab countries could solve this problem by situating Israel's military frontiers on the Jordan and the Suez Canal while at the same time adopting other lines of demarcation for its geographical limits. Though not a simple matter, this would be a negotiable question. I do see less clearly the distinction proposed between territorial and community frontiers.

Now we are back to Mendès-France's strong objection to my settlement plan. Traditionally, a classic type state is a monolithic structure where nation, territory and defense are one. The new international realities are such that for most countries the line of defense is different from geographic lines. Are we in agreement on this point?

Of course.

As for the Near East where the communities of nations, cultures, religions and languages are so different and so enmeshed, one more step is necessary. It will be necessary in the more or less distant future, when the horrible memories and fears of our wars have been forgotten, to rekindle the notion of a state, adopting it to the geo-political realities of this part of the world.

I understand. But how is it possible to put these ideas to work?

Technically, there would be a very simple way which eventually will be used to normalize the Near Eastern situation. But first peace has to be achieved between Israel and its neighbors, the closest of which is Jordan. Hussein's proposal, whatever has been said about it, is an excellent basis for discussions to lead to a concrete settlement of the problems between the two countries. For the agreement to be successful both governments must determine two different borders between the two countries, one for defense, the other for administration. This is not impossible and I suppose that everything else remaining equal, one can reasonably hope to reach this goal.

And then what?

There still remains a concern over the political and national status of the Arabs settled on the frontiers of Israel and the Jews in Transjordan or in the other Arab territories.

What do you have in mind for them?

Simply the right to choose their nationality. The Arab from Haifa, the Jew from Hebron will have the opportunity to be citizens of the Jewish State or the Arab State according to their free choice and without having to change their place of residence.

How do we go about this?

I think it is a matter of general interest and, in principle, a great idea. It is surely in Israel's interest to lighten the load which the exploding Arab birthrate is putting on its population. It is in its interests to soothe the moral condition of its Arab citizens by not forcing on them a nationality which they do not want. For their part the Arabs would like to consolidate their strength by regaining those Arabs of Israel who would like to opt for Jordano-Palestinian nationality. They will be happy not to create an issue over the Jewish minority which could and does live in their state. This would be a good way to separate the notion of state from its geographical dependence, on the eve of an era when the globe is becoming smaller and smaller and frontiers more and more meaningless. This would be a good way to discredit the out-dated notion of a Moloch-State, of a monolithic state created for war and death rather than for peace and life. I am not a prophet, but I can announce with certainty that this central idea will finally come to fruition, and not just in the Near East. Obviously a treaty on nationality will have to be ne-gotiated, signed and put into effect between the Jewish State and the Arab State.

Does not such a situation already exist?

I have told you that I am not a prophet. I am speaking of a reality which already exists in Jerusalem. The city is part of the State of Israel, but its Arab citizens (who vote in the municipal elections just as the Jews do) have the choice of being citizens of Israel or remaining Jordanian citizens. The vast majority have remained Jordanian citizens settled in a territory under the administration of Israel. It is simply a question of normalizing this situation, beneficial to all, and to give it legislative expression authorized by a Jordano-Israeli treaty on nationality.

There remains the Jerusalem question.

While I am writing these lines this Easter week, Hussein tells an American newspaper that Jerusalem will remain the capital of the State of Israel, thus recognizing an existing fact.

But he also says that Jerusalem will be the capital of the Palestinian province of his united kingdom.

There again his proposal rests on a fact: the existence in Israel of more than a million Arabs who consider Jerusalem their political and spiritual center. Indeed, Jerusalem is the seat of autonomous religious institutions, the Christian patri-archs, the Moslem Grand Council. As all capitals do, it has its embassies and its consulates which enjoy extra-territorial status.

Would it not be in Israel's interests to house in its capital a Palestinian assembly and a Transjordanian provincial gov-ernment by guaranteeing them extra-territorial status if this were the condition for peace? It is likely that the Jewish super-nationalists will demonstrate once more their con-genital blindness by opposing the idea. It is certain that the vast majority of the nation will accept it, including the important Gahal faction, if this were the condition for peace.

You would have the Jordanian flag flying over Jerusalem?

Every day of the year I see the flags of the United States, Great Britain, France and of twenty other countries and international organizations such as the United Nations, UNESCO, the Red Cross, the Vatican and many more waving in Jerusalem. I am rightfully pleased. Tomorrow the Egyptian, Syrian, Lebanese, Iraqui and Algerian flags will wave in Jerusalem's skies as well as those of all the other Arab and Moslem countries. Then why not the Jordano-Palestinian one belonging to our closest neighbors? As for the municipal status of Jerusalem, several years ago Teddy Kollek proposed essentially pluralistic regulations which would protect everybody's interests and susceptibilities.

To complete Jerusalem's story I repeat that this city has the mission, in the future, of being the federal capital of a reconciliated, pacified, renewed Near East. I say this to my nationalistic friends: the Jordanian flag in the skies of Jerusalem is but a beginning. Ought not they to accustom themselves to the true grandeur of their city?

Then peace is imminent?

I have repeated that I am not a prophet. Tomorrow a new crisis can shatter the tangible results acquired by the efforts I have just described. A change in positions or in the present local and international balance of power could compromise everything and force the armies to fight their absurd and idiotic war once more. I hope that this new madness will be avoided and it surely will be if we want it to be.

Peace now? I hope so and what is more I believe that it is possible. Nothing can resist the firm resolve of a united will. The dialogue between Mattatias Mizrahi and Ahmed Benghanem continues. It teaches us that dreams and utopias, committed to men's wills, can become triumphant, historic realities.

ANDRÉ CHOURAQUI
Jerusalem, Easter 1972

Photographs 1, 2, and 3 courtesy Israel Government Tourist Office
Other photographs courtesy the United Nations